Chronology of Housing
in the United States

Chronology of Education in the United States (2006)

Chronology of Public Health in the United States (2005)

Chronology of Communication in the United States (2004)

Chronology of Transportation in the United States (2004)

Chronology of Energy in the United States (2003)

Chronology of Labor in the United States (2003)

Chronology of the Stock Market (2002)

Dominating the Diamond: The 19 Baseball Teams with the Most Dominant Single Seasons, 1901–2000 (2002)

A Tale of Two Leagues: How Baseball Changed as the Rules, Ball, Franchises, Stadiums and Players Changed, 1900–1998 (1999)

Crossing the Plate: The Upswing in Runs Scored by Major League Teams, 1993 to 1997 (1998)

Life and Death in the United States: Statistics on Life Expectancies, Diseases and Death Rates for the Twentieth Century (1997)

The Best of Teams, the Worst of Teams: A Major League Baseball Statistical Reference, 1903 through 1994 (1995)

Presidential Elections in the United States: A Statistical History, 1860–1992 (1995)

The Evolution of Baseball: A History of the Major Leagues in Graphs, 1903–1989 (1992)

Chronology of Housing in the United States

RUSSELL O. WRIGHT

McFarland & Company, Inc., Publishers
Jefferson, North Carolina, and London

HD
7293
.W76
2007

LIBRARY OF CONGRESS CATALOGUING-IN-PUBLICATION DATA

Wright, Russell O.
    Chronology of housing in the United States / Russell O.
Wright.
       p.   cm.
    Includes bibliographical references and index.
    ISBN-13: 978-0-7864-3033-8
    softcover : 50# alkaline paper ∞

    1. Housing development — United States — History —
Chronology. I. Title.
    HD7293.W76   2007
    363.50973'0202 — dc22   2007013514

British Library cataloguing data are available

Cover photograph: Aerial view of suburbia in Paradise, Nevada
(©2007 Thinkstock)

Manufactured in the United States of America

McFarland & Company, Inc., Publishers
  Box 611, Jefferson, North Carolina 28640
    www.mcfarlandpub.com

To Ruth Naomi Wright Bainbridge

ACKNOWLEDGMENTS

This is my eighth book in this series of chronologies, and what I have previously called the Wright writing company once more was the key to completing this book.

My wife, Halina K. Wright, in addition to supplying research material from the Internet, the *Los Angeles Times*, and our local libraries, served as editor of the manuscript.

My daughter, Terry Ann Wright, applied her expertise in Microsoft Word to create the manuscript, including the index. Her experience with the Internet enabled her to supply information of all types, including finding and ordering (at much reduced prices) otherwise obscure books containing just the right piece of additional information being sought. The Internet can provide nearly any piece of information needed for a book of this type, but it is truly useful in the writing process only when it can be accessed via an expert researcher such as Terry.

CONTENTS

INTRODUCTION

Housing in the sense of shelter from the environment has always been a key element in the survival of the human race. The exact form of the shelter has varied greatly over time, but in most of the world for the last 10,000 years, when humans tended to settle into villages and communities rather than pursuing a nomadic life, the form of the shelter has been replaced in importance by issues such as water supply, sanitation, and the common defense. As governments developed, they became concerned with the adequacy of these three issues when considering housing for the people they governed.

As far as the form of the shelter was concerned, the first building codes can be found in the Code of Hammurabi circa 1760 B.C. But the Greek and Roman Empires had city planning activities focusing on those ever-present problems of water supply, sanitation, and defense. In Europe of the 13th Century, city walls provided safety from nomadic looters in the countryside. The demand for such urban housing increased in many areas as the centuries went by, leaving water supply and sanitation as the issues most defining adequate housing.

The 19th century brought the Industrial Revolution, the single most significant historical factor affecting the demand for and location of housing. People flocked to the cities in large numbers to find work. Many lived in inadequate conditions relative to water supply and sanitation, but the availability of jobs became the prime and nearly only issue in determining housing demand.

Where the Industrial Revolution was initially most well established, such as in Great Britain and Western Europe, the housing issue was most complex. Settlers seeking a better life in many ways began to emigrate from these regions by the early 1600s to what would become the United States. Housing from the standpoint of available land and lumber to build shelter with

1

suitable water supplies and sanitation was relatively easy, but local wars involving different countries claiming parts of the emerging United States, and conflicts with the Native Americans already here, created severe problems in terms of defense (military forts were built in the United States up to the beginning of the 20th century).

Finally, the Industrial Revolution arrived in the new world in the early 1800s, bringing its common problems of overcrowding in the cities. But most other problems related to water supply, sanitation, and defense faded away on a national basis. The history of housing in the United States then became mostly involved with the preference of living in the cities or outside, and the development of the techniques of the mass production of housing which the majority of citizens could afford to own. The most complex history of housing in the United States took place after the arrival of the Industrial Revolution circa 1825, as the following overview will show.

An Overview of the History of Housing in the United States

There were two basic periods in the development of housing in the United States, with each period covering about two hundred years in duration. The periods were 1600–1825 and 1825 to the present. In these periods, the country grew from a mostly rural nation to one that is primarily urban, but one with the people living mainly in the suburbs in large metropolitan areas. The most complex period came after 1825.

The final result of the total development is shown well by revisions to the 2000 census near the beginning of 2003. These showed 106.3 million occupied housing units in the United States, of which 29.8 percent were in central cities, 50.4 percent were in suburbs within defined metropolitan statistical areas, and 19.8 percent were outside the defined metropolitan statistical areas. These outside areas were mostly rural, but they also included some of each of the other two categories. Thus, as of 2000, more people live in suburbia in the United States than in the other two categories (central city and rural) combined.

The rapidity with which the nation changed from a rural country to an urban country is well shown by considering the changes in the number of people engaged in the farming profession. In 1820, about 72 percent of the workers in the nation were engaged in farming. By 1900, only 37 percent were so engaged. People had left the farms to work in the varied occupations of the Industrial Revolution. Such jobs were usually in or near the big cities, which were rapidly being interconnected by the new railroads crossing the country (the transcontinental railroad was finished in 1869). By 1980, less than 3 percent of the workforce was employed on farms. Much better equipment and techniques accounted for some of this 96 percent drop in farm employment between 1820 and 1980, but most of these people simply left rural areas to live in urban areas.

The movement of the population (and its housing requirements) was initially from rural to city areas before 1825. Then a movement from the central cities to their suburbs slowly developed and eventually became a rushing tide in the twentieth century. In the beginning of the twenty-first century the movement to suburbia has captured the majority of the people in the nation, as noted above, and is still continuing.

Many critics have decried this somewhat isolating movement, but it has clearly been driven by both technological (e.g., the development of streetcars, trains, automobiles, buses, trucks, and extensive new highway construction and improved methods of building houses) and political and cultural issues (e.g., the Civil War, giving away of federal government land, the entry of the federal government into financing of all kinds into the housing market, and the desegregation decision by the Supreme Court in 1954). Riding on top of all of these issues has been the desirability of the United States as a prime destination for immigrants from all over the world for the last 200 years. All of these items have contributed to the rise of suburbia from a rural nation as is described in detail in the chronology that follows this Introduction.

The Development of Housing from 1600 to 1825

When the primary groups of settlers arrived starting in the 1600s, the country was essentially a gigantic but sparsely inhabited forest from the Eastern Seaboard to the Mississippi. Beyond that were huge and mostly empty plains up to the Rocky Mountains, and then the country turned down to another seaboard on the Pacific Ocean. France and Spain had large claims in the western part of what would become the United States, but land was plentiful even before acquisitions from both of these countries in the 1800s.

Early towns and communities in the 1600s had problems with the understandably resentful Native Americans from whom land was being taken. In spite of such problems, the growth of settlements and farms in the United States went on at a rapid rate. Settlers and new immigrants were easily convinced to move to a nation seemingly offering endless amounts of land and lumber. The initial prime industry in such a country was agriculture, and most people lived in a rural setting.

Housing densities were relatively small, even in the forming cities. Thus, rudimentary water supplies and sanitation systems were able to handle the initial housing demands. The conflicts with Native Americans and other countries who had claimed parts of the United States were resolved as the boundaries of the new country became more generally agreed to by other countries, and the Native Americans were pushed ever farther west as new settlers arrived.

In New England, emphasis was placed on model cities and communities rather than model houses, with the city common area or village green exemplifying this aspect of housing. Philadelphia was billed as the "city of brotherly love," being built in neat squares and rectangles encompassing various neighborhoods which would cooperate with each other. They still retained their identities until they were integrated into the city of Philadelphia in the middle of the 1800s. In the South, huge plantations with gigantic manor houses copied their distinctly English heritage.

Thomas Jefferson, in the late 1700s, before he became vice president of the United States in 1796, stressed the idea of the model family farm, with the farmer reigning over his plot of land and farmhouse in cordial relations with the other farmers surrounding him. Jefferson was a leading advocate of requiring the states, including his home state of Virginia, to give up their claims to land in the "Ohio Territory" (some claims extended west to the Pacific Ocean), and ceding them to the federal government. This effort succeeded in spite of the actions of many land speculators, and in 1785 surveyors began to measure the Ohio territories to prepare them for sale to provide funds for the new government of the United States. The manner in which the surveyors measured and laid out the land dictated the typical town plots of land sold to settlers who came in the 1800s. But Jefferson's model farm idea was soon overwhelmed by the Industrial Revolution.

In essence, early housing needs in the United States reflected the rural nature of the country and were easily met by the large amount of land and building materials available. But the rush to the cities caused by the Industrial Revolution, the immigrant tide, and the Civil War produced a movement to an urban society that has not ceased through 2006.

The Second Period of Housing in the United States from 1825 to the Present

The second period of the development of housing in the United States encompasses by far the most complex period in the history of housing. In 1825, the Erie Canal opened in upstate New York between Lake Erie and the Hudson River near Albany (and then on to New York City) amid much ballyhoo. Derided as "Clinton's Ditch" after the New York governor who persisted mightily in getting the canal built, the Erie Canal was a huge success and other states set out immediately to copy it. New York City rapidly became the prime port in the United States and its population grew substantially.

Ironically, in the same year as the birth of the canal, an event that would cause the future demise of the Erie Canal and others like it took place in Hoboken, New Jersey. A man named John Stevens operated the first experimental steam locomotive in the United States (they were already operating in Great Britain). Thus, 1825 can be taken as the year the Industrial Revolution began its prime impact in the United States. Two years later the Baltimore & Ohio railroad (that became the famous "B&O") was incorporated, and the railroad began construction one year later in 1828. Significantly, the railroad was incorporated instead of following an existing plan to build a canal from Baltimore west towards Pittsburgh to compete with the Erie Canal.

For the rest of the 19th century the railroad was king in the United States. It was the prime reason so many workers left the farm in that period and moved on to the jobs of the Industrial Revolution. The railroads themselves employed more workers by 1900 than anyone but the rapidly declining agriculture industry (a decline noted above), and the railroads were certainly the motive force behind the creation of industries in the United States in the 19th century. Major industries like the oil business bloomed in the late 1800s, and automotive manufacturing followed soon after in the early 1900s. The diverse manufacturing base established in the United States almost completely replaced the agricultural industry that had dominated the efforts of the workers of the United States in its first two hundred years. The country moved from a rural to an urban one, and housing needs changed accordingly. For a time, the railroads also facilitated the movement of people from the center city to the suburbs.

As poor minorities filled the cities, upper class housing tended to build outward along road and trolley commuter lines from the major cities and rail centers in the country, with New York City and Chicago at the top of the list. Existing residents of the United States found new immigrants moving to the big cities with them once the potato famine in Ireland in the 1850s started a rush of immigrants that grew ever larger in the rest of the century. This started the era of the tenements and all that followed in the years after 1825.

The key pressures affecting housing needs in the United States after 1825 were almost exactly the opposite of those operating before 1825. On one hand, the Industrial Revolution drove people to the cities in search of jobs. In addition, unprecedented levels of immigrants supplemented this movement. The first wave peaked in the early 1900s after beginning in the 1850s, but the United States still receives more immigrants than anywhere else in the world continuing through today. Their prime destination is generally the major metropolitan areas where many of their prior countrymen have settled before them. Hence the demographics of cities continued to change substantially.

Another key pressure in the 19th century was the fact that the United States grew in size dramatically with the acquisition of the Louisiana Purchase in 1803, and the once–Spanish lands north of the Rio Grande that were won from the relatively new Republic of Mexico in the late 1840s. The establishment of a republic in Texas in 1836 led to its annexation by the United States in 1845. After Texas defeated Santa Ana in 1836, the Mexican government was no more able to express its will in the area above the Rio Grande than were the Native Americans who were being pushed aside in the rest of the United States. The result was that the United States now had a lot of land to fill west of the Mississippi, and many steps were taken to entice new settlers into the region. In addition, the discovery of gold in California in 1848 attracted 80,000 new immigrants to the area in the following year. There were pressures both for filling the existing cities and urging citizens to go west. These pressures continued at varying levels from the 1820s through today. But the city pressure eventually won out as the country first had more people living in urban areas than rural areas, and then most of its people living in suburbia as noted above.

Housing development in the United States after 1825 was greatly affected by the Civil War of 1861–1865. The result of the war added about four million newly freed slaves to the number of residents migrating throughout the United States (there were about 31 million people in the United States at the time of the Civil War). Many were attracted to northern cities to escape the residue of slavery. Washington was an initial target where rumors abounded that they would receive benefits directly from the government that in their view had set them free. There was another peak in migration to cities like Detroit shortly after 1900 where jobs (the least desirable like spray painting) were available to blacks in the new automotive industry. The migration of blacks north continued through the 1920s and 1930s when the south was especially impoverished, and the demands of the defense industry for World War II into the 1940s kept the trend flowing.

Ultimately the big cities of the northeast and Midwest and Los Angeles contained large black (and other poor minority immigrant) populations. In Los Angeles and other cities in the southwest, Latinos became the dominant members of the minority populations. After the desegregation decision by the Supreme Court in 1954, the school districts of the inner cities contained predominantly minority groups as white families fled to the suburbs ("white flight"). The particular minority groups changed, but minorities remained predominant. For example, the Los Angeles school district gradually changed to having many blacks after World War II, but by 2005, the school district was 73 percent Latino, 12 percent black, 9 percent white, and 7 percent other (mostly Asian). Programs from the 1960s meant to help blacks get into college were not working properly by 2005 because the racial mix had changed so dramatically.

Housing for these groups was of the tenement type typical of public housing in the Northeast and Midwest, but of the type known as low cost housing in the west. Minorities began to be employed by the cities to teach the mostly minority students or process their welfare applications and control their typically long life on the welfare rolls. Although different minorities were involved after 1950, much of this activity had its roots in the Civil War and its displacement of blacks to other areas.

The Civil War produced a quite different group looking to migrate from the defeated south. These were ex-soldiers of the Confederacy (and their supporters) who fled what they saw as the humiliations (and abuses) of Reconstruction. They accepted the enticements to move west to possibly find an independent lifestyle more similar to what they were used to. They became ranchers, cowboys, and hunters and eventually even workers in the oil fields of Texas and Oklahoma. Some became farmers in the diminishing agricultural industry, because it was what they knew. Along with settlers from other regions in the Oklahoma Land Rush of 1892, they became the Okies from the Dust Bowl of the 1930s who migrated on to California.

They met their own housing needs on the lands they were awarded or their employers provided housing in the areas in which they chose to work. No tenements here, although much of the housing some were forced to use was substandard by any measure.

Immigration as a Key Driver of Housing Developments

The United States has long been known as a nation of immigrants, but truly massive immigration into the United States began after 1850. Until 1890, each state was originally responsible for processing immigrants to its shores. In New York City alone, about eight million immigrants were processed through its Castle Garden facility (originally Castle Clinton) in the Battery. Most were from Western and Northern Europe. Between 1880 and 1890, the leading country of origin was Germany, followed closely by Ireland and Italy. By 1890, there were more Germans living in New York City than in Hamburg, Germany.

As the wave of immigrants continued, it became clear that the federal government would need to become involved in the process, and it opened Ellis Island in the New York Harbor on January 1, 1892. Over the next 40 years or so, over 10 million more immigrants passed through Ellis Island.

Other cities on the East Coast (Boston, Philadelphia, Baltimore, Charlestown, Savannah, and Miami) accepted many immigrants over that period, not to mention New Orleans in the South and San Francisco on the West Coast. It is estimated that in the 50 years from 1880 to 1930, over 27 million immigrants entered the United States with about 20 million (or 75 percent) entering via the port of New York City (the most popular destination of steamship companies).

The impact of immigration has been enormous. The population of the United States in 1880 was just over 50 million. More than 5.2 million immigrants (about 10 percent of the existing population in 1880) entered the country in the next 10 years. In that same period, the population of the United States increased by 12.8 million. This means that new immigrants, ignoring the children born to them after they arrived, accounted for 41 percent of the increase.

The present influx of immigrants into the United States accounts for about one-third of the ongoing yearly increase of population, but a decade's worth of immigrants today (about 10 million people) accounts for only about 0.3 percent of the population at the beginning of the decade. This is 30 times less than the 10 percent represented by a decade's worth of immigrants in 1880–1889. That is why the impact of immigrants in the late nineteenth century was so substantial on the United States and its housing requirements.

About 3.7 million immigrants were admitted to the United States between 1890 and 1900. This made a total of almost nine million new immigrants between 1880 and 1900, a period in which the population of the United States increased by 26 million. That means about 35 percent of the increase was due to new immigrants, even when ignoring the children produced by these new immigrants in the meantime.

The two decades' worth of 9 million new immigrants was 14 percent of the average population of the United States between 1880 and 1900.

The foreign-born percentage of the total population in 1900 was 13.8 percent, and this rose to 14.7 percent in 1910, a percentage that subsequently has never been equaled. The percentage fell steadily to 4.7 percent by 1970, but then began to regularly increase again, reaching 11.8 percent in 2003. Germany was the country of origin at the top of the list from 1880 through 1920, but Mexico has been at the top of the list in the past four decades (Germany was still second as recently as 1980).

The 27 million immigrants who entered the United States between 1880 and 1930 (20 million through New York Harbor alone) were part of a population increase of about 73 million during that period. This wave of immigrants was 37 percent of the population increase in the United States, again ignoring the children produced by the new immigrants and the fact that World War I in 1914 produced a negative attitude towards immigration in the United States. This attitude resulted in a number of restrictive laws against immigration being written in the early 1920s. The percentage of the foreign born in the total population (about 15 percent in 1910) dropped every decade from 1910 to 1970.

If one were to carefully select years between the 1860s and early in the second decade of the 1900s about 50 years later, one would find that nearly 50 percent of the about 60 million increase in population in the United States during that period could be attributed to new immigrants.

The immigration flood peaked at Ellis Island in New York Harbor in 1907, when about 1.25 million immigrants were processed. For comparison, less than 1.1 million immigrants were admitted (legally) to the United States as a whole in 2002. The total population of the United States in 1907 was about 87 million, compared to about 290 million in 2002.

In terms of the impact on housing, one key problem in the 1850–1920 period was that the immigrants tended to stay where they disembarked. This put the peak pressure on New York City. The fact that the immigrants stayed where they arrived was due partly to the fact that they found countrymen (and jobs) there, and partly due to the fact that many had no resources to move farther into the United States.

New York ballooned into by far the largest city and metropolitan area in the nation, and huge tenement buildings arose to handle housing for the new immigrants (and other migrating residents in the country following the Civil War). Other large cities had similar problems, but New York had by far the largest problem, and what happened to tenements there was a model for the whole country.

Discrimination against new immigrants was also common. In Boston where many Irish arrived, the acronym NINA (No Irish Need Apply) was widely applied to both jobs and housing. Later new housing developments would carry restrictions that no houses could be sold to anyone having Irish ancestry. This discrimination helped push the new immigrants into the tenements of Boston.

New York City was overwhelmed by its new immigrants. And housing for them took the form of tenements, as well. The word originally meant simply subdividing and subletting properties, but it came to mean an incredibly crowded apartment building. The buildings typically rose five or six stories high from a twenty-five-by-hundred foot lot, with four or more families per floor (including grandparents, other relatives, and even boarders). A typical apartment contained only 325 square feet. Tenants shared sinks on the landing and privies in the basement or rear yard. There were many windowless rooms, with light and air entering the structures only at the narrow ends.

Reformers passed laws in New York City in 1867, with major revisions in 1879 and 1901, to improve light, air, and plumbing in the standard tenement. Other large cities such as Chicago, and cities along the northeast coast, followed the New York laws as a model. The 1901 version of the law was especially extensive and caused a revolution among landlords. But they subsequently lost in every court, including the United States Supreme Court, which issued a ruling in 1906.

The reformers stressed that the crowded and unsanitary living conditions led to high rates of tuberculosis, diphtheria, typhoid, and scarlet fever. Further, the infant mortality rate in the tenements was among the highest in the western world. The new laws greatly improved conditions in the tenements, but still left living conditions there very marginal. The original immigrants slowly improved their living conditions over the following years, but there were always (and still are) new immigrants ready to take over latterday tenements to gain a foothold in their new country.

The March to the Suburbs in the United States

Against the background of the items in the overview listed above, the real story of housing development in the United States is the story of the march to the suburbs over the last 200 years. Suburbs are not new in history, although for about the first 4,500 years encompassing the development of cities in history, the most desirable place to live in a city was near the central core, especially in a walled city. Thus, the initial suburbs developed in the United States tended to become slums and areas of low social status (ignoring the occasional estates of rich men built far from the city in terms of hours of travel time by the transportation means then available).

But the notable thing about suburbs established in the United States from about 1815 onward was that they became very desirable places to live in order to escape the congestion and pollution of the center city (and the presence of undesirables in terms of class, ethnicity, and race). The transition was triggered by the development of new methods of transportation, which made traveling to the city to work a small enough part of the workday to permit living outside the city while working within the city.

These new methods of transportation included the steam ferry, the omnibus, the commuter railroad, the horse car, the elevated railroad, the cable car, the electric trolley, and finally the automobile and buses. As the transportation methods improved, armies of land developers brought property along the rights of way and greatly encouraged the movement of people from the city to single-family detached residences built on the land owned by the developers in the suburbs. It was the combination of transportation improvements and avid land developers that created the huge movement to the suburbs that continues today.

Within large cities there was a general movement outward from the core as commercial businesses, tenements, and other housing for immigrants (and other undesirables such as blacks) began to fill the older downtown areas. But the suburbs as we understand them now did not really begin until residents began to settle in relatively remote areas and commute to work in large cities. These became commuter suburbs, and an excellent early example was the town of Brooklyn Heights, which grew in Brooklyn, then a separate place from New York City (then mostly Manhattan) that was just across the East River at the head of New York Harbor. The advent of high-speed steam ferries in 1814 transformed Brooklyn Heights (and Brooklyn) over the next several decades.

Brooklyn—The First Substantial Commuter Suburb

As steam ferry service expanded after 1814 to the point that ferries were available every five or ten minutes during the working day (at a cost of two cents), living in relatively bucolic Brooklyn Heights and commuting to the ever growing but highly congested city of New York became very popular. By 1870 about 50 million passengers per year (about 150,000 every working day) were traveling on the various ferry lines. But the very success of Brooklyn as a commuter suburb turned it into a major city on its own. Brooklyn grew from 1,603 people in 1800 (New York then had a population of 60,489) to 806,343 in 1890 (an increase of 500 times) as it became the third largest city in the country from 1860–1880 (until passed by Chicago in 1890— largely because of the annexation of south Chicago in 1889). New York had grown to 1.5 million people by 1890 (an increase of "only" 25 times), and the political combination of the two cities in 1898 (along with what we now know as Queens and the Bronx) gave rise to a colossus of 3.4 million people in 1900 (twice as large as Chicago and 2.7 times as large as Philadelphia). Brooklyn was no longer a suburb of New York in any sense.

Scores of other ferry-based suburbs arose around New York Harbor in the 1800s. Other cities in the United States followed, and even San Francisco Bay was used by such commuters building homes in Oakland and Alameda across the Bay. But nothing approached the degree of ferry commuting between New York City, on its way to becoming the busiest seaport in the world, and its suburbs in Brooklyn and northern New Jersey.

The Growth of Commuter Suburbs amid New Means of Transportation

Steam ferries were actually limited in application as only cities where waterways were available in the proper locations could make use of them. However, the development of the omnibus (a horse-drawn semi-stagecoach operating on a regular transit schedule) in France in 1828 could be applied to nearly any city. It was adopted in New York City in 1829, then in Philadelphia in 1831, Boston in 1835, and Baltimore in 1844. Typically, a city gave a small businessman already in the livery or freight business an exclusive franchise to operate along an existing street in exchange for a promise to maintain certain minimum standards of service.

By 1850, omnibuses had become big business, which was creating heavy congestion in the central cores of cities. New York City alone had 683 firms operating within its boundaries by 1863, and average waiting times on some corners were as low as two minutes, with one intersection on lower Broadway claiming to have a coach available every 15 seconds. The cars were a boon to business, but were generally uncomfortable riding over the rough cobblestones found in most cities. The typical twelve-passenger coach averaged only about five miles per hour, not much faster, although certainly less fatiguing, than a brisk walk. Not many commuter suburbs developed from the omnibus as a result of its limitations, but it did create what has been called the riding habit among an influential group of urban citizens. This habit proved very useful when the steam railroad began commuter service (rather than just long-distance service) starting in the 1830s.

The railroad transformed city commuting habits in the United States as it transformed nearly every other aspect of life in the nineteenth century. As routes expanded and prices fell, more and more working class people began to use the railroads to commute, especially as land developers began to tie their new developments to stations on the commuter lines. Once yearly commuter fares fell to as low as $30 yearly, the much more comfortable railroad ride became financially competitive with the omnibus. Railroad suburbs appeared everywhere.

The success of the railroads gave birth to the idea of operating cheap horse-drawn cars on rails that promised greater comfort and speed than the omnibus. By 1852, a grooved rail had been developed that lay flush with the pavement of the street. The horse-drawn streetcar, known simply as the horsecar, became immediately popular. The use of rails not only made greater speeds possible, it permitted a single horse to pull a 30- to 40-passenger vehicle that had more room and comfort. The cost of a ride was cut in half compared to the omnibus, and the omnibus rapidly disappeared. The tracks for the horsecar radiated outward from the center of the city, and land developers quickly located along the routes and began selling land to homebuilders. Once again it must be stressed that the actions of land developers, quickly recognizing the increase in the value of land connected to the city via new methods of transportation, were as important as any other factor in the rise of the suburbs.

New York City, as the nation's largest city, soon had by far the most horsecars and track mileage. By 1860, track mileage was 142 miles, and ridership was 36 million or about 100,000 per day. The result was a real estate boom in upper Manhattan as commuters could now stay within reasonable commuting times to their jobs without resorting to the steam ferries. Horsecar lines could be established almost anywhere in contrast to the relatively limited number of commuter railroads.

Horsecars also made the prime contribution to the development of integrated transportation systems. Omnibuses could provide cross-town service, railroads relatively long distance commuter service, and ferries could provide cross-waterway services. By the mid–1880s, there were 415 street railway companies in the United States running on 6,000 miles of track, and carrying 188 million passengers per year. This set the stage for the electric streetcar to follow. They were so important to the growth of suburbia that they will be discussed in separate sections to come.

Together with the improvements in transportation that developed in the nineteenth century came a cultural phenomenon that stressed the desire for a stand-alone house with a yard in the suburbs as the ideal residence for the common man as well as the wealthy. Catherine Beecher, Andrew Jackson Downing, and Calvert Vaux were among those who wrote about the desirability of this ideal, and starting in the 1850s planners were developing suburbs that reflected these ideas.

City streets had traditionally been laid out in a gridiron or checkerboard fashion in the early United States. Philadelphia was one of the first and probably most famous to adopt what actually was a style that was very old in origin, going back to the Greeks in about 450 B.C. This system simplified surveying, minimized boundary disputes, and maximized the number of houses that could be built on the standard 25 foot wide by 100 foot deep lots (later to be infamous for the tenement buildings that were jammed upon them). One developer who later submitted a grid plan for New York City admitted that the grid system greatly facilitated the buying, selling, and improving of real estate. The entire nation was basically laid out in the same grid system starting in the late 1700s, which divided each square mile into quarter sections of 160 acres. These were later subdivided further giving rise to the "40 acres and a mule" promise claimed by freed slaves. Most ordinary new suburbs were also laid out in the gridiron fashion.

As a reaction to this square, gridiron layout, developers of affluent suburbs designed them with curved roads and much open space and trees.
Llewellyn Park in northern New Jersey was one of the first to open in the
1850s. It featured locked gates and a gatehouse, and utilized basic railroad
commutation to Manhattan. Thomas Alva Edison was one of its residents
for many years. It was clearly only for the wealthy (and still is), but it started
a trend.

Frederick Law Olmsted, the creator of Central Park in New York, built
many such suburbs after the Civil War, the most famous of which was Riverside, built nine miles west of Chicago in the late 1860s. Riverside was the
first suburban station on the Chicago, Burlington, and Quincy Railroad. As
beautiful as it was, Riverside failed financially (partly because local investment was drained by the great Chicago Fire of 1871), and went bankrupt in
1873. Garden City on Long Island was another planned suburb for the
wealthy that did not work out as initially planned around this time, but
Llewellyn Park, Riverside, and Garden City were often mentioned together
as examples as the ultimate in planned suburban retreats for the wealthy at
the end of the nineteenth century.

During the same period, railroad commuter lines for the super rich were
developed along the main line of the Pennsylvania Railroad as it headed west
from Philadelphia. The term "main line" developed from this exclusive series
of suburbs with a meaning of anything especially rich and elegant. Chicago,
growing rapidly in the 1800s due to its position as the railroad hub in the
nation, had a similar upscale railroad suburb in Lake Forest, and New York
City developed the same type of railroad commuter suburbs in Westchester
County, just north and east of Manhattan. Bronxville was the crown jewel
of this development.

But as beautiful and notable as all these railroad suburbs were, they were
occupied by only a tiny fraction of the nation's population. The key transportation improvement that had the greatest impact on the movement of the
middle class to the suburbs between the end of the Civil War in 1865 and
the beginning of World War I in 1914 was the electric streetcar or trolley
(named after the apparatus used to supply electric power to the trolley).
Only the automobile would have a greater impact when it arrived in the twentieth century.

The cable car would enjoy a brief vogue in the 1890s, but only the electric trolley would displace the horsecar and the pollution effects of the
100,000 horses in the nation by 1885 necessary to pull them. Frank Sprague,
who worked with electricity when he was in the Navy, and who briefly
worked with Thomas A. Edison in Edison's famous laboratory, developed
the first successful trolley system in Richmond, Virginia, in 1887. Railway
investors and operators poured into Richmond to inspect the system, and

by the turn of the eighteenth century into the nineteenth, Sprague's company was supplying half the streetcar systems in the United States, and 90 percent of them were using his patents.

The electric streetcar was an immediate success. Faster and larger than the horsecar it replaced, and with no horses to feed, the average fare dropped from a dime to a nickel. By the end of 1903, there were 30,000 miles of electrified railways in the United States. Even as early as 1890, there were about two billion passengers a year riding on street railways in the United States. This figure was twice that for the rest of the world combined.

People began using the cheap and comfortable trolley for family excursions. Ridership on weekend and holidays exceeded that of regular weekdays. Amusement parks were built and the end of trolley lines to encourage such ridership (Coney Island in Brooklyn was the largest such park). John Wanamaker in Philadelphia used the trolley line to establish his department store as the commercial center of the city by 1900, and other such retailing names as Gimbel, Rich, Marcus, Hudson, Goldsmith, Woodward, and Lathrop followed his example. The electric streetcar, traveling as fast as fourteen miles per hour (three times the speed of the system it replaced) created a new surge of suburbanization.

Trolley lines in the United States had a major advantage over those in Europe in this respect. In Europe fares were higher to gain profits and zone fares were typical (payment according to distance traveled). In the United States one flat, low fare with free transfers was common to encourage greater ridership and thus profits based on mass usage. Thus, even as trolley lines extended well beyond city limits, the cost of travel to the city was the same. Real estate developers were busy at work along all trolley lines.

Some trolley operations were simply vehicles to make profits by the increase of land values in areas where the tracks were extended, rather than by profitable operation of the trolley system itself. Vivid examples near the turn of the century were the system operated in Oakland, California, by F. M. "Borax" Smith, an entrepreneur who made his fortune selling borax as a cleanser and then turned to real estate; Henry E. Huntington and his "big red cars" in Los Angeles; and Senator Francis G. Newlands in Washington, D. C. These men were only the very big tip of a very big iceberg in which trolley systems were operated by speculators in land who increased the value of their land in a sort of self-fulfilling prophecy by directing trolley lines to serve their properties. Such a combination was forbidden in Europe, but it worked extremely well in the United States in terms of creating millionaires who in turn created more and more suburbs. But these were generally suburbs for the common man, not just for the wealthy.

Improvements in Building, Selling, and Financing Housing

While technological improvements in transportation by the end of the nineteenth century greatly expanded the physical areas in which housing could be located, during the same era there were substantial improvements in the methods of constructing and selling houses that also played a great role in the march to the suburbs, especially for middle-class families. The most important step in new construction techniques was the development of the so-called balloon frame house, a technique that made possible the building of large numbers of houses with relatively inexperienced builders (including persons who built their own houses).

For the first two hundred years in the United States, basic log cabin construction was widely used in frontier areas, but the standard colonial house was the New England frame house. This house was usually made of oak using a post-and-beam construction method. In this technique, the weight of the house rested on thick horizontal beams held up by bulky vertical posts. Much labor and skill was needed to set up the basic frame. The completed house was very durable, but getting the building process started required experienced craftsmen.

In 1833 in Chicago, an architect named George W. Snow (or perhaps the credit goes to Augustine Deodat Taylor, active around the same time) developed a new building technique called with derision the balloon frame. As with many such inventions, people came to laugh but stayed around to copy. The construction technique was used to build St. Mary's Catholic church, the first Catholic Church built in Chicago. The balloon frame spread across Chicago, then across the Ohio Valley, and ultimately to the East, where it was known as Chicago construction.

The balloon frame used relatively thin 2-by-4 inch studs (actually 1.5 inches by 3.5 inches, but called 2-by-4 studs since they began to be used in construction) nailed together in such a way that every strain went against the grain. The posts were placed 16 inches apart, and spread the stress of the house over a number of studs producing an overall construction of great strength, far beyond the capacity of one seemingly fragile stud. In addition, the wall units could be framed on the ground by nearly anyone and simply raised into place. This eliminated the bulky members of the New England frame house, simultaneously eliminating the need for several laborers with some carpentry skills to set up the basic house. A method for rapid mass construction of houses had been developed.

With only limited carpentry skills being required as well as literally no heavy lifting, two men could erect a balloon frame house as quickly as twenty could erect the previous heavy frame model. This meant many common laborers could erect their own homes, and many did. This process was greatly assisted by the development of the machine-made nail in place of the previously expensive hand-wrought nail. When the machine-made nail proved capable of meeting the stress requirements, houses could be built with nails costing only 3 or 4 cents a pound compared to 25 cents per pound for the hand-wrought nail.

By the 1850s and 1860s, home building rapidly became an industry rather than a specialized craft. Land speculators continued to do their thing by buying farmland and subdividing it into lots. Individual families and small contractors then built houses on the lots from a few common designs. Entrepreneurs and lumber companies developed kits that could be delivered to a nearby railroad depot and taken out to a lot to build a complete home. Magazines and pattern books began to include plans for homes, and with lots available for as low as $150 in many places before 1900, even a working man with average wages could afford to own a lot for building his own house. In 1871 in Louisville, Kentucky, lots were selling for $50 cash down with the remainder payable over as long as 5 years. An agricultural downturn after the Civil War until 1900 made more farmers anxious to sell their land, and the rise of building and loan associations during the same period helped more people finance their homes. The pattern was clear: move outward from the center of the city to find cheaper land to build your house, then commute rapidly back to the city via the trolley to work. Everything came together by 1900.

Studies showed that immigrants, especially those who spread across the nation by leaving New York, tended to prize home ownership by higher rates than native American whites. This was because the immigrants could never hope to achieve what they saw as the financial security offered by home ownership in the countries from which they emigrated. They seized the chance to do so in the United States, even if it meant doing without higher education for their children, or the convenience of paved streets or other such amenities in their neighborhoods. To them, owning their own home was the epitome of success in their new land.

Blacks were not able to share in this experience. Racial discrimination plagued them from the time they left the plantation life of the south after the Civil War until well into the twentieth century. Home ownership was explicitly barred to blacks in most suburban developments. Even after such discrimination was declared illegal, the effect of it lingers even today in many places. One attraction of suburban life to many whites in this era was that the suburbs were mostly free of blacks and other undesirables from the center city.

Great fortunes were made in land development speculation, although most of the houses were actually built primarily by individual small developers. The richest man in the United States was John Jacob Astor of New York. Most people who have heard the name would connect it with furs and the fur trade. But the aggressive Astor, who arrived as an immigrant in 1883 at the age of 20, with only twenty dollars in his pocket, only made his first fortune in the fur trade (among other such activities). His prime fortune resulted from his purchase of land that was outside New York City proper starting in 1810. He added to his holdings in the financial panic of 1837, ruthlessly foreclosing on mortgage holders who couldn't keep up on the payments during the downturn.

By 1840 Astor had accumulated a fortune of $20 million, a huge amount at the time, most of which was based on the increase in value of his land holdings. Shortly before he died in 1848, Astor was quoted as saying if he had it to do all over again, he would buy every square foot of real estate in Manhattan. Many individuals or syndicates tried to follow his example by buying and subdividing huge tracts of property on the edges of large cities and selling them for home building. The prime developer had the city engineer lay out the land in typical gridiron fashion as the developer pressed the city to supply services including paved streets to the development. He also pressed the local trolley lines to extend their services to the development.

One of the nation's biggest such developers was Samuel Eberly Gross of Chicago. Between 1880 and 1882, he not only laid out 40,000 lots and developed 16 towns and 150 subdivisions, but also built and sold 7,000 houses. Some of the houses were priced below $1,000, and all of them cost less than $5,000. Gross was an exception, as most developments were still the work of a multitude of small contractors. The result was housing availability for the common working man at a scale undreamed of in Europe or anywhere else in the world.

The Age of the Automobile and Road Building

As the twentieth century opened, the march to the suburbs was well established in the United States. The stage was set for the transportation development that would establish the suburbs as the predominate mode of living in the United States by the end of the twentieth century. That development was the automobile (and the trucks and buses that followed along with it). In conjunction with a massive program of highway building that took place from the first decades of the 1900s through the end of the century (being driven to a peak by the 1956 Highway Act), the automobile (and bus) became the dominant mode of transportation in the United States. More people lived in the suburbs than in rural and city areas combined by 2000. Further, the combination of the automobile and the bus essentially drove the trolleys and commuter railroad systems into bankruptcy by 1950. Any public transit systems such as subways and light rail (and even via buses) that still survive in the United States do so only due to governmental subsidies.

Automobiles were still a novelty in 1900, but when Henry Ford announced the Model T in 1908 and subsequently sold them in the millions, at one time producing over half the cars built in the entire world during the teens as he improved on his perfection of the moving assembly line, the car quickly overcame its novelty status. Deliberately building cars for the common man, by 1924 Ford had the cost down to $240, making it possible for a working man to buy a car with less than three months of labor (compared with 22 months in 1909). In 1923 the state of Kansas had more automobile owners than either France or Germany, and the state of Michigan had more than Great Britain and Ireland combined. The car was now a necessity for the entire middle class.

A massive road-building program was necessary to support the growth in the use of the cars. Municipalities were generally glad to undertake this effort because automobiles were initially seen as an excellent non-polluting replacement for horses and horsecars, and were much more flexible than trolleys and commuter railroads in terms of getting shoppers into stores. A notable event concerning cars versus railroads took place in 1917, when President Wilson, who incidentally was the last president to ride to his inauguration in a carriage rather than a car, got into a furious battle with the railroads. The railroads were used to doing as they pleased, as they had been doing for much of the prior century. Wilson was concerned with delivering men and supplies to ports on the East Coast to be transported to Europe during World War I, a battle the United States had just entered. But the railroads acted as if cooperating with the president of the United States was beneath them. Wilson forced through the Adamson Act early in 1917, giving Congress the nearly complete authority over railroads it had long sought. The immediate effect of the act was to bring the eight-hour day to the railroads to avoid a crippling strike. The railroads responded by suing in the Supreme Court, but even after the act was upheld, Wilson had to seize control of the railroads at the end of the year to stop the endless bickering of the different railroad companies between both themselves and the government.

In contrast, the automotive industry was doing all it could to help in the crisis. To ease the burden on the overloaded railroads, the automotive industry agreed to drive 30,000 trucks, intended for service in Europe, directly from Midwest plants to the East Coast. The winter of 1917 was unusually severe, and crews went out to clear snow drifts as the trucks bumped along clearly inadequate roads. The story was the same during the rest of the war. The railroads were grumpy and uncooperative, while the automotive industry did all it could to help.

Congress noticed the difference. The year 1916 represented the peak point for railroad track mileage in the United States (254,036 miles). From 1917 onward, the total shrank by about 50 percent by 2000. The railroads received more burdensome regulation and taxes from 1917 onward, while the automotive industry received more and more government-built roads. It wasn't until the 1970s that the railroads got some regulatory help, but it was too little and too late to make the railroads an industry competitive to cars and trucks.

Many critics have complained about this seemingly unequal treatment as a cause of what they see as super-congestion in cities and suburban sprawl outside due to the triumph of the car as the preferred method of transportation in the United States. But others point out that the supreme arrogance of the railroads in the early decades of the twentieth century (and before) meant that they brought the beginning of their troubles upon themselves. Their excellent performance in World War II could not undo decades of neglect (and in some cases revenge) by a government that was angry at being ignored for so long.

Real estate developers were among the most vigorous promoters of building new roads as they quickly recognized that land values immediately increased along the path of a new or improved roadway. Even in the late nineteenth century, before the age of the automobile, new road surfaces had been developed to replace the ancient use of cobblestones. First came macadam, a kind of crushed stone named after its inventor, but it was too lightweight to stand up against heavy usage. Next came asphalt, another European development, and then came concrete as its quality of production greatly increased at the end of the 1800s.

In addition to new materials, a new thought process was applied to streets within a city. They were no longer open spaces but rather arteries to carry automobile traffic. Parkways were developed everywhere with limited access and no grade crossings to impede the traffic on the parkway. Soon expressways and elevated drives joined the ever-growing network of roads around all major cities in the United States.

In rural areas, groups such as the National Grange Association lobbied for better roads between the farmer and his markets. The Federal Road Act of 1916 offered funds to states that organized highway departments, and in 1921 the Road Act of that year designated 200,000 miles of roads as primary roads eligible for funds on a fifty-fifty matching basis. In addition, the Road Act of 1921 created a Federal Bureau of Public Roads to plan a highway network to connect all cities of 50,000 or more. Roads were seen as the most flexible way to interconnect the states stretching across the nation, and when

Adolph Hitler built his famous autobahns in Germany in the 1930s for obviously military reasons, the defense department of the United States saw a clear reason to continue and increase its support of road building at home.

The first freeway system in the United States is generally regarded to be the Arroyo Seco Parkway (later called the Pasadena Freeway) opened in California in 1940. It would become the beginning of the most extensive freeway system in the world, and although its original intent was to draw shoppers into downtown Los Angeles, one of its prime results was to draw homebuyers to the suburbs, greatly raising land values in Pasadena along the way. The lesson was not lost on builders and developers who became avid supporters of more freeways.

The value of highway construction passed one billion dollars for the first time in 1925, and it never fell below that figure again, except for a few years in the Depression and World War II. Gasoline taxes imposed at the pump, starting in 1919, provided state revenues for road building, and even in the Depression road projects were popular "make work" programs. There is no way to separate the growth of highway construction from the growth of automobile sales in the United States during the twentieth century, but it is clear that the popularity of the car and the individual independence it gave its owner was the driving force behind the combination.

Housing Developments in Kansas City and Los Angeles Before the Depression

Before the Great Depression drew the federal government into the housing market, large growth (and overbuilding) took place in the United States as typified by the actions of land developers in Kansas City and Los Angeles.

Developers such as Jesse Clyde Nichols in Kansas City and Harry Chandler in Los Angeles made their mark as the most significant developers of their time. Nichols was noted more for the quality of his Country Club development in Kansas City in 1930 than for quantity (even though he also built about 10 percent of the housing in the Kansas City area in the first half of the 1900s). But Harry Chandler was noted for the massive size of his developments in Los Angeles, although not necessarily for the quality. Real estates booms were common in Los Angeles, as it became the permanent boomtown of the twentieth century. The discovery of oil in the area fueled several booms, but where developers did not find oil, they turned to another source of wealth — real estate.

Harry Chandler, who had to leave Dartmouth College in New Hampshire for health reasons, came to Los Angeles in the early 1880s seeking a drier climate for a lung ailment. He started delivering newspapers in 1883 and soon gained control of large areas of newspaper circulation in the city. In 1894 he married the wealthy daughter of publisher Harrison Grey Otis, and Chandler soon thereafter became the owner of the *Los Angeles Times*. He was a progressive reformer with his newspaper, but he also found time to head a syndicate of rich investors who accumulated almost 50,000 acres of ranchland in the San Fernando Valley between 1903 and 1909. The syndicate, including Harry E. Huntington of "Big Red Cars" fame, then arranged to have water brought to the dry valley from Owens Lake via a 200-mile aqueduct. After the Pacific Electric Railway also extended transit service to the valley, the land the syndicate had purchased for less than $3 million was now worth about $120 million.

The syndicate immediately moved on to bigger investments in the Tejon Ranch, and Harry Chandler became the biggest and most powerful land developer in the state of California (as well as the publisher of the biggest newspaper in the West). The ability of the syndicate to convince the City of Los Angeles to acquire the water rights to the Owens Lake and float a bond issue was the key to their profits. But the resulting homes built on the large tracts increased the population (following an annexation in 1915) and gave a large impetus to the economy of the city. It was a classic win-win situation of the type that greatly increased the suburbanization of the United States.

The future design of Los Angeles was set in 1926 when local voters chose to fund a bond issue to build a massive road system to interconnect the suburbs that had grown around the very successful trolley system built in the Los Angeles basin. At the same time voters declined to fund a new central rail and trolley station that was proposed as part of a prior plan to eliminate congestion between the trolleys and cars by building subway tunnels into the downtown area. These decisions laid the foundation for the huge freeway system now existing in Los Angeles.

The voters followed the recommendations of civic leaders who were in favor of the road system because it would cause real estate values to rise throughout the entire Los Angeles Basin. The trolley system would cause values to rise primarily along trolley lines, and they might rise so far along those lines that only high density housing would be profitable rather than the single-family house. By choosing to favor the development of single-family houses across the entire basin, the civic leaders set Los Angeles on the path to huge decentralized subdivisions connected by the car and freeways, a path that the entire nation would eventually follow.

Incidentally, the great housing boom of the first three decades of the twentieth century featured houses that were built following plans published in the most successful magazine of that period, the *Ladies' Home Journal*. Soon colonies of *Ladies' Home Journal* houses sprang up everywhere, with the bungalow being the most popular style. President Theodore Roosevelt was quoted as saying of Edward Bok, the publisher of the *Journal*, that "Bok is the only man I ever heard of who changed, for the better, the architecture of an entire nation, and he did it so quickly and so effectively that we didn't know it was begun before it was finished."

The Impact of the Entrance of the Federal Government into Housing Policy

While the age of the automobile drove the creation of new suburbs in the 1920s and very early 1930s as described above, the Great Depression of the 1930s caused a major crisis in the housing market, just as it did in every other aspect of life in the United States. The crisis forced the federal government to take action in the housing area with results that reverberate in a major way through today, 70 years later.

The federal government had stayed out of the private housing market to date, except for some brief activities involved with building war workers' housing in the latter part of World War I, but the great housing boom that came to an end with the Great Depression of the 1930s caused the federal government, in the person of President Franklin Roosevelt, to get involved. It did so with effects that are still of great importance today, and the housing market has never been the same since the 1930s. The primary effect was in the financing of the building of houses and housing developments, and this further drove the nation to more suburbanization, although that was not the specific intent. Today, even in the hottest markets of what may or may not prove to be a housing bubble waiting to be popped, the comment is made that people are not buying an apparently highly priced house; they are buying a monthly mortgage payment. This means simply that as long as even people with relatively low down payments available can manage the monthly payment, the price of the house is irrelevant. The huge financing industry that exists today is a legacy of the actions of the federal government in the 1930s.

In April 1933, as Franklin Roosevelt was beginning his famous first 100 days in office (he was the last president to be inaugurated in March of the year following his election), the Home Owners Loan Corporation (HOLC) was created (it was signed into law in June 1933). Together with the Emergency Farm Mortgage Act passed a month earlier, the HOLC established the concept of long-term, self-amortizing mortgages with equal payments spread out over the life of the loan. Mortgages had been for five or ten years and previously had to be refinanced, possibly in periods of tight money. Under HOLC, mortgage terms were extended to about 20 years (now 30 or even 40), and when the term was over they were fully paid off.

The HOLC program was very successful. It also established a standard system for making appraisals across the nation, but this aspect of the process was blamed by some for codifying the practice of redlining, where housing in areas with black residents or those of other ethnic groups were appraised at lower values because the neighborhoods were thought to be in danger of the type of decline that would ultimately decrease housing values. This appraisal technique would be carried over to the Federal Housing Administration (FHA) and would in essence bar blacks and other ethnic groups from participating in the suburban housing boom for a good part of the rest of the twentieth century.

The Federal Housing Administration (FHA) was created with the adoption of the National Housing Act of June 1934. The act was to provide assistance to the housing market by providing financing and other standards to help draw private industry back into the home building process. The real primary purpose of the act was to get people back to work, as it was estimated one-third of all unemployment was involved with the building trades in some manner. The FHA (and its later counterpart for veterans, the Veterans Administration or VA) insured loans made for home construction and sale. But whereas loans had previously been made for one-half or two-thirds of the appraised value requiring a typical down payment of 30 percent, the FHA offered loans to 93 percent of appraised value (the VA later would go to 97 percent), reducing the down payment to less than 10 percent. Further, the loan terms were extended to 25 or 30 years, greatly reducing monthly payments.

The FHA also created nationwide standards for home construction. Homebuilders and buyers relied on FHA approvals as a seal of good quality. With the FHA and similar federal government programs in place, housing starts rose steadily from 93,000 in 1933 to 619,000 in 1941. They continued to grow after World War II, exceeding one million yearly. The FHA was immensely successful in meeting its goals of reviving home building, stimulating home ownership, and reducing unemployment. However, meeting these goals helped stimulate the move to suburbia to assure FHA services could be achieved in terms of having housing that the FHA decided was safe to insure. The core of inner cities continued to decline, and blacks and other ethnic groups were unable to obtain FHA insurance for homes in inner city or mixed-race areas. Thus, the racial divide in housing continued to grow. It might have done so in any case, but the good intentions of the entrance of the federal government into the housing market (and associated areas like highway construction) have proved to be of great assistance to the (mostly white) march to the suburbs, but of little or even negative value to racial minorities and the poor.

The great housing boom of the twentieth century did not affect all Americans equally, even if in many cases the harm has not been intentional. A definite bias between housing certain levels of society has existed in the United Stated since colonial times, and it still exists today. How to provide suitable housing for those who cannot (or will not) provide for themselves in spite of all well-meaning government programs to help is, and continues to be, a problem without solution in the United States (and in many other parts of the world as well).

The Great Divide in the Provision of Housing in the United States

In the early days of the pilgrims in Massachusetts in the seventeenth century, then as now one of the most liberal states in the nation in terms of social welfare, the term "public neighbors" was used to describe those who were in need of assistance for a variety of reasons beyond their control or beyond their ability (or desire) to address. Poor people were no strangers to the Pilgrims who had left behind cities full of the poor in their escape from England.

Initially the reaction to the new poor in the United States was a sense of Christian obligation to help, but this soon evolved into a community obligation, and civic leaders were empowered to warn off those potential new community inhabitants who might become a burden to the community. Almshouses and poor houses soon followed, both as a method to care for the poor and to essentially locate them away from the general public. By the eighteenth century the general sense of providing help for the poor had evolved into a sense of reforming the poor. Then it was a small step to dividing the poor into the deserving poor and the undeserving poor. However they were helped, or not helped, the poor inevitably ended up clustered together in slums in undesirable parts of the community.

The huge influx of immigrants in the second half of the nineteenth century, together with the influx of newly freed slaves from the south, created huge tenement districts in the larger cities for those who were poor (and most were). Reformers in New York City passed laws in 1867, 1879, and 1901 to alleviate conditions in the tenements, but the newest concept to come out of New Deal policies was the Housing Act of 1937, which intended to build public housing for the poor as had been done in Europe for much of the past 50 years.

But as was the case with many New Deal programs, the chief intent at the time was to reduce unemployment, and although many public housing units were built (130,000 units in 130 projects across the nation were underway by 1941), after World War II the priority of public housing was very low. By 1980, public housing accounted for only about 1 percent of the ever-booming United States housing market (compared with over 40 percent in England).

Part of this difference was due to the fact that because of constitutional issues, the construction of public housing in the United States had to have voluntary local involvement, including the decision as to where such housing would be located. The inevitable result was that public housing was located primarily in already racially segregated areas. Suburban areas generally declined to be involved. That heightened the already large wall between suburban areas and their core cities in terms of segregation based on race and class.

An additional irony of public housing was that it was originally intended for the deserving poor, people temporarily down on their luck who needed a brief respite to be able to rejoin the middle class. By the 1960s, however, this policy had changed because of the nature of the demand for such housing, and all long-term welfare recipients were admitted to public housing. The result was that public housing became the shelter of last resort, the permanent home of the underclass. No matter what good intentions existed originally, public housing became synonymous with crime, gangs of black youths roaming the projects, and segregation and isolation. On the one hand the policies of the federal government in the twentieth century greatly benefited those who joined the flight to the suburbs (and continues to do so). On the other hand, the policies of the federal government can be said to have contributed to the concentration of the poor in the inner cities, while those who were better off fled to the refuge of the suburbs.

The Post–World War II Explosion of the Suburbs

The demand for houses for the returnees from World War II hit unprecedented levels, and that demand was most notably met by large developers who had gained experience in building large numbers of temporary homes during the war for defense workers. Probably the operation that had the greatest impact on the building of massive developments, both in the number of houses built and the techniques used to build them, was the company formed by Abraham Levitt and his sons William ("Bill") and Alfred. The Levitts ultimately built more than 140,000 houses, and the techniques they developed to build (and finance) them cheaply became the model for developers across the nation.

Their biggest and most famous project was finally named simply Levittown. It began in 1946 when the Levitts acquired 4,000 acres of potato farms near the town of Hempstead, Long Island, close to New York City. After the land was bulldozed and cleared of trees, trucks dropped off building materials in intervals of 60 feet. Each house was built on a concrete slab with asphalt floors and walls of composition rock-board. Plywood was widely used and other lumber pieces were pre-cut and delivered to the site by a lumberyard. The workers at the site used new power tools and non-union work rules to assemble as many as 30 houses daily at the peak of production. The Levitts produced their own concrete, grew and cut their own lumber, and bought their appliances from wholly owned subsidiaries.

Levittown was only 25 miles east of Manhattan, and was initially limited to veterans, who stood in line to apply months before the first 300 houses were occupied in October 1947. The first 1800 houses were available for rental at $60 per month with an option to buy after one year of residence. Nearly everyone eventually bought because the total mortgage payment was less than the rent since the Levitts had built so cheaply. By 1949, the houses were offered for sale only.

Levittown ultimately consisted of 17,400 houses with 82,000 residents. The typical Cape Cod house had 750 square feet with two bedrooms, with expansion easily possible in the attic upstairs or even outward into the yard. Some dubbed the Levittown house as the Model T of the housing industry, both in terms of being priced within the reach of the average man and in terms of being intelligently and simply designed so that it readily served a number of needs. The Cape Cod went for $7,990 and the more expensive Ranch for $9,500. More importantly, there was no down payment, no closing costs, and no hidden extras. The FHA and VA had made production advances that comprised the largest line of credit ever offered to a private homebuilder. Bill Levitt reduced the paperwork for buying, financing, and titling to a transaction that took only an hour to complete. He also offered a built-in Bendix washer and a built-in eight-inch television as sweeteners. The Levitt operation was so efficient that it was reported that Levitt undersold his competition by $1,500 and still made a profit of $1,000 per house. One architectural critic commented that Levittown houses were much more social creations than they were architectural ones. The homes transformed the detached, single-family house from being merely a dream into a practical reality for thousands of middle-class families.

Other critics complained about the esthetics of Levittown, as they have similarly complained about the esthetics of many elements of suburbia. But as suburbia has been, Levittown was a smashing success with people looking for homes. Other Levittowns were built near Philadelphia, and they proved to be as successful as the original. Levitt's building and financing techniques were copied across the country as large developments went up everywhere. One notable element of these developments was their relatively low density. Levittown, for example, even with houses stretching away as far as the eye could see, had a density of 10,500 people per square mile, about half that of the streetcar suburbs circa 1900.

Another notable element was the absence of blacks in these new suburbs. Levittown, which refused to sell to blacks for two decades after the war, reached a population of 82,000 in 1960 without a single black anywhere in the community. This approach was essentially supported by the FHA, which did not want to insure homes in mixed-race communities. As the Levitts said: "We can solve a housing problem, or we can try to solve a racial problem. But we can not combine the two."

The automobile became the preferred method of transportation in the nation, greatly aided by the National Highway Act of 1956, which provided freeways and expressways across the entire country. This suited the move to the suburbs, which assumed the ownership of one or more cars per family to get around. By the 1980s, some analysts were announcing the end of suburbia in the classical sense. Suburbs had been defined as rings around a central city core, but now suburbs were essentially merging together without a definable central core. They stretched over many miles, connected primarily by the automobile and the freeway.

Everything in the nation now focused on the automobile. Motels, restaurants, shopping centers, gasoline stations, and so forth. Even factories appeared in suburbia, and commuters moved from one part of the suburbs to another to work, shop, and go home without ever entering what could be called a central city. Many critics decried what they saw as the isolation and homogeneity of the suburbs and the damage life on wheels did to the environment. But the critics notwithstanding, people chose to live in suburbia because they found life more amenable there, regardless of the comments of what they saw as snobbish critics.

Many critics saw the disappearance of great cities in the move to the suburbs, especially as individual homes developed home entertainment and information capabilities centered on television and the Internet. But other critics questioned the need for so-called great cities. In their opinion, such cities belonged to the nineteenth century, not the twentieth. This feeling was supported by the fact that 18 of the nation's largest cities in 1950 lost population over the next three decades. Further, in 1970, for the first time in history, the census of the United States showed a nation with more suburbanites than either city dwellers or rural dwellers (today, the suburbanites outnumber the city dwellers and rural dwellers combined). Finally, the 1980 census showed that of the 15 largest metropolitan areas in the United States, only Houston, at number 15, had a larger city population than suburban population. Their suburbs dominated all other large metropolitan areas. Relatively small cities in terms of physical area, such as Boston, Pittsburgh, and St. Louis, had more than 80 percent of their metropolitan population in their suburbs. Even the largest metropolitan area, New York–New Jersey, had 54 percent of its metropolitan area population in its suburbs, and the next largest metropolitan area, Los Angeles, had over 66 percent of its metropolitan population in its suburbs. Los Angeles trailed New York–New Jersey for largest suburban population by about 13 percent, even though in largest overall metropolitan population Los Angeles trailed by about 30 percent. No matter how it was calculated, or where one looked, the United States was a suburban nation.

Some analysts argue that the urge to own a detached home of one's own is not uniquely American, but the ability to do so on a large scale because of the relatively low cost of building and financing a house and the high availability and low cost of real estate to put it on are factors that are uniquely American. Essentially, many people in the world have similar housing dreams, but only in America can they be realized so readily by so many.

Another aspect of housing that can be said to be uniquely American is the fact that Americans readily are willing to leave the community nature of large cities in preference for focusing on their own homes as the center of their lives. Further, few nations have had the substantial diversity of population as has the United States over the centuries, especially including the migration of former slaves (now citizens) after the Civil War. This has introduced a racial element into the abandonment of central cities for the suburbs as the central cities filled with minorities and the poor. Thus, the suburban sprawl so often decried by critics is on one hand simply the result of Americans preferring to own their own homes and to own them in areas of relative racial homogeneity (which incidentally helps to preserve real estate values).

The 1954 Supreme Court decision creating integration of schools played a major factor in these processes, but it may have simply speeded up what would have happened in the decades after 1950 anyhow. Americans, on a per capita basis, are quite wealthy compared to the rest of the world and can readily afford to finance their own homes. Relatively cheap land and the balloon-frame house have made these houses relatively cheap, the car has made it possible to live nearly anywhere, and actions of the federal government in terms of income-tax policies, depreciation rules, highway building, and the provision of housing financing have all supported the move to the suburbs as might be expected in a nation based on a capitalist economic model. Thus, many factors have combined to create a nation that is basically composed of two almost equal (in terms of population) groups — those who live in the suburbs and those who do not.

The Future

Predicting the future of any enterprise is fraught with danger because one doesn't know what developments may come along that completely change the dynamics of what has been happening in the past. Who in the 1940s could have predicted the invention of the transistor, and the subsequent development of semiconductors and solid-state computers? Could anyone even as recently as 1980 have predicted the impact of the Internet and the cell phone? Many people who wrote about housing trends in the 1980s predicted the end of the suburban trend either because of a strict definition of what a suburb actually consists of, or because of such things as increasing oil shortages producing increased gasoline prices, and the "failure" of such trends as telecommuting or increased use of the Internet (these "failures" never happened).

But the growth of suburban sprawl continues even as housing prices climb dramatically. Among things no one could have forecast was the even more dramatic growth of mortgage lenders who would make loans on terms that were literally unheard of in the recent past, and an interest rate environment that has the Federal Reserve continually raising short-term rates while long-term rates (such as on mortgages) refuse to budge. Many critics of the Fed find it hopelessly out of date. They accuse the Fed of aiding or even creating the stock market bubble of the 1990s, and then reacting poorly to the popping of that bubble by creating a real estate bubble in the early years of the twenty-first century. By 2006, the jury was still out on the question of whether a real estate bubble existed or not, but the Fed did lower interest rates to historic lows, creating a frenzy in the mortgage market where lenders seemed willing to make almost any deal to get people to take out a mortgage on which the lender would collect fees. As noted before, people began buying monthly mortgage payments instead of houses, and the sale prices of the houses became nearly irrelevant.

Now the Fed seems unable to push long-term interest rates back to normal levels, and the nation is watching an inversion develop in which short-term and long-term interest rates are nearly equal. This situation has historically forecast a recession that will drive short-term rates down again. But it may reflect yet another new development of globalization. It may mean that so much cash is available globally that long-term rates in the United States stay low as this cash pours into mortgages in America. In essence, mortgage rates are ignoring the nearly frantic efforts of the Fed to increase short-term rates, the only rates the Fed can control. Market forces, perhaps much stronger than any prescribed government forces, control long-term rates. As long as these rates stay relatively low, the prices of houses will continue to grow and the media will be filled with advertisements for the "best mortgage rates and terms ever."

Thus, the future of housing is the United States is continued sprawl. Suburbs will merge together without the identification of a core city. Already many suburbs have taken the role of a core city in that large industrial parks fill every day with workers in various commercial enterprises, and then at night these enterprises are dark as the workers go home to a nearby or distant suburb. All movement is by car (or perhaps by limited bus lines), and no one ever approaches a core city. The homes of the commuters serve as electronic entertainment centers, and trips out to the movies or theaters or even some sports arenas are made within the extended suburbs without the need for visiting a central (still often congested from a traffic standpoint) core city. Those who say the suburbanization of the United States is over on the basis that a suburb requires a core city by definition may be correct by a strict application of this definition, but it is the already existing suburbs that are growing (often into each other) rather than growing around cities.

Perhaps more important is the fact that the cities which do manage to keep from shrinking do so with an additional influx of (mostly poor) immigrants. Thus the future of American housing is one of cities full of poor minorities whose housing is sub-standard (except when compared to what the immigrants left behind) while the streets are paved with gold only in the suburbs. With more Americans living in suburbs than in city and rural areas combined, the future will trend more and more toward a country divided into those who live in the suburbs and those who do not. There are great differences in the cultural lifestyles of the two Americas, including the critical area of the quality of the high school education available in each area and the likelihood of high school graduates being able to or desiring to go on to higher education.

In many ways, these developments in housing have greatly affected American politics, and will continue to do so. The red-state, blue-state phenomenon named after the presidential election eve practice of the major television networks showing states in a red color if won by Republicans and in a blue color if won by Democrats, is primarily an issue of the major cities versus the rest of the country. Basically, all of the major cities vote overwhelmingly Democratic, while the rest of the country votes Republican by varying margins. The manner in which this affects voting results in presidential elections is described in the Appendix.

Summary: Key Elements of Housing since the 1930s

Although housing has been developing with a suburban twinge for a large part of the previous 200 years, housing in the United States took a dramatic turn in the Great Depression of the 1930s and after. Housing starts had hit an all-time low shortly before Franklin Roosevelt came to power in 1932. The construction industry was literally flat on its back, and Roosevelt, who was determined to get people back to work, decided that the major emphasis would be placed on the construction industry. Not only did this industry employ a large percentage of the people in the United States, many of the jobs were simple enough that almost anyone could do them.

He put his brain trust to work to develop a program that would get the unemployed back to work with hopefully a minimum infusion of government funds. The brain trust came up with what became the Federal Housing Administration in 1934. This was the single most important development in the housing industry in the United States. The FHA completely redid the way mortgages were repaid (amortization), coming up for the first time with the concept of complete amortization, i.e., once the mortgage payments ended, the mortgage was fully paid off. This may sound like a self-evident statement, but in fact, many mortgages prior to this time were not completely paid off after the mortgagee made what were the "last" of the payments due to the lender. That caused many people to default on their mortgages in times of tight money or unemployment, such as in the Depression.

The FHA also came up with the concept of relatively low down payments (i.e., considerably less than 20 percent) and stretched out payment periods (i.e., more than twenty years, instead of five to ten years). The FHA basically acted as the insurer of last resort for mortgages, but did not actually put up any money of its own, which was the kind of program Roosevelt was looking for. With FHA insurance, builders started building homes again and buyers began buying them. Into the 1960s, the FHA never ran a deficit and returned millions of dollars to the U.S. Treasury. It is a record unmatched by any federal agency.

Ever since the beginning of the FHA, it has been the magic wand for increasing housing construction. New lending sources such as the Veterans Administration added to the power of government guarantees, and today many private insurance companies have added to the mortgage insurance market. With the development of exotic mortgages in the early years of the twenty-first century, housing appreciation, especially in California, has reached highs never dreamed of before. Some observers have commented that it seems quite logical that the availability of capital on easy terms has become the single biggest driver in the housing market in a capitalistic society.

Certainly the people who first established the FHA had no idea of how far and how fast the concept would grow and become the single biggest factor (plus or minus) in the health of the housing market. In combination with the decisions of the Federal Reserve on setting interest rates, the entire housing market can be said to depend on the financial decisions made by both the Fed and mortgage lenders.

The next key element driving housing construction primarily took place in the 1940s, both before and after World War II. The entry of the United States into World War II created a great demand for housing workers who were building the weapons and munitions necessary for use by the United States and its allies in the war. With so many men in the war, many women became factory workers ("Rosie the Riveter") and needed appropriate, safe, and inexpensive housing to be able to live where the war factories existed. Many building contractors learned for the first time how to build houses on a mass production basis. Previously the housing industry was primarily a craft business with many, many small builders building five to six homes a year. During World War II, contractors learned to build thousands of homes in a short time. This required truly a revolution in terms of how houses were built and the materials used to build them.

Also, during the war, the Navy especially was known for its Seabees which was the name given to their fighting Construction Battalions. C.B. rapidly became Seabee, and these men learned how to build in a hurry, often under fire, airfields, bridges, and many other construction items needed to go along with the invading forces. Many men with construction experience, who were almost like knights of medieval time, joined the Seabees at an advanced age (30s and 40s) because they saw it as an adventurous business that could use older men rather than the youngsters who were doing the fighting. William Levitt, probably the most known of the builders using mass construction methods after the war, joined the Seabees and he credited them for his development of building methods and use of modern materials in building. Levitt left the Seabees at the age of 38 and immediately turned to building Levittown, which was the most famous and influential housing developments probably ever built.

After World War II was over, Levitt led the men returning from the war in constructing houses on a huge scale for the servicemen and women returning from the war. In conjunction with the housing hearings held in 1947–1948 under the aegis of Senator Joseph McCarthy, which uncovered many problems with antiquated building codes and industry traditions that enriched certain individuals who acted as middlemen and provided essentially no service except driving up costs. These hearings publicized these problems, which were subsequently discussed in many leading magazines, and McCarthy even turned over material from his hearing committee to local attorneys general who arrested some of the middlemen for grand larceny. This publicity helped get rid of these problems and let people like William Levitt go to work revolutionizing the way that homes were built (and financed).

Levitt built nearly 20,000 homes in his first Levittown and sold them for prices far below anything anybody else was asking. Many contractors paid Levitt the ultimate compliment of imitating what he was doing and the housing crisis of just after World War II was quickly solved. (As an aside, one of the local bureaucrats in Levitt's area originally refused to give him a building permit on general principles. The bureaucrat had never heard of houses being built without basements before, but Levitt was putting the houses on a cement slab to make them faster to construct as well as cheaper, and in his view, eliminating a needless element. Levitt often liked to say the ancient Romans never had basements, and who was he to question the ancient Romans. Again, newspaper publicity about the bureaucrat's general principles made them quickly withdrawn.)

So the two fundamental revolutions of the 1930s and 1950s period were those produced by the FHA and William Levitt. Since that time, there has been much fine-tuning of both the FHA concepts and those of William Levitt, and things today are quite different from the way they were in 1950. They are different in a great sense, and things are much better today in the housing business than ever, but the basic elements that revolutionized the entire housing industry were contained in the words "FHA" and "William Levitt."

In the simplest possible statement about the future of housing in the United States in the years following the beginning of the twenty-first century, the future of housing in this country and its impact on the life of the nation will simply be "more of the same." The people of America have been voting with their feet for more than two centuries to show that they prefer the suburban lifestyle regardless of the complaints by many self-appointed critics of what they see as the various defects of such a lifestyle.

CHRONOLOGY OF HOUSING

This chronology tracks the development of housing in the United States from the time the initial settlers began arriving in the early 1600s until the present day (2006). An overview of the development of housing in the United States during this period is presented in the Introduction. Because suburbs are such a big piece of the story of housing in the United States, it should be noted that the word traces its origins back to the 1300s, while the idea or concept can be found in writings as early as 500 B.C. In the United States, suburbs of the established cities of Boston, Philadelphia, and New York were created well before the Revolutionary War of 1776. Suburbs are not, and were not, unique to the United States. But as with many other things in the history of the United States, suburbs were ultimately developed to an extent and in a way in this country that was never dreamed of elsewhere.

1637 — Boston selectmen were granted the formal power by the State of Massachusetts to screen visitors to their town to keep out those considered undesirable. This was part of the warning off process that was common in New England. It was meant to keep out people of different religions (Solomon Franco, Boston's first-known Jew, was warned out of Boston in 1649) and people who might require public assistance because of their financial condition.

This policy was an outgrowth of the sense that the commonwealth had a moral obligation to help those needing assistance, but it wanted to be sure these were only people who deserved such assistance. It was also an outgrowth of the fact that the Puritans considered the community the prime element in everyone's lives. Every town had its meetinghouse, and in 1635 a law was passed forbidding new houses to be built more than half a mile from the meetinghouse. The law turned out to be unenforceable, but it demonstrated the desire of the state to keep communities small and compact to make shared cooperation more readily attained.

1677— A map of New England made by John Foster showed miniature houses and churches to identify settlements created by the English, but showed only trees to mark Indian settlements. This was indicative of the feeling of the English settlers that the Indians never truly owned any of their lands because they never attempted to settle them. The English accepted deeds from the Indians for their settlements, but the English considered this a mere formality and not a recognition that the Indians ever held title to their lands under the definitions of English law (which required a settlement process). The Indians basically believed that nobody — or rather everybody — in their tribe owned the land that the tribe used in common. Many future battles and even wars would be fought over this issue.

1719— Real estate developer John Saniford offered housing lots at Barton's Point overlooking Charlestown, the Charles River, and a large portion of downtown Boston. In a sense it was the first planned suburban development in the United States.

1739— The Shippen Brothers began to develop and sell house lots on land they owned close to what was known as Society Hill in Philadelphia, the first classical suburb development in that city. Two years later, Ralph Asherton created a second suburb when he sold off his 80-acre estate in small building lots in an area called the Northern Liberties. It would be annexed to the city of Philadelphia in 1854.

September 30, 1785— A surveyor named Thomas Hutchings, the first man appointed geographer of the United States, began to survey the Ohio Territories at the point where the Ohio River crossed the western boundary of Pennsylvania and the northern tip of what was then the state of Virginia. The prime purpose of the survey was to measure the land in identifiable blocks so it could be bought and sold or exchanged by the new nation of the United States. The land lying between the eastern states and the Mississippi River was the major asset of the new country.

Hutchings used a 22-foot length of chain that had been invented by the English mathematician Edmund Gunther for the purpose of surveying. The chain permitted areas to be measured in acres, and today nearly every major city in the western United States (i.e., west of the western boundary of Pennsylvania) has city blocks that are some multiple of Gunther's chain. Basic units were created in what were called townships (after the New England model) measuring six miles on each side. The 36 square miles were alternately split into 36 smaller units each measuring one mile on each side, and these were sold by the square mile or section. The alternate townships were sold whole.

The one square mile sections each contained 640 acres. Four of the sections were to be reserved by the local government for the maintenance of public schools. Other sections were often further subdivided when used for purposes of defining building lots, so that a quarter section was 160 acres. It was the concept of further dividing the quarter section by another quarter that led to the demand of "forty acres and a mule" which the slaves freed by the Civil War in 1865 felt they had been promised.

The measuring system finally extended across the entire United States, helped by the Northwest Ordinance of 1787 and the Homestead Act of 1862. Local townships and counties everywhere were based on some multiple of the system. Ultimately, the building of cities and even the suburbs was based on this system, and they were initially laid out in a gridiron fashion that originally featured some further subdivision of the basic plan. Some suburbs first attracted attention because they were laid out with curved streets rather than the rectilinear fashion of the gridiron technique.

January 1801— The Philadelphia water supply system, designed by Benjamin Latrobe, began operation during this month. The system included an aqueduct and a distribution arrangement of wooden pipes through which water was pumped by a steam engine. Frederick Graff was appointed system engineer in 1805, and he served for 42 years, during which time he was acknowledged as the leading water system expert in the United States.

When Graf ended his tenure in 1847, Philadelphia had a population near 120,000. Only New York, Baltimore, and Boston were larger (New York was a colossus of almost 500,000 by then, while the other cities were closer to Philadelphia in population). But the annexation of some of its prime suburbs in 1854 vaulted Philadelphia to become the second largest city in the nation by 1860, with a population of over 565,000. The same basic water system expanded as necessary to serve the merged city. The Philadelphia water system was considered a model for cities of its type and size, and it was a good example of what cities needed to do to support housing growth in their area. When the system was put into operation in 1801, Philadelphia had an un-annexed population of only 40,000.

1811— New York City was laid out in gridiron fashion where all streets meet at right angles to all other streets and otherwise run parallel to each other as they run in north-south and east-west directions. This system dated back to about 450 B.C., but fell into disuse for about 1500 years after the fall of Greece. It reappeared in the 16th century, and was used in mapping the western territories in 1785 (see entry for December 30, 1785). It was adopted in Philadelphia in 1682, in Savannah in 1733, and in planning for the nation's new capital in 1791 (superimposed in this case on radial streets running out from the center).

The use of the system in the nation's largest city was certainly one of the most notable dates in its evolution, and it was there that the man who proposed the plan, John Randel, frankly admitted that such an arrangement greatly facilitated "buying, selling, and improving real estate." The system also maximized the number of houses that fronted on a given street and minimized the number of legal disputes. It led to the standardization of lots in New York (and other cities) that were twenty-five feet wide by 100 feet deep. These lots became infamous because of the crowded tenements that were built on them to attempt to house the influx of immigrants and others that overwhelmed New York City after 1850 (see entry for 1867).

1814— Regular steam ferry service began between New York City (then consisting only of what we know today as Manhattan) and the town of Brooklyn just across the East River at the easternmost tip of Long Island. The ease of access to the relatively bucolic area of Brooklyn from the congested streets of Manhattan turned Brooklyn into the first major commuter suburb in the United States. Additional ferry lines were established as the 1800s progressed, and Brooklyn became a place of feverish real estate development because land prices there were much cheaper than in Manhattan.

Detached single-family residences were the highlight of the housing developments in Brooklyn, as they would be in future suburban developments. Hezekiah Beers Pierpoint was the first speculator to take advantage of Robert Fulton's development of the steam-driven ferry, and Edwin Clark Litchfield followed him. But Brooklyn became a victim of its own success as a suburb, becoming the fourth largest city in the country before it was annexed by New York City in 1898. By then it was no longer a bucolic suburb but rather a major industrial city on its own.

1829— Abraham Bower introduced the omnibus to New York City (and the United States) by beginning a transit service along Broadway. The idea was copied from a transit system started in Paris on January 30, 1828. The omnibus was a sort of stagecoach pulled by horses that operated on a regular schedule within a city. The city government would grant a franchise to a single company to operate along specific streets in exchange for a promise to maintain certain standards of service. Rides on the omnibus ranged from four to ten cents a day, and the service supported those who wished to work and shop in the city while living in the suburbs.

The omnibus caught on quickly in the United States, and by 1853 New York City alone had 683 licensed coaches representing 22 separate firms competing for the business. At some street corners, the average waiting time for a coach was less than two minutes. But the large 12-passenger coaches were uncomfortable to ride in on the cobblestone city streets, and although they were widely used, the omnibuses were susceptible to ready replacement if a more competitive system were to appear. They did give the public the riding habit, as one analyst stated, and when the horsecar and then the trolley came along later in the century, the omnibuses quickly disappeared.

1833 — St. Mary's Catholic Church was built in Chicago. It was the first Catholic Church built in Chicago, but much more significantly it was identified as the first building in the United States to be built with what became known (at first with derision) as the balloon frame. The invention of this form of construction was truly revolutionary, and the balloon frame was an important factor in the great housing boom in the United States over the next 175 years.

Before 1833, houses in the United States (other than the log cabin) were generally constructed in the New England-frame house style. The frame house required thick oak beams that rested on other thick beams to support the weight of the house. This construction required trained craftsmen to assemble, and a number of men to raise the initial beams into place.

The balloon frame house used so-called 2-by-4 (actually 1.5 inches by 3.5 inches) relatively thin studs nailed together in a way that spread the stress over many thin boards rather than relatively few bulky members as in the tradition frame house. The house was easy to construct, and many sections could be nailed together on the ground and later easily raised into place. The use of the balloon style was greatly facilitated by the development about 15 years earlier of the machine-made nail which cost only about 3–4 cents a pound compared with 25 cents a pound for hand-wrought nails.

The invention of the new building style is credited alternatively to lumberyard owner George W. Snow or to carpenter-architect Augustine Deodat Taylor (although there is some dispute about the inventor as noted in the appendix). Either way, the balloon style spread over Chicago and the Ohio Valley, and then to the East Coast, where it was called the Chicago style. Other than simply making the overall construction of a house much easier than before, the balloon style permitted a relatively untrained worker to undertake the task. This permitted ordinary workers (i.e., inexpensive workers) to build large housing developments quickly (and cheaply). It also permitted an individual to buy his own lot and then to construct his own house from plans supplied by sources such as general magazines. The *Ladies' Home Journal* was a prime supplier of such plans over the next century, and Sears & Roebuck supplied everything needed to build your own house, including plans, during much of the same time.

The balloon frame house created an easy way for working individuals to become homeowners as new means of transportation constantly became available for the workers to make the connection between their jobs and the cheap land lying outside of major cities. In this way, the balloon frame house was as responsible, or more so, than any other technological or financial innovation for the flight to the suburbs in the nineteenth and twentieth centuries.

1837 — In the financial panic of 1837, John Jacob Astor, considered the richest man in the United States before the Civil War, added greatly to his accumulation of real estate north of Canal Street in Manhattan by ruthlessly foreclosing on those property owners who were temporarily unable to keep up with their mortgage payments. Astor was known for his successes in the fur trade, but the bulk of his estimated $20 million fortune in 1840 was due to his land speculations in Manhattan that he had started after 1810.

Before he died at the age of 85 in 1848, Astor was quoted as saying, "Could I begin life again, knowing what I now know, and had money to invest, I would buy every foot of land on the Island of Manhattan." Most of Astor's fortune was made after he was nearly 50, and most of it resulted from the flight to the suburbs of his time.

1841 (Beecher) — A book titled *Treatise on Domestic Economy, For the Use of Young Ladies at Home and at School* appeared in 1841. It was written by Catherine Beecher, a member of the famous Beecher clan that included seven minister brothers (of whom the most known was Henry Ward Beecher), and sister Harriet Beecher Stowe, who wrote *Uncle Tom's Cabin*. Catherine Beecher was the eldest child in the family, and she believed strongly that women were morally superior to men. However, she felt women should help their husbands by developing homes of piety and purity that would produce a happy home life for the family.

Her book became an immediately popular success that was often used as a textbook. It went through dozens of reprintings in the next three decades. Beecher set out the proper protocol for every household activity, recommending which rooms should be used for what, and laying out the ideal house in the process. She pushed for large houses with parlors, dining rooms, separate sleeping areas, and indoor plumbing including privies. Beecher even included plans for houses in her book, and had five chapters on yards and gardens.

Beecher subsequently wrote articles for *Harper's New Monthly Magazine*, and among other books she co-wrote with her sister Harriet (in 1869) *The American Women's Home, or the Principles of Domestic Science*. In all her writings Beecher stressed the division of husband and wife into homecare (women) and the business life (men). Women could best achieve the goal of providing a proper, restful home life for the family with a house in the suburbs. Women followed her counsel, which had a sense of the proper god-fearing life about it. It was another supporting element in the move to the suburbs.

1841 (Downing)— In the same year that Catherine Beecher wrote her semi-religious book *Treatise on Domestic Economy* (see listing above), a landscape architect named Andrew Jackson Downing published the first American book about landscape gardening. His *Treatise* on the subject, which would go through eight editions and 16 printings in the next four decades, was another literary push favoring houses in the suburbs, but only if they were properly landscaped per his instruction.

Downing had inherited a nursery operation from his father, but its failure in 1847 almost drove him into bankruptcy. His landscaping work and his writings eventually made him solvent, and he featured the English cottage and the villa in his housing plans. He became the editor of a journal of rural art and good taste called *The Horticulturist*, and in 1850 he wrote *The Architecture of the Country House*. This book, which was reprinted nine times, expressed the idea that the nuclear family "was the best social form," and thus the "individual home has a great social value" for a nation. The home, of course, was best placed in the countryside.

October 12, 1842— After decades of complaints about the quality of the water in New York City, the New York state legislature in 1834 authorized the city to plan an aqueduct and water distribution system. On October 12, 1842, a day celebrated by parades and the ringing of church bells, the city system bringing water from the Croton River was officially opened.

The new system not only improved the quality of the drinking water but also the quantity. This permitted the installation of more flush toilets, and in three years more connections to the city sewers were permitted. This was followed by the construction of more sewers. It was a typical story in many cities of the time, but often there was a longer gap between the introduction of improved water supplies and the construction of improved sewage systems.

New York City reached a population of over 500,000 in 1850, three times larger than the next most populous city (Baltimore). New York grew nearly seven times larger by 1900, achieving a population of 3.5 million after its 1898 annexation of nearby suburbs (especially Brooklyn). An influx of immigrants, led by the Irish fleeing their potato famine in the 1850s, also contributed to the much higher city population in 1900. This immigrant influx, together with the shift of the national population to the cities following 1820 (when the Industrial Revolution arrived), led to desperate attempts to house the growing population. This created the tenement abuses of the second half of the nineteenth century. Other cities had similar problems, but those in New York City were by far the greatest, and the city became the model for the rest of the nation in trying to correct these tenement problems.

July 27, 1844— The Long Island Railroad opened a train run to Boston by way of Long Island and a steamboat transfer back to the mainland at Stonington, Connecticut. The line was successful, and the Long Island Railroad began to establish commuter runs for suburbs well away from New York City. Railway suburbs were soon appearing everywhere offering comfortable (but expensive) commuting to New York and other cities. This was another major step in transportation innovations that supported the concept of moving to the suburbs of major cities while commuting to work and shopping in the cities.

1852— Alphonse Loubar developed a grooved rail that lay flush with the pavement on which it was installed. This was a major innovation in that previous attempts to lay rails on which horse-drawn vehicles could be run resulted in rails that protruded six inches above street level and greatly interfered with other traffic. The use of rails on which coaches could run was an obvious way to combine the best features of the railroad and the omnibus (see entry for 1829), but the protruding rails were an untenable problem until 1852.

Three years later in 1855, the horsecar was beginning to replace the omnibus on the major routes in New York City. Horsecars offered a much smoother and faster ride than the omnibus, and by the 1860s the horsecar was expanding to other cities in the United States (and around the world). Larger vehicles holding 30 or 40 passengers could be pulled by a single horse on the low-friction rails (the omnibus typically held only 12 passengers), and the higher speed permitted longer commutes into more distant suburbs, a fact quickly noted by real estate developers.

By 1860 there were 142 miles of track in Manhattan and horsecar ridership was up to about 100,000 per day or 36 million per year. Upper Manhattan was now accessible to commuters to an extent that initially slowed the steam ferry exodus to Brooklyn (see entry for 1814). Further, the horsecar permitted the first truly integrated transportation system in the United States. The horsecars permitted rapid service radiating from the center of a city. Passengers could use omnibuses to go cross-town, the steam ferries permitted travel across nearby waterways, and the steam railroads permitted longer distance travel.

By the mid–1880s, 415 street railway companies in the United States were operating 6,000 miles of track and carrying about 188 million passengers per year. All of these operations were contributing to the developments of suburbs in the cities in which they were based.

1854— The City of Philadelphia consolidated its major suburbs into one large city within the boundaries of Philadelphia County. In percentage terms, it still stands as the largest such consolidation in American history (a consolidation involves the absorption of one municipal government by another, whereas an annexation involves the addition of unincorporated land around a city into the city).

Philadelphia grew from an area of 2 square miles to 130 square miles, and quadrupled its population in one stroke. In this way the city greatly benefited from the prior growth of its suburbs, but of course new suburbs immediately began to grow around the newly consolidated city. At the time, the consolidation made Philadelphia the largest city in the world in terms of area, but this distinction lasted for only five years. Philadelphia would never add to its area again, and in fact would lose a few square miles after 1950.

1856— Llewellyn S. Haskell, a wealthy drug merchant, completed with eight partners the accumulation of about 400 acres of property on a slope of the Orange Mountains in northern New Jersey, about 13 rail miles from New York City. The Delaware, Lackawanna, and Western Railroad provided an easy commute to the city and its numerous steam ferries. Haskell then proceeded to build what could be called the first truly picturesque suburb in the United States. The site of what he called Llewellyn Park was heavily wooded with rolling hills and sparkling streams plus a beautiful view of Manhattan.

Haskell had selected Alexander Davis Jackson to prepare the site plan. Jackson was a known architect of the time who had designed many palatial homes for wealthy patrons, including one for Edwin Clark Litchfield in Brooklyn (see listing for 1814). Davis was a close friend of Andrew Jackson Downing (see listing for 1841), and Haskell considered Davis to be the "Michelangelo of his time."

Llewellyn Park featured two new elements in its design: curvilinear roads and a natural open space of 50 acres at its center. Only residences (no industrial activities) were permitted, and these had lots that averaged more than three acres. No fences were permitted in order to maintain the view. Only the wealthy could afford to live there, a circumstance that remains true today. Architect Davis moved there after his retirement, and famous inventor Thomas A. Edison lived there for most of his active life. Llewellyn Park was also the first known development to feature a gatehouse to keep out nonresidents, an item that became common in the United States as more planned developments for the wealthy emerged in subsequent years.

1857— Calvert Vaux, who had become a close friend and partner of Andrew Jackson Downing (see listing for 1841) in 1850, near the end of Downing's life, published a book titled *Villas and Cottages* based on work he had done with Downing. The work contained 39 designs for houses that had been built in the Hudson River Valley in New York. Vaux, born in England, became a major influence on suburban architecture in the United States after 1850. He collaborated with the famous Frederick Law Olmsted in 1856 on the design of Central Park in New York City, and later collaborated with others on the design of various parks and museums in New York and Chicago.

Vaux especially disliked the formal gridiron plan of the layout of many new communities. He pushed for more imaginative designs. Vaux, together with Downing and Beecher (see listings for 1841) had much to do with ultimately turning suburbs from the less desirable areas they had been at the turn of the century into places that were far more attractive for living than the congested and dirty cities.

August 27, 1860 — Frederick Law Olmsted, the nation's prime landscape architect in the middle of the nineteenth century, designed Central Park in New York City and much of the grounds of the U.S. Capitol. He was greatly in favor of green spaces in cities, but not of the movement to the suburbs per se, and he issued a warning in a letter to a friend that proved to be an accurate vision of the suburban growth to come in the United States even up to today.

Olmsted foresaw that if no attempt was made to improve the cities, and people just left them for the suburbs, then the decay of the cities would eventually move out to the suburbs. The elegant villas being built on what were then the edges of New York City, primarily to the north of Manhattan, to escape the squalor of the city, would themselves by ultimately invaded by that same squalor as the city continued to be left behind by its citizens who also wanted to escape their unpleasant living conditions. The fashionable villas would go up for sale, but the only buyers would be those who wanted to build public housing. The properties would inevitably deteriorate, and it would turn out that the property risk in terms of value would be as great as if the owners had remained in their decaying neighborhoods in the city. Olmsted noted that this problem was not only occurring in New York City, but in the suburbs of Brooklyn (then a separate city from New York), Jersey City, and on to the suburbs of Philadelphia and Boston.

Today, nearly 150 years later, many so-called inner ring suburbs that once drew inhabitants from the inner city have become rundown and unfashionable. Olmsted could not foresee the development of zoning laws and horizontal suburbs (edge cities) that would seal off or no longer surround inner cities, but many conventional suburbs that surround inner cities have fallen into undesirable status, and the central cores of their inner cities have become third-world cities. This effect was most notable in the suburbs surrounding

Boston, Cleveland, Pittsburgh, Detroit, and St. Louis in the 1970s, with the inner first ring of 21 suburbs surrounding Detroit losing 19 percent of their population between 1970 and 1990, a net loss of nearly 170,000 people. The city of Detroit lost 32 percent of its population or 486,000 people in the same time, but the first ring decline showed that Detroit's closest suburbs were declining along with their original inner city.

May 20, 1862— The Homestead Act of 1862 was written by Congress and soon signed into law by President Abraham Lincoln. This piece of legislation was later called one of the most important in the history of the United States. It ultimately made available 270 million acres of public domain land (10 percent of the area of the United States) to private citizens to be claimed and settled. The passage of the act was made possible by the secession of the southern states due to the Civil War and the resulting absence of their lawmakers in Congress.

Under the law, a homesteader had only to be the head of a household and at least 21 years of age to file a claim on a 160-acre parcel of land. To "prove up" their claim, they had to live on the land for five years, building a home, making improvements, and farming the land. Total filing fees of only $18 was all the money required, and two neighbors who would vouch for the homeowner at the end of the five-year "proving-up" period were all that was additionally needed to receive ownership of the land.

Of course, five years of hard work and sacrifice were also involved, but the homesteader could become a landowner, something out of the question for many immigrants in their home country of origin. Subsequent applicants included many such newly arrived immigrants, but also farmers without land of their own in the crowded East, single women, and newly freed slaves, all of whom saw the chance of a lifetime to own property.

The Homestead Act remained in force until 1976 (1986 in Alaska). When it was finally repealed, very little land was left in the West for homesteading. The Taylor Grazing Act of 1934 substantially ended homesteading in the United States except for Alaska. However, after the act was initially passed in 1862, a series of land runs or rushes took place in the United States to claim the previously public lands. The most famous of these was probably the Oklahoma Land Run of 1889 (see listing).

1867— The New York Tenement Law of 1867 was enacted. It was one of the first housing codes in the United States. It applied only to New York City, but as New York had by far the largest tenement facilities in the nation, it became a model for all other cities with large tenement installations.

The law became known as the Old Law to differentiate it from new laws enacted in 1879 (and amendments in 1888 and 1889) and especially in

1901. Each new law was somewhat more stringent than the one before, but a law with real teeth and substantial changes (including indoor plumbing) was not established until the law of 1901 (see listing).

The Lower East Side of Manhattan was most famous — or infamous — for its incredibly crowded tenements. The area was originally laid out from farmland in the late 18th century into lots 25 feet wide by 100 feet deep. This was very suitable for the single-family row homes that were built on the lots in the early 1800s. But as New York dramatically increased in population in the 1840s and 1850s due to the arrival of immigrants, the homeowners moved to the more fashionable north of Manhattan. Builders then began to convert the single family homes into dwellings for multiple families, including buildings five to six stories high meant for 20 families or more on the 25 × 100 foot lots.

The influx of Irish fleeing the potato famine and Germans fleeing the German Revolution of 1848 drove the population of New York to increase by 65 percent in the 1840s (from 312,710 to 515,547) and 58 percent in the 1850s (from 515,547 to 813,669). Both groups settled in the Lower East Side, the Germans occupying an area that became known as Kleindeutschland ("Little Germany"). As early as 1843, the Association for Improving the Conditions of the Poor described these early tenements as defective in many ways, including size and arrangement, water supply, warmth and ventilation, with yards, sinks, and sewage in generally bad condition. Similar surveys in 1864 by an activist group called the Council of Hygiene and Public Health found that 495,592 people lived in tenements in New York City. This was more than half the population of the entire city. In the Lower East Side, the population density was 240,000 people per square mile, which the council proclaimed to be probably the highest level in history to that point.

A typical five story tenement housed 20 families in three-room apartments laid out four to a floor, two in front and two in back. Reached by an unlighted, wooden staircase running through the center of the house (it was at least a source of ventilation), the average apartment contained only about 325 square feet for the seven or more people occupying the three rooms (only one of which was officially designated a bedroom). The front room of each apartment was the sole room that received light and ventilation, although some bedrooms had casement windows opening into the hallway. There was no toilet, shower, or bath, nor for that matter necessarily any water supply running directly into the apartment. The "privies" for each building were located in the back yard, and may or may not have been connected to a local sewer, depending on the situation.

The 1867 law required at least one privy per 20 people with connection to a local sewer as available. It also required one three-foot square transom over each interior bedroom door for light and ventilation. A subsequent law in 1879, as amended in 1888 and 1889, required all rooms to have access to air, and required flush toilets in the back yard with individual compartments to which each tenant had a key for his particular compartment. More substantial changes (including indoor plumbing) came with the law of 1901 (see listing).

1868— The famous architect and historian Frederick Law Olmsted, who is primarily credited with the development of Central Park in New York City in 1856, started the development of Riverside near Chicago. Olmsted was probably the most known landscape artist in the United States in the period after the Civil War. Olmsted was basically a protégé of Andrew Jackson Downing (see listing for 1841), and was partnered at Riverside with Calvin Vaux (see entry for 1857), who had collaborated with Olmsted in the building of Central Park.

Riverside was nine miles west of State Street, a major artery in Chicago, and was the first suburban station on the Chicago, Burlington, and Quincy railroad. Many suburbs were being developed near Chicago at the time due to the large number of railroads that were running into Chicago as the nation's basic train hub. But Riverside was intended to be the crown jewel of them all. Emery E. Childs headed a group of Eastern investors that created the Riverside Improvement Company in 1868 and gave Olmsted and Vaux the freedom to develop the ideal suburb.

The 1600-acre site featured curvilinear roads rather than the gridiron design, and had large lots and many other special features. Olmsted had planned a limited access highway to Chicago to permit an easy carriage commute to compete with the railroad, but he could not obtain approval from the necessary officials outside Riverside. In essence the development was an artistic but not a financial success. The great Chicago Fire of 1871 and the rebuilding of the city absorbed all available funds in the area. The financial panic of 1873 then produced bankruptcy for the Riverside Improvement Company. Olmsted, who later became a great critic of what he saw as unplanned suburban development and the neglect of cities, felt Riverside represented the proper attempt to create suburbs that would function as an urban compromise with the city.

August 7, 1869— The magazine *Harper's Weekly* carried an article about the competitive bidding for almost 9,000 acres of land available near the town of Hempstead on Long Island, about 20 miles east of New York City. The winning bidder turned out to be millionaire Alexander T. Stewart, whose huge dry-goods store built in 1846 at the corner of Broadway and Chamers streets in New York City is often thought to be the world's first department store.

Stewart and his architect, John Kellum, developed a housing tract named Garden City on the site. Stewart built a railroad spur at his own expense to the nearby Long Island Railroad to ease the commute to New York City (and to increase the value of the land). Stewart also knew that the high price of commuting by rail (about a dollar a day) would restrict his development to the well to do rather than the working class.

Garden City was laid out in gridiron style, but there were a number of natural features incorporated to break up the gridiron in many places. The most notable feature of Garden City was the size of its streets and individual lots. They were about five times the typical size of a New York City or Brooklyn block in terms of the area enclosed.

But another departure from normal proved to be the undoing of the development. Stewart decided to lease the houses on an annual basis rather than sell them. He wanted to control the admission of residents to his development to be sure there was no decay in the community due to persons of what he considered poor character. The plan did not succeed, and the death of Stewart in 1876 foreclosed any possibility of turning the development around. By the 1890s only thirty leased homes existed in Garden City, and it was not until houses were offered for sale that the community began to grow.

May 20, 1871— Reflecting the tenor of the times, an advertisement in the *Louisville Courier* noted that land for sale was a "Splendid opportunity for speculative investment. No other locality promises to be so profitable." In this era of the nineteenth century, speculation in real estate was unusually high as the mounting pressure of the flight to the suburbs made speculators of even common working people.

October 1871— The Grand Central Terminal in New York City began operation. This marked the beginning of a mass exodus of businessmen from New York City to the suburbs, where they exchanged well-kept lawns and opulent residences for the hurly burly of the city. By 1898, major (and minor) passenger railroads were discharging 118,000 commuters per day into Grand Central Station. The suburbs boomed around New York City as they did in other railroad commuter cities such as Philadelphia, Chicago, and Boston. Most of these suburbs featured upper class and wealthy residences that clustered in close proximity to their specific railroad station. Such suburbs reached their peak around 1920 when travel by automobile began to replace travel by train.

October 8, 1871— A blaze that became known as the Great Chicago Fire of 1871 started rather innocently about 9 P.M. on this Sunday evening, in a cow barn at the rear of a cottage occupied by the Patrick O'Leary family at 137 DeKoven Street. The stories about Mrs. O'Leary's cow kicking over the milking lantern notwithstanding, no one is sure how the fire started, but by the time it had spread across Chicago the following Monday, 300 people were dead, 90,000 were homeless, and property losses totaled about $200 million.

Fires originating in the poorer sections of big cities have been with us since the time of the Roman Empire, and Chicago had averaged about two fires a day during the year before the great fire, including 20 fires in the preceding week. It had been a very dry summer, and a strong wind drove the fire straight into the center of the city, where it split unpredictably into several parts and burned through a good part of Chicago during Monday. By early Tuesday morning some rain began to fall and helped extinguish the fire.

To some extent, the danger of fires was a natural hazard of living in the city, especially where there was much flammable debris spread about some parts of the city, and even many streets, sidewalks, and bridges were made of wood (as they were in Chicago). But the Chicago Fire of 1871 was on a much larger scale than had been seen before, and it would not be until the San Francisco earthquake of 1906 and the fire that followed it (see listing) that losses on such a level would be seen again.

The so-called burned district encompassed an area about four miles long and an average of about three-quarters of a mile wide. That came to about two thousand acres and included 18,000 buildings and roughly a third of the property valuation of the entire city. About one-half of the loss was insured, but the financial collapse of many insurance companies after the fire cut the actual insurance payments to a half of their face value. Ironically, the O'Leary cottage was found safe and sound standing in front of the ashes of its burned-out cow barn. The final estimate of the loss of life of less than 300 was considered relatively small, when it was considered that there was a fire in rural Peshtigo, Wisconsin (near Green Bay), the same night that killed about 1,500 people, the greatest loss of life in America due to a fire.

Also notable were the parts of Chicago that did not burn. The famous stockyards and other heavy industry were generally south or west of the burn area and were untouched. Railroad depots downtown were consumed, but the rail infrastructure was generally unharmed. With Chicago still at the center of railroad connections and thus markets, the city was rebuilt by 1875 with little remaining evidence, if any, of the great fire of four years before. The city went to great lengths to encourage investors in such places as New York to get in on the ground floor of opportunities that were opened by the rebuilding process, and many investors did so. The result was a rather quick — and nearly complete — recovery from the Great Chicago Fire of 1871.

1874— Merchant John Wanamaker of Philadelphia bought an old rail freight depot at 13th and Market streets in downtown Philadelphia. He began developing a new kind of store with low prices, departmental organization, money-back guarantees, and large-scale advertising. Others of the time tried similar approaches, but Wanamaker took them to the extreme while depending on the successive transportation developments of the era to bring him customers from the suburbs and return them home again. The development of the trolley (see entry for February 2, 1888) was what he needed to put him over the top. By 1900 Wanamaker's Department Store was the commercial heart of downtown Philadelphia, and others in other big cities were copying his success by making major use of the trolley. No single development did more to tie city and suburb together until the ascendancy of the automobile in the 20th century.

1879— Henry George published his historical book *Progress and Poverty*, which sold millions of copies all over the world, and caught the attention of George Bernard Shaw and Leo Tolstoy abroad. George felt that the solution to the problem of ongoing prosperity for land developers and other capitalists among the ongoing poverty of ordinary wage earners was a single tax on land. This tax would raise enough to run the government with enough left over to help everyone.

George spent the rest of his life writing and lecturing on the single tax and similar reform issues. He ran for mayor of New York City in 1886 on a reformist platform with a single tax program, but he lost the election, finishing behind the Tammany Hall candidate, Abraham Hewitt, but ahead of Republican candidate Theodore Roosevelt. In 1897 he planned to run again, but died just before the election. *Progress and Poverty* was rated one of 13 books that changed America, according to Eric Goldman in the *Saturday Review* in 1953, but the specific idea of a single tax on land never was realized.

1882— Demonstrating how the actions of land developers drove the flight to the suburbs in the nineteenth century, Samuel Eberly Gross of Chicago, in just two years ending in 1882, laid out 40,000 lots, developed 16 towns and 150 subdivisions, and built and sold more than 7,000 houses. Following the same principle of the saying that stocks and bonds are not bought, they are sold, the suburbs bloomed in the nineteenth century not because buyers happened to pass that way, but because the suburbs were developed and aggressively sold to potential buyers by speculative real-estate developers.

1883— The city of Philadelphia opened its first cable car system. The cable car was yet another form of urban transportation that helped commuters reach the suburbs. It had been developed in the 1870s in San Francisco by Andrew Smith Hallifield, who adopted the English coal mining technique of moving coal cars by attaching them to a large cable. This system seemed an ideal way to get cable cars to climb the high, steep hills of San Francisco by grasping a large underground cable.

The system was soon copied by other cities like Philadelphia, Chicago, and New York. The cable car reached its peak by 1890 with 283 miles of track in operation in 23 cities nationally, with a total of 373 million passengers being carried per year. The cable car system used a steam engine to continuously operate the underground cable to which cars, operating in tracks as did the horsecar (see entry for 1852), were attached by a grip to move along the street.

The advantage of eliminating the horse required for the horsecar was soon outweighed by the large initial cost needed to install the underground cable, and the inefficiencies of the cable. These included only one speed of operation at all times, and occasional difficulties in disconnecting from the master cable. The cable car soon faded due to competition from the trolley (see listing for February 2, 1888).

1886— Pierre Lorillard IV, whose great-grandfather founded P. Lorillard and Company (the oldest tobacco company in the United States), used his family fortune to complete Tuxedo Park on his family's land in the town of what would become Tuxedo. The name was derived from the name "Tucseto" which Indians had given to the largest lake in the area. Tuxedo Park was 40 miles north of New York City and west of the Hudson River.

Lorillard and architect Bruce Price used about 1,800 Italian and Slovakian laborers to build about twenty miles of roads, a gate, a clubhouse, and three dams in what was essentially a resort that attracted a number of the financial, industrial, and social leaders of New York City of the time. Over the next thirty years more than 250 houses and stables were built in Tuxedo Park, together with what we would now call infrastructure. But the millionaires resort suffered greatly with its residents in the stock market crash of 1929, and slowly declined thereafter, although the town still remains alive today.

Many people think of Tuxedo Park as the first gated community to exist in the United States, but that distinction belongs to Llewellyn Park, New Jersey, completed in 1856 (see listing). Tuxedo Park still has its gatehouse and a private police force to provide security for the residents who do live there today. According to *Forbes Magazine* of November 2004, about 10 percent of houses built in the United States before 2000 that cost upward of $500,000 were situated in gated communities. But for houses built between 2000 and 2003, the number jumps to 17 percent. People who can readily afford it will pay a high price for security.

Some critics complain about the homogeneity and exclusion of gated communities, but others reply that the doormen in certain apartment buildings in Manhattan achieve the same effect. Apartment buildings on the Upper East Side, for example, are just as exclusive as any gated community, or maybe more so, and the doormen at these apartment buildings serve the same function as do the gatekeepers in gated communities. People of all origins live in these buildings, as is the case in gated communities. Their prime common bond is that they are very wealthy and can afford to pay to be effectively left alone.

Tuxedo Park has two other distinctions, one much better known than the other. First, many people would guess correctly that Tuxedo Park gave its name to the tuxedo or the dinner jacket. Originally created for the Prince of Wales (who became King Edward VII), the idea of the English dinner jacket was brought to Tuxedo Park by James Potter, who happened to be a friend of the Prince of Wales. In the highly closed and artificial atmosphere of Tuxedo Park (a perfect example of the Gilded Age of the end of the nineteenth century in the United States), the first Autumn Ball at the Tuxedo Club in October 1886 featured the introduction of dinner jackets (satin in this case) that eventually replaced the traditional white tie and tails as the appropriate dress for highly formal occasions. The dinner jacket became known as the tuxedo after its debut in Tuxedo Park.

Second, Tuxedo Park was the residence of Alfred Loomis in 1940, a multimillionaire investment banker who was also a talented amateur scientist. Loomis was known among serious scientists of the world for the private laboratory he built in Tuxedo Park in the 1920s. On September 29, 1940, a group of scientists, including two from Britain, gathered in the mansion owned by Loomis in Tuxedo Park. The two British scientists had come to show the then top-secret cavity magnetron, a key element in developing radar systems to defend Britain from German bombers. Loomis, who had been conducting private studies in the area, and who had influential friends in Washington who in turn had the ear of President Roosevelt, became the prime mover in establishing the MIT Radiation Laboratories at the Massachusetts Institute of Technology. Many historians feel the work done there on radar played a bigger role in winning World War II than the much more famous atomic bomb.

Loomis essentially had nothing to do with the Radiation Laboratories after providing the impetus to get them started, but none of his wealthy neighbors had any idea of the key part he played in World War II. It was perhaps going from the frilly to the sublime in terms of the historical significance of Tuxedo Park, but few knew of the part Loomis played compared to the history of the Tuxedo. Among the frilly elements connected with Tuxedo Park was the fact that the daughter of Bruce Price, the architect of

Tuxedo Park, was named Emily Price. She became known as Emily Post, the name she assumed to write her famous books on etiquette.

February 8, 1887—The Dawes Allotment (Severalty) Act attempted to facilitate the assimilation of Native American Indians into white culture by applying a version of the Homestead Act of 1862 (see listing) to Indian tribal lands. But by attacking a central tenet of Indian tradition, i.e., common ownership of tribal lands, the act ultimately failed to achieve its objectives as do most well-meaning laws that seek to overturn ancient traditions in the name of the greater good of assimilation.

The prime effect of the act turned out to be the reduction of Indian tribal holdings from 138 million acres in 1887 to 78 million by 1900. Most of the lost acreage was deemed as surplus and opened to sale to non–Indians, including homesteaders. This essentially set the stage for the Oklahoma Land Run of 1889 (see listing).

March 6, 1887—The price of a promotional train ticket from the East and Midwest to Los Angeles plunged to exactly one dollar as part of a fare war between the new Santa Fe Railroad and the established Southern Pacific Railroad. It was part of a real estate boom in Los Angeles, and the two railroads were competing to carry customers to the Los Angeles area. People were coming to settle in the area as a result of intense promotion by the Santa Fe Railroad, and speculators, who had most recently been profiteering in Iowa and Kansas and who smelled money to be made anew in California, were also pouring into the region.

The boom peaked during the summer of 1887, but not before carrying over to San Diego, 120 miles to the south of Los Angeles, where the number of registered businesses tripled between 1886 and 1887, as did the price of land. Unusually heavy rains and floods during the rainy season brought the boom to an end by the spring of 1888, but in the long run it was more like a pause in the rush to speculate in Southern California real estate than an end (see Henry Huntington listing for 1901).

February 2, 1888—Franklin J. Sprague successfully ran streetcars powered by electricity over his electrified test system in Richmond, Virginia. Sprague had previously worked with Thomas Edison in his laboratories at Menlo Park, New Jersey, where a test model of an electrified streetcar was operated. But Edison at the time was more interested in electric street lighting than transportation. Sprague left Edison in 1884 to form his own company.

Others had tried electrified streetcars, especially after the development of the electric motor and the alternator in Germany by the late 1870s. But there were problems with an 1885 system tested in Baltimore (named the Ampere) in that small animals were often electrocuted by the third rail supplying the crucial electricity connection. Other systems tried in Cleveland and Alabama about the same time failed for other reasons. Sprague operated an experimental system in New York City, then contracted with the city of Richmond in 1887 to provide a system for the entire city.

Sprague's system used a small four-wheeled carriage that provided electrical power to the cars using a flexible connection to an overhead cable. This carriage was called a troller, and the word was corrupted in trolley, and that became the popular name for the electrified streetcar. The trolley would revolutionize urban-suburban travel, and would produce an even greater surge in real estate housing development in the suburbs than had all of the prior transportation developments up to then.

Spague's initial test system used 12 miles of track and forty streetcars. In the summer of 1888, officials from the Boston streetcar (horsecar) system, which had 2,000 cars and 8,000 horses, came to Baltimore to visit Sprague's system. They were considering replacing their horsecars, and especially the horses that pulled them while leaving tons of manure behind, with a cable car system (see entry for 1883). The officials were impressed with Sprague's system, but decided against it in discussions among themselves because they feared it could not handle the overload if a traffic jam resulted in putting all of the cars on the line out on the road at once.

Spague heard about the objections, and assembled all of the Richmond cars together at night after the line had ceased operating for the day. He got the Boston officials out of their hotel to witness that the line could operate with such a load. The officials decided to replace their horsecars with Spague's system. Six months later the horsecars were gone in Boston and the trolley had taken their place. Other cities soon followed Boston's example. By the turn of the century, street railway mileage had passed 22,000 miles (compared with 8,000 in 1890), and only 1 percent was powered by horses (compared to 75 percent in 1890). Sprague was equipping half the electrical systems in use, and 90 percent were using his patents.

The trolley was typically bigger and faster than the horsecar or cable car, and required no major investment in animals, feed, and stables, or in underground cables. It also was cheaper to operate and the typical fare was soon reduced to five cents. Where the horsecar required on the order of 100,000 horses nationally to operate in the late 1880s, together with their manure and associated diseases, trolleys required no animal power of any sort. The horsecars quickly disappeared, and the trolley would be the major type of transportation in the cities (and the suburbs) until the automobile and bus took over by 1950.

1889— The city of Chicago annexed about 133 square miles of what are now mostly the far reaches of the South Side of Chicago. At the time, only about 225,000 people lived in the area that was primarily rural in many places. But within 30 years, more than one million people lived in this part of Chicago. Chicago added another 38 square miles by 1930, but after that only small additions occurred before Chicago joined the long list of Midwestern and eastern cities that lost population to the south and far west after 1950.

March 23, 1889— President Benjamin Harrison issued a Proclamation that opened two million acres of unassigned lands in Oklahoma for settlement under the provisions of the Homestead Act of 1862 (see listing). These lands were considered by many to be the best public lands (previously in Indian Territory) now available in the United States, and many groups across the entire United States started planning to make claims. The Homestead Act permitted settlers to receive title after a five-year period of living on and improving the land, and impoverished farmers, common laborers, professional men, and politicians all sought a way to eventually claim ownership of the prime land.

By late spring of 1889, a large number of would-be settlers were camped in Kansas border towns. Other "boomers," as they were called, came from the south and west to camp along the other borders of the Oklahoma Territory. Sites along the Santa Fe Railroad that had been built through the Oklahoma Territory in 1886-87 were considered choice spots as later town sites, and many settlers planned to enter the race by way of the railroad, which cost them dearly in some cases as the Supreme Court later defined this as an illegal entry. Others entered the territory early and hid out until the official time. They were known as "sooners," a nickname later applied to sports teams at the University of Okalahoma.

United States troops were supposed to monitor the run, but they were generally too few in number and too spread out to do the task effectively. At noon on April 22, 1889, an estimated 50,000 people began the rush across the borders of the Oklahoma Territory. Some hardy single women were included, but blacks had to hold back and then come in after the initial rush. All were later known as "eighty-niners." Claimants determined the location of their choice based on surveyors' cornerstone markers, planted a stake indicating their claim, and then rushed to the land office to register their claim.

The day was incredibly chaotic, but within about nine hours, an estimated 11,000 agricultural homesteads were claimed among the two million acres available. The area became officially known as the Oklahoma Territory in 1890, and as other adjoining Indian tribal lands were opened to settlement, the territory became the 46th state of the union — Oklahoma — in

1907. Ironically, only a little over 25 years later, many Okies would lose their land to the Dust Bowl of the Great Depression and begin a forced exodus to California.

1890— The Census of 1890 was the first to observe a generally continuous string of white settlements across the United States from both east to west and north to south. Thus, it was called by many as the census that showed the frontier had disappeared in the United States. The nation was now a settled country, although its overall population density was still quite low and there was plenty of space between settlements for new ones.

January 1, 1892— The federal government officially opened its immigration station on Ellis Island in New York Harbor, just off the coast of New Jersey. Prior to this date, the individual states bore the responsibility for processing immigrants, but as New York was the prime destination of immigrants in this era, the city was overwhelmed and the federal government finally stepped in to help.

Over the years, Ellis Island was enlarged from its original 3.3 acres to 27.3 acres by using landfill from the ballast of ships, the excavations for the New York subway system, and similar places. About eight million immigrants had been processed through New York Harbor prior to the existence of the Ellis Island facility, and another 12 million were processed through Ellis Island from 1892 to 1954 (mostly by 1920), when the job was taken over primarily by the numerous airport arrival facilities throughout the United States.

The Introduction contains substantial detail on the role immigration played in increasing the population of the United States, and accordingly, the role immigration played in increasing the population of New York City and producing a housing crisis and the tenement laws of 1867 and 1901 (see listings) and afterwards. The immigrant flow mostly from Europe into the United States through the nineteenth century has been called the largest mass human migration in the history of the world. Actually, the immigrant flow continued well past 1900, and 1907 was the peak year for Ellis Island, with just over one million immigrants processed. The peak day was on April 17, 1907, with 11,747 immigrants processed.

The first person processed through the Ellis Island facility was a 15-year-old Irish girl named Annie Moore, who happened to be celebrating her 15th birthday at the same time as she entered Ellis Island. She was given a $10 gold Liberty coin (an impressive amount of money for a new immigrant at that time) in recognition of her being the first person to be registered there, probably the most valuable birthday present she received that day. Millions of immigrants later, Ellis Island is a museum that is part of the Statue of Liberty National Monument. The museum attracts two million visitors annually.

June 6, 1892 — Although not as important in the development of the suburbs as the trolley and its variations, elevated trains began operation in
Chicago. The elevated trains were called the "L" in Chicago, and still are.
In New York, they were called the "el," and eventually that designation
became preferred on the East Coast. The elevated train is one form of rapid
transit, while the subway is another. The distinction between mass transit
and rapid is that rapid transit has its own right-of-way and thus is not subject to the traffic jams of regular transportation. However, rapid transit is
limited to transportation along its right-of-way, just like the railroad. In
fact, rapid transit is simply the adaptation of the railroad to operation in the
middle of a city.

The first el in New York City began running in July of 1866. It used
cable-drawn cars, and then steam locomotives, which were objectionable
because of their smoke, but by 1893 the el was carrying a half-million rid-
ers a day. This level of traffic convinced Chicago to try an "L" of its own,
which began operation on this date (June 6, 1892). But what was notable
about the Chicago L was that it became electrified in 1895 (New York did
not do so until 1896). Further, in 1898, Frank Sprague (see entry for February 2, 1888) developed a multi-unit control system for use in electrifying
any kind of train. Every electrified rapid transit system and electrified railway system in the world today uses a variation of Sprague's 1898 system.

1893 — The first subdivision of Chevy Chase, Maryland, a planned community just outside the boundary line of Washington, D.C., opened to residents. Senator Francis G. Newlands planned Chevy Chase as an elegant
suburb of the nation's capital. Senator Newlands quickly grasped the importance of the invention of the electric trolley by Frank Sprague (see entry for
February 2, 1888), and in 1888 Newlands received a charter for his Chevy
Chase Land Company to operate a transit system between Chevy Chase and
the capital.

Newlands went on to develop Connecticut Avenue in the capital, buying land with his associates along the route it would serve as he went. He
sometimes shifted the direction of the route slightly to punish landowners
he felt were holding out for excessive prices for their land. Finally, after completing the glamorous thoroughfare, Newlands deeded it to the nation's capital and the state of Maryland. Then he installed his trolley line along the
avenue to connect his holdings in Chevy Chase to desirable places within
the capital.

His Chevy Chase housing development had restrictions that insured
only prestigious homes would be built within the community. For most of
the rest of the century, Chevy Chase would remain an enclave for the upper
class in the Washington, D.C., area. Senator Newlands was one of the first

of many entrepreneurs who would use their trolley transit franchises to strike it rich in the field of housing development.

1896— The Rural Free Delivery Act greatly improved mail delivery to the suburbs and rural areas, and in only a few years the expansion of mail-order businesses followed. Included in these businesses were a number of companies offering build-it-yourself plans and materials for homes.

June 4, 1896— In the early hours of the morning in the city of Detroit, Henry Ford, a farm boy in the Detroit area who had a mechanical "green thumb" and used this talent to get work in Detroit, knocked down some bricks on the wall of a shed in his backyard, thus making room to get his experimental car (later called a Quadricycle) out of his shed and onto the street. Henry Ford had built his first car.

He sold the car, little more than a motorized bicycle with extra seating, for $200 in the fall and started to build an improved model. Almost exactly seven years later, the Ford Motor Company would be formed (following some earlier failures), and the world would eventually adopt the Model T automobile in 1908 as the first hugely successful mass-produced car. The car would go on to have the greatest effect on American housing of any transportation development, and it would provide the final link between Americans and their much-loved suburbs by the end of the twentieth century.

January 1, 1898— By far the largest consolidation in absolute terms in American history took place when New York City (then the largest city in the nation), Brooklyn (then the fourth largest city), Queens, Staten Island, and what is now known as the Bronx merged together (the largest consolidation in percentage terms happened in Philadelphia in 1854 — see listing). The city of New York grew from 44 square miles to 299 square miles, and the 1890 population of 1.5 million grew to 3.5 million in 1900.

The city of New York grew only slightly in area in the twentieth century, and after reaching a population peak of about 8 million in the 1950–1970 era, the city lost population with the other big cities in the east and mid-west sections of the country as part of the flight to the "sun belt." But thanks to immigrants again surging into New York, the city stopped its population loss in the last two decades after plunging to almost 7 million in 1980. By the turn of the century in 2000, New York was back to slightly more than 8 million inhabitants and slowly growing.

1900— At the end of the nineteenth century, two-thirds of American urban residents were still tenants rather than homeowners, most of them living in

tenements of some sort. The movement of these residents out to the suburbs locally and in distant states, as the population of the cities in the east
and mid-west declined both in relative and absolute terms compared to the
rest of the nation, would become the story of the 20th century.

1901— Henry E. Huntington, a former co-owner of the Southern Pacific
Railroad, formed a land development company in 1901 to exploit the Big
Red Car transit line he assembled between 1890 and 1910. The Big Red Car
lines were basically trolley lines, but the cars were somewhat larger and faster
than the typical trolley, and as they operated primarily between communities rather than just within they were called interurbans.

Huntington's transit operation was named the Pacific Electric Railway
Company, and it operated literally across the entire Los Angeles Basin. The
line was too far flung to make high profits from its basically short-haul passenger business, but it criss-crossed potentially lucrative land developments,
and that was where high profits were available. Huntington's land company
included Moses Sherman and Otis and Harry Chandler, all of whom would
be involved in great land developments in California in the next decade, and
the company selected and promoted various sites, aided by Huntington's
analyses of weekend patronage of his transit lines. This was the beginning
of the Los Angeles sprawl that developed during the 20th century, but the
later land developments that flowed out of Huntington's initial efforts
dwarfed anything that Huntington was able to do (see Harry Chandler entry
for 1905 and the Los Angeles-Owens Valley Bond issue).

April 12, 1901— The Tenement House Act of 1901 brought new changes
to the building of tenements in New York City (and elsewhere after being
widely copied as previous laws in New York City had been — see listing for
1867). The new act required indoor plumbing with one toilet for every two
families (usually 20 families occupied one five story building with four apartments and thus four families per floor). The act also improved natural lighting conditions within the building, essentially outlawed any more tenements
being built on 25 foot-wide lots, and mandated changes to already existing
tenements. The 1901 law became known as the "new law," and a Tenement
House Commission was established to survey conditions in the city's tenements and insure the laws were being appropriately applied.

Landlords objected vigorously to the 1901 law, especially the part requiring indoor plumbing. They went to court, lost at the state level in 1904, and
eventually lost in the United States Supreme Court in 1906. The tenements
were still small and very crowded, but now they had minimally acceptable
levels of sanitation and ventilation. Battles between tenants and landlords
would go on through the rest of the century, and in New York City, which

had more tenants than anywhere else, these battles would go on through rent strikes and rent control issues of higher or lower intensity in a seemingly endless procession.

1903— The combined trolley and real estate operations of F. M. "Borax" Smith in Oakland, California, reached their peak in the year of 1903. Smith had made a fortune selling borax as a cleanser, and he used the proceeds to buy a controlling interest in a number of electric railway companies in the East Bay Area of San Francisco in 1893. Oakland was the largest city in the East Bay, and by 1903 his Oakland Transit Company was operating 75 miles of track and carrying 30 million passengers each year.

Smith had realized early that rather than just operating a trolley line, higher profits were to be made from speculating in real estate developments where land prices rose as transportation developments (such as the arrival of a trolley line) made the land more accessible to population centers. Smith had already built a real estate syndicate that was doing very well because it knew just where new trolley lines would run, thanks to the fact that Smith also owned the trolley service.

In 1903, Smith felt at the peak of his powers and created a commuter trolley line called the Key System. It was intended to take on the powerful Southern Pacific Railroad in the Bay Area. Smith did not expect to make any money from the commuter line, but rather from real estate speculation along the route of the line, as he had done before. But as most such entrepreneurs eventually do, Smith had overreached himself by taking on the Southern Pacific. By 1913 he lost control of his empire in a sea of red ink.

November 1905— The City of Los Angeles successfully passed a bond measure to build a $25 million aqueduct to bring water from the Owens Valley in the Eastern Sierra Mountains to Los Angeles. The 238-mile aqueduct was completed eight years later (see entry for November 5, 1913), but controversy raged around it for decades (and goes on to some extent even today).

Many hands were in the pot of this project, but the prime mover was Harry Chandler of the *Los Angeles Times*. Chandler was born in New Hampshire, but left Dartmouth College there for health reasons before graduating. He came to Southern California in 1883 for the drier climate and got into the newspaper delivery business so effectively he soon controlled the circulation of the *Times* in large parts of the city. In 1894, Chandler married the daughter of Harrison Grey Otis, owner and publisher of the *Los Angeles Times* since 1884.

Chandler headed a syndicate of rich investors (including his father-in-law), assembling over 47,000 acres of land in the San Fernando Valley between

1903 and 1909. The land there was relatively cheap because it lacked a supply of water. Other investors in the syndicate included transportation king Henry E. Huntington (see entry for 1901) and Moses Sherman, who later developed much of Hollywood.

The syndicate, with the help of the *Los Angeles Times*, pressured the city to build the aqueduct to the Owens Valley. They supposedly created a false drought by creative use of rainfall numbers and by emptying water from city reservoirs into its sewers at night and then drawing attention to the low water levels. Facing restrictions on watering their lawns and gardens, voters passed the bond measure on Election Day of 1905.

With the completion of the aqueduct, and the extension of a line for the big red cars of Huntington's Pacific Electric Railway, the land assembled by the syndicate rose in value from less than $3 million to about $120 million. The investors went on to form other syndicates, and Harry Chandler, together with inheriting the *Los Angeles Times*, became the most influential land developer in the state, if not the entire west. The basis of his fortune at his death in 1944 was not the newspaper but rather the land bought in the early 1900s that was annexed into Los Angeles in 1915 (see entry for November 5, 1913).

1906— Burton E. Green formed the Rodeo Land and Water Company, and subdivided 3,200 acres of land north of Santa Monica Boulevard in Los Angeles. In 1914 this development would be the basis for the incorporation of the City of Beverly Hills. This was part of the constant real estate boom in Los Angeles in that era, which made Los Angeles the growth city of the twentieth century in the United States.

April 18, 1906— The city of San Francisco was hit by a massive earthquake at 5:13 A.M., and then was essentially destroyed by a fire caused by the earthquake that burned for four days. Decades later it was estimated that 3,000 people died from all causes in the earthquake and fire, although at the time the estimated death toll was placed at as low as 300. But many victims were trapped in the so-called South-of-Market tenements that collapsed in the earthquake and then immediately caught fire. So it is not surprising that on-the-spot estimates of deaths were hard to make. Property damage was also later estimated at $500 million, more than twice the $200 million caused by the Great Chicago Fire of 1871. Also, 300,000 people were left homeless after the San Francisco earthquake and fire in 1906 compared to 90,000 left homeless after the Chicago fire in 1871 (see listing).

Damaging earthquakes in the United States are generally limited to California northward through Alaska, with by far the most people likely to be affected living in California. San Francisco has been called the "City That

Waits to Die" because it sits almost literally on top of the San Andreas Fault that runs through California from the south to the north and on into the Pacific Ocean just a few miles south of San Francisco. The San Andreas Fault is considered geologically active, and thus a repeat of the 1906 earthquake could occur at any time. However, that fact has little or no effect on people who choose to live in or near San Francisco or the Silicon Valley to the south.

Some of the most expensive housing in the nation is in the San Francisco Bay area and in the Los Angeles area 500 miles to the south, where earthquakes are also common. But there are much better building codes in existence in the state now than there were in 1906, and officials have learned how to respond to the truly few serious earthquakes that occur every generation or so (five deadly earthquakes in the 20th century, for example). There are actually about 5,000 earthquakes yearly in the Los Angeles region that can be measured on the high technology listening equipment now available, but the general public does not feel most of these. Few of the 5,000 cause any damage, even to the extent of a can falling off a grocery shelf.

Earthquakes in California, hurricanes along the Southeast coast, tornadoes in the Midwest, and wildfires and floods in many places are all evidence that people generally pay little or no attention to the occurrence of natural disasters when choosing a place to live. Wildfires and mudslides have caused far more deaths and property damage over the years in California than the much more heralded earthquakes, but the state has grown steadily over time to become by far the most populous state in the nation. Natural disasters are things that happen to someone else.

The San Francisco earthquake of 1906 was felt from Oregon in the north to Los Angeles in the south to mid–Nevada in the east. It affected an area of about 375,000 square miles, about half of which was in the Pacific Ocean to the west of San Francisco. The region of destruction in California ran about 400 miles long by about 25–30 miles on either side of the fault. Many trees near the fault were uprooted or broken off. Many buildings collapsed in the city, and a major aftershock at 8:14 A.M. on April 18 caused the collapse of already damaged buildings. This is typical of large earthquakes, and often results in many deaths among dazed residents who are out and walking around after the initial shock.

Fires continued to ignite and spread throughout the day of April 18. They went on in this fashion through April 20 in spite of the dynamiting of some mansions to attempt to form a firebreak. Firemen were greatly hindered by a lack of water. Finally on April 21, a combination of 3,000 volunteers armed mainly with knapsacks and brooms helped a few firemen stop the fire at 20th and Dolores Streets and began to turn the tide. On the 23rd Governor Pardee announced the beginning of the rebuilding of San Francisco now that the fires and earthquake appeared to be over. Three hundred thousand people were homeless, but the army had been on hand since the beginning and efforts moved rapidly and efficiently to help find shelter for and feed the homeless.

1908 NAR—A National Association of Real Estate Exchanges (NAREE) was formed in Chicago. It became the National Association of Real Estate Boards (NAREB) in 1916, and in 1974 took its present name of the National Association of Realtors (NAR).

The association lobbied for favorable governmental treatment for the real estate industry and won a big victory in the 1920s when home mortgage interest was made deductible from income taxes. This action gave what has become a huge government subsidy to the home building industry in the United States. The National Association of Realtors ultimately became the largest trade association in the United States.

1908 Sears, Roebuck—Sears, Roebuck, and Company, which had been founded in 1886 and became prosperous by doing much business by mail, issued a catalog called "Book of Modern Homes and Building Plans." Sears bought several lumber mills to support its catalog business, and by 1911 also entered the mortgage business to help its customers build their homes. Subsequent analysis suggests the mortgage business was even more profitable than the do-it-yourself house building business. Sears built its business by easy credit, but the crash of 1929 eventually drove Sears out of the business by 1940.

Estimates of the number of houses sold by Sears during its years in the business run from 50,000 to over 100,000 (there were eight million new housing units built in the United States in the 1920s alone). There were enough different models that Sears houses turned up in various places across the nation. Many other companies competed in this market, but the Depression in the 1930s and the shortage of materials during World War II drove many of them out of business. After World War II the mass production companies like the Levitt brothers of Levittown fame (see October 1947 listing) took over.

March 13, 1908—The first circulars describing the new Ford car, the Model T, were sent out to Ford dealers. The new car would be available in October, so the dealers were given plenty of time to clear their stocks of older models. The Model T had many advanced engineering features, but was priced only at $825, a very competitive but not spectacularly low price (it eventually would sell for less than half that price). Orders poured in, and by May of 1909 Ford had to stop accepting new orders because the factory output was committed for the rest of the year.

Henry Ford had deliberately set out to build a car that would be efficient, reliable, and yet cheap enough for the common man to own and operate. He had succeeded on all counts, and now he would turn his attention to learning how to mass-produce the car so he could fill the incoming orders as well as drive the price even lower. He succeeded in meeting that goal by an even greater margin than he at first expected. Ford would almost single handedly make the automobile a ubiquitous part of American life and real estate developments would be built around access by car instead of simply access by trolley.

January 1, 1910— The first formal move into Henry Ford's new Highland Park Plant took place on this date. This was the plant in which Ford perfected the moving assembly line, and where he announced the famous "five dollars a day" wage in 1914. It is hard to over-emphasize how dramatically Ford brought the car to popularity in the United States — and the world. In the sales year of 1923 Ford sold over 2 million cars, accounting for 57 percent of all cars sold in the United States, and about half of all cars sold in the world. When Model T production ceased in 1927, almost 16 million of the cars had been produced, and the price dropped from $950 in 1910 to $290 in 1924. Car ownership had become nearly a necessity for the middle class.

Ford became an almost senile tyrant, and his refusal to change the Model T or listen to any other suggestions from his staff (including his son) nearly ruined his company. General Motors, led by its Chevrolet division, took over the sales lead in cars by offering much more flexibility in its available models by the end of the 1920s and afterwards. But it was Henry Ford who put the nation on wheels and established a relationship between the car and the public that became the main thrust of the flight to the suburbs after the 1920s.

November 5, 1913— The Los Angeles Aqueduct, running 233 miles from the Owens River Valley in the Eastern Sierra Mountains to the San Fernando Valley (then just outside the Los Angeles city limits), held its opening ceremonies after eight years and $25 million were spent in its construction. The chief engineer of the project was William Mulholland, but there were a number of others who pulled the political strings in the background to get the bond issue passed in November of 1905 to begin the project (see entry).

There are numerous stories of deceit and chicanery involved with the aqueduct, but the prime villain in this respect was probably Harry Chandler (see entry for 1905). He used the influence of his father-in-law's ownership of the *Los Angeles Times* to create a phony drought and convince the residents of Los Angeles to pass the bond measure while he and his partners were accumulating land. Their land would soar in value when the project was completed. It was estimated that Chandler's group bought for less than $3 million land in the San Fernando Valley that would later be worth $120 million.

Chandler and his associates went on to use the leverage of the water from the Owens River Aqueduct to greatly increase the area of Los Angeles by annexation, including the "great annexation" of 1915 that essentially tripled the size of the city at the time. The purpose of acquiring all of this land and its water supply was to eventually build row upon row of single-family detached houses in the greater Los Angeles Basin. In later decades, aqueducts were built from the Colorado River to Los Angeles, and from the San Francisco Bay area and the northern California water supply to Los Angeles. The Los Angeles Basin is essentially a desert. Without these water supplies, most of the massive Los Angeles suburbs, and the city itself, would not exist.

1915—A writer named Graham R. Taylor wrote a book that was the first to discuss industrial suburbs. He pointed out that the truck, part of the revolution of vehicles based on the internal combustion engine, was permitting the shifting of factories from the core of cities to the edge of the city. This led to suburbs (eventually called edge cities many decades in the future), where people could both live and work and move within the suburbs with the assistance of the car, which also permitted movement laterally to streetcar lines.

The number of trucks grew from 158,000 in 1915 to 3.5 million in 1930 (and ultimately more than ten times that number later in the century). The ease of movement by truck (eventually including deliveries of goods to one's front door) meant warehousing and distribution centers could also move to the edge of big cities. In this way, trucks played as significant a role in the flight to the suburbs as did the car during the rest of the twentieth century.

1916—An ordnance established in New York City became the first zoning law in the United States. Such laws theoretically served the interest of all citizens by limiting land speculation and congestion. They were meant to preserve residential areas from invasions by industrial properties, and to maintain property values accordingly. But once it was found that zoning laws could serve purposes that were desirable to haves versus have nots, zoning laws spread rapidly across the nation.

By 1926, an additional 76 cities had adopted zoning laws similar to the one in New York City, and by 1936 about 85 percent of all cities (a total of 1,322 cities nationally) had zoning laws. Zoning became a tool to keep poor people and undesirable industries out of areas generally populated by the well-to-do. Accordingly, it also became a tool for the suburbs to keep the areas of the central city they found to be disagreeable from infringing on the suburbs. Even commercial land owners in the core of cities found zoning to be a way of getting permission to build commercial enclaves that were more profitable than any kind of housing would be for the (generally) poor residents of the inner city. Zoning thus became a legal way of segregating people by race and class in terms of where they lived.

March 5, 1917— This was inauguration day for the beginning of President Woodrow Wilson's second term. Wilson was the last president to ride in a carriage to his inauguration; future presidents would ride in cars. Wilson was furious at the railroads on this day because he had signed legislation averting a strike in January that would cripple his planned entry into World War I in April. The strike issue was the eight-hour day, and after it was approved, the railroads had sued in the Supreme Court to block its implementation. Wilson subsequently won in court in March, but he had continuing problems with the arrogant railroads, and he had to seize control of them by the end of 1917 to insure shipment of men and materiel to East Coast ports and thence to Europe.

The automobile industry, on the other hand, was extremely cooperative, and offered to drive over 30,000 trucks being built for the war effort from Detroit to the East Coast ports, even though the roads were hardly adequate for the task. From this time onward, Washington supplied billions of dollars for new roads over the next several decades, while railroads received mostly harsher new regulations. The automobile industry benefited greatly from this governmental support, and Americans found more reasons to buy cars to drive wherever they wanted whenever they wanted. Other forms of mass transit waned, and additional land was opened to home building with the car (and trucks) capable of reaching directly to and between the most distant suburbs.

June 1918— In a significant reversal of prior practice, Congress appropriated $110 million to begin two programs for housing war workers who were being attracted to areas building munitions of all sorts for the war effort (the United States had entered World War I in April of 1917). The two programs, the Emergency Fleet Corporation of the United States Shipping Board and the United States Housing Corporation, were rather late in getting implemented because there was a great dispute in Congress over an action of the government to get involved in the housing market, especially a market that would feature rental units.

Prior to this date, in the history of the country, the issue of housing was considered an individual issue, or at the most, an issue for the states. Because of the late start (the war ended only five months later in November of 1918), only 25,000 units were built under both plans. The houses were later sold to private developers, and by the early 1920s the federal government was out of the housing business. It would not get involved again until the advent of the Great Depression in the 1930s.

1919— Edward Bok retired as editor of the *Ladies' Home Journal* after 30 years at the helm. The magazine had been the most successful magazine in the United States during the early decades of the twentieth century, as well as the most successful in the world. It was the first magazine in the world to reach more than one million subscribers, and by 1919 when Bok retired, the magazine had a circulation over two million. *The Saturday Evening Post*, another member of the powerful magazine combine published by the Curtis Publishing Company, which also published the *Journal*, later surpassed the circulation of the *Journal*. But no magazine had a greater impact on housing design and construction in the first half of the 20th century than the *Journal*.

Since 1895 the *Journal* had been publishing plans for new houses costing from $1,000 to $5,000. The houses featured a new developing style of home in the twentieth century. The old-fashioned parlor and front porch were being eliminated, and even the wealthy were adopting new styles to respond to the tendency towards servantless homes. The suburbs had greater space available for suburban living, and the growing use of the car with which people could move around gave less importance to the basic design of the home. Frank Lloyd Wright and his followers emphasized one-story homes with low-slung roofs, with a return to basic simplicity, culminating in his prairie house (leading to the ranch house of the following decades). All of these styles and ideas were carefully chronicled by the house plans shown in the *Ladies' Home Journal* from the turn of the century onward.

Entire colonies of *Ladies' Home Journal* houses sprang up around the nation. By 1919 the bungalow had become popular as an unpretentious dwelling one-and-a-half stories in size that still seemed horizontal in design and reflected the larger average size of building lots. The basic unit contained about 800 square feet and was in easy reach of the middle class. Plans were available from advertisers for one dollar per package.

At first architects complained that the *Journal* was taking the bread out of their mouths, but finally Stanford White was quoted as saying in 1906 that Bok "has more completely influenced American domestic architecture for the better than any man in his generation." Even former President Theodore Roosevelt said approvingly, "Bok is the only man I ever heard of who changed, for the better, the architecture of an entire nation, and he did it so quickly and so effectively that we didn't know it was begun before it was finished." Few people today recall the impressive contribution made by

Edward Bok and the *Ladies' Home Journal* to the development of housing in the United States in the first half of the twentieth century.

1920— Douglas Fairbanks completed what for a decade or so was the most famous house in California, if not the United States. On the base of an old hunting lodge in what was then the nearly wilderness area of Beverly Hills, not far from downtown Los Angeles, Fairbanks and his architect built Pickfair, a home for himself and his wife, Mary Pickford. They were essentially the king and queen of Hollywood at the time, and Pickfair was their castle (supposedly with the first private swimming pool in Los Angeles).

Over the next dozen years, famous visitors including Prince George of Britain dined at Pickfair, but President Coolidge declined Mary Pickford's offer in 1927 to use Pickfair as a summer White House. Alas, fairy tales do not fare well in the real world, and trouble surfaced between Fairbanks and Pickford in the early 1930s, and they split up in 1936. For the next three decades, Pickford reigned alone over a series of charity picnics. She died in 1979, and Jerry Buss, owner of the Los Angeles Lakers, bought Pickfair in 1981. By then, much more grand mansions had arisen in Beverly Hills, and the probate judge who approved of a sales price of just over $5 million, marked down from $10 million, observed that "it must be a tear-down."

By 1990 termites were in residence at Pickfair, and the house was indeed a teardown. Subsequent owners built other mansions on the site, confirming that in California real estate (as elsewhere), the house is nothing and the land is everything. Will Rogers, the famous humorist of the 1920s and 1930s, happened to be the first mayor of Beverly Hills, and he joked that the biggest part of his job was telling tourists how to get to Pickfair. Rogers died in an airplane crash in 1935, and Pickfair as a magic castle expired not long after.

1922 HOSI— Architects Donn Barber and Whitman S. Wick of the Home Owner's Service Institute (HOSI) were sponsored by the Better Homes in America organization to build a modern replica of a seventeenth-century home on public grounds near the White House in Washington, D.C. The rise of do-it-yourself homes (see listings for Sears, Roebuck in 1908 and Edward Bok in 1919) attracted the attention of regular architects who felt the homes were poorly designed and who felt they were missing out on potential fees. Among other organizations, architects founded the Home Owner's Service Institute.

Marie Meloney, editor of *The Delineator*, a magazine for women with a circulation of over one million, founded the Better Homes in America organization. The house chosen for replication was the birthplace of John Howard Payne, who wrote the sentimental ballad "Home Sweet Home" in 1822. The song contained the classic line, "Be it ever so humble, there's no place like home." Politicians (supposedly originally Herbert Hoover) used the slogan, "Nobody sings songs about a pile of rent receipts" to promote home ownership campaigns. Ironically, Payne wrote the song while he was in Europe in 1822, and he lived most of his life abroad.

It happened that Herbert Hoover chaired the National Advisory Council for the Better Homes in America organization while he was secretary of commerce, and he had business in mind as well as helping the Republican Party woo women voters who had voted for the first time in 1920. Construction of housing was a big business in the 1920s, and it was the collapse of the construction industry that led to many New Deal programs in the 1930s, including the creation of the Federal Housing Administration (FHA). The FHA was the most significant and substantial single program assisting housing during the rest of the twentieth century.

1922 Nichols— Jesse Clyde Nichols began the housing development known as the Country Club District in Kansas City. The district would eventually contain 6,000 homes and 160 apartment buildings with 35,000 residents. Nichols was estimated to have built as much as 10 percent of all the homes in the Kansas City area in a career that ran from 1906 through 1953. His prime achievement was the Country Club District, which featured curving roads, large lots and expensive homes. It was considered the prime place to live in Kansas City, and made a major contribution to the claim in the 1930s that Kansas City was one of the most attractive cities in the world.

October 1922— A black-tie dinner for about 200 guests was held in the famous Willard Hotel, just across the street from the White House in Washington, D.C. The dinner was held under the auspices of Thomas H. "Chief" MacDonald, who was chief of the Bureau of Public Roads for the United States. MacDonald had come to Washington to take the position in 1919 when he was 38 years old. He remained in the post for 34 years until he was 72, avoiding mandatory retirement several times because he was so highly regarded by Congress.

From 1919 until 1953, MacDonald was by far the most important figure in the nation in terms of building both federal and state highways. He developed close working relationships with his counterparts in the individual states and representatives of the various manufacturing groups involved in building roads, as well as the automotive industry. MacDonald knew how things worked in Congress, and eventually all members came to depend on his advice on matters to do with road building and road locations. The black-tie dinner in October of 1922 was just one of many events to which members of all these groups were invited to be informed of the actions of the Bureau of Public Roads.

MacDonald's efforts expanded roads across the United States, and helped developed the concept that roads were a key to national security in permitting the rapid movement of troops and equipment to nearly anywhere in the country. This concept was a key to the National Highway Act of 1956 that built a network of first-class roads across the nation. The act was also one of the key steps in establishing the automobile (and truck and bus) as the dominant means of transportation in the country, which gave the suburbs their final claim on preferred housing.

1924— The Immigration Act of 1924 essentially marked the end of mass migration to the United States after the huge surge of immigrants in the later 19th century and the beginning of the 20th century before World War I. Quotas were set based on the census of 1890, and total annual immigration was held to 164,000 (down from numbers near one million before World War I). The Immigration Act also provided for the examination and qualification of immigrants at United States consulates overseas.

Legal immigration into the United States today is back near the one million mark annually, although the prime source of immigrants is now Mexico and other countries south of the border of the United States, as well as immigrants from Asia. In the 20th century, the percentage of the population of the United States that is foreign-born peaked near 15 percent in 1910, fell steadily to 4.7 percent in 1970, and then climbed steadily to just over 9 percent by the end of the century.

1925— Writer and sociologist Harlan Douglas (sometimes spelled Douglass), in his book, *The Suburban Trend*, said, "It is the city trying to escape the consequences of being a city while still remaining a city. It is urban society trying to eat its cake and keep it too." Douglas was among those who believed, especially after World War I, that cities were inherently evil places, full of crime and disease and dirt. The suburban trend was the best way to escape the intrinsically dehumanizing effects of the city.

Douglas forecast that less than 15 percent of women would commute to jobs in the city, and would spend most of their time driving their husbands to and from the train station, driving their children to and from school and their music lessons, and driving to and from varied shopping locations. In a sense, as early as 1925, Douglas described the soccer moms that became politically popular at the end of the century. Douglas believed that the decentralization of the suburbs would be far superior to the old-time centralization of the cities.

1926— The future design of Los Angeles was set when voters chose to fund a bond issue to build a massive road system to interconnect the huge suburbs that had grown up around the city and its extensive trolley system (see listing for 1901 and Henry E. Huntington's Big Red Cars in the Pacific Electric Railway Company). At the same time voters declined to also fund a new central rail and trolley station that was proposed as part of a prior plan to eliminate congestion between trolleys and cars by building subway tunnels into the downtown area. These decisions set the stage for the huge freeway systems that would be built in the Los Angeles Basin, and would also greatly limit the growth of downtown.

The voters essentially gave up the biggest mass transit system in the world (in terms of track mileage, which reached 1,114 miles) to favor roads and the automobile. The civic leaders in the city greatly favored the highway plan, but they were not necessarily objective because they had interests in land whose value would be greatly increased by the road network. The trolley lines also increased land values, but only along the lines themselves, and there was fear high-density development would result from increased land values near the trolley lines. The single-family house had always been favored in the development of Los Angeles and its huge building tracts, and the network of roads would raise land values throughout the entire basin where huge quantities of single-family homes would be interconnected by the many roads. Los Angeles thus set out on the road to decentralization, and many communities across the nation eventually followed its lead.

November 13, 1927—The Holland Tunnel opened to traffic. The tunnel ran about 100 feet under the Hudson River between Jersey City, New Jersey, and Canal Street in lower Manhattan. The tunnel was a result of the growing automobile and truck traffic (at the turn of the century Hudson River ferries were carrying 30 million vehicles per year between New Jersey and New York), and it was a sign that vehicular transportation was the wave of the future. The Lincoln Tunnel, built in 1937 (see entry for December 22, 1937) further confirmed this realization.

Tunnels per se were not new, but a vehicular tunnel would require a much larger diameter than usual, and would require venting to prevent carbon monoxide poisoning of the occupants of the vehicles, especially if they were stuck in traffic. A revolutionary two-duct ventilation system was designed for the Holland Tunnel, and vehicular tunnels still use it all over the world today. A new financing system was also used for the Holland Tunnel that permitted the surpluses from the tunnel to finance Staten Island-New Jersey bridges as well as the Lincoln Tunnel built in 1937. In many ways the Holland Tunnel was a breakthrough that confirmed the importance of automobile and truck transportation that did so much to support the suburbanization of the United States.

1929 — Christine Frederick, a well-known editor, writer, and consumer advocate and consultant in the areas of home economics and housing, wrote her most famous book, *Selling Mrs. Consumer*. Frederick had written previous books on how to run households and kitchens more efficiently, operated a laboratory in her Long Island home for testing foodstuffs and household items of all types, was a consulting editor to the *Ladies' Home Journal* (see listing), and the home economics editor of the Butterick Publishing Company magazine *The Designer*.

Frederick dedicated her book to Herbert Hoover, the secretary of commerce at the time she wrote the book, saying "the founding and furnishing of new homes is a major industrial circumstance in the United States." Frederick's book was published by the Business Bourse, of which her husband was the president. Frederick was very much a businesswoman, and her book spoke of progressive obsolescence to avoid the negative connotations of planned obsolescence in developing new products to sell to "Mrs. Consumer" for her new house. Frederick was an active proponent of better consumer credit so consumers could more readily furnish their houses.

1931 — At the International Conference for Modern Building held in Brussels, an attempt was made to show maps for the world's great cities, using the same scale and standard symbols for various city zones such as business districts, factory zones, slums, suburbs, and so forth. The map for Los Angeles attracted much comment. It dwarfed those for all other cities, taking up much of the wall space set aside for the comparison.

Richard Neutra, a Los Angeles architect, was present at the conference, and he reported that many attendees were puzzled at "business zones that seemed to stretch for hundreds of miles along endless traffic boulevards which cut through unoccupied or agricultural areas. Cottage suburbs and satellite garden cities ... seemed to extend amorphously over three hundred square miles on this monster map. Multi-story slums seemed ... anomalously absent." The Europeans could not decide if the metropolis was a paradise or if a type of blight existed there which did not fit the classical descriptions.

Fifty-six years later in 1987 in his book *Bourgeois Utopias*, author Robert Fishman joked that this latter question was still unanswered, but Los Angeles of 1931 was the first city to be built for automobiles and to have a network of freeways-to-be to support them. That was why Europeans were unable to understand the map of the city.

Los Angeles was planned around the single-family residence early in its growth, and it stayed that way as it went from a town of 102,479 in 1900 to a city of 319,198 in 1910. It hit 576,673 in 1920, and passed one million in 1930 (it was about 1.25 million in 1931 when its map caused such a stir in Brussels). As New York and Chicago had been the growth cities of the nineteenth century in the United States, Los Angeles was the growth city of the twentieth century. Los Angeles passed Chicago in population as the 1980s opened, becoming the second largest city in the United States as its population passed three million. In city terms Los Angeles at four million is now about half as big as New York, but in metropolitan area terms, New York is near 18 million and Los Angeles 12 million.

Author Fishman describes Los Angeles as a "Suburban Metropolis." This is the ultimate suburb in the sense that suburbs in Los Angeles were no longer a peripheral growth around a core city, but rather they constituted the entire area itself in terms of serving the single-family residences of which Los Angeles was primarily constructed. Its fate was sealed in 1926 when preference was given to freeways over public transportation (see listing), and it now represents the end of the traditional suburb in the United States in Fishman's opinion (see listing for 1987).

July 22, 1932 — President Herbert Hoover signed the Federal Home Loan Bank Act (Public Law 304), which was intended to establish a credit reserve for mortgage lenders and thus stimulate the moribund housing market. But the terms and conditions of the act were so strict that of the 41,000 applications made under the law by individual homeowners in the first two years, precisely three were approved. It was an unfortunate example of the old joke that banks loan money only to people who don't need it. Needless to say, the act did not reverse the decline of the real estate market. Further, the Reconstruction Finance Corporation (RFC) created to issue bonds to banks to help them issue mortgages was accused of bailing out bankers who were friends of RFC directors.

1933 Housing Starts — In 1933, in what by many statistical measures was the bottom of the Great Depression, housing starts were only 93,000, still the lowest mark on record in the United States. As recently as 1925, starts had peaked at 937,000 to mark a decade of expansion and overbuilding. Housing starts fell every year after 1925, and by 1930 they had fallen to 330,000, nearly only a third of what they had been in 1925. Starts dropped to 254,000 in 1931, 134,000 in 1932, and to the record low of 93,000 in 1933, a 90 percent drop from 1925.

However, the stock market crash of 1929 had foretold (not caused) a coming recession, and between the spring of 1930 and the summer of 1932 the stock market fell by 66 percent. This completed a drop of 92 percent from the stock market's high reached in September of 1929. Thus, the real stock market crash came between April 1930 and July 1932, rather than in October of 1929. Relatively few people realize that the big drops sustained by the stock market in October of 1929 were recovered in the next six months.

On April 17, 1930, the stock market was within 4 percent of the value it held just before the infamous Black Thursday of October 1929. In the spring of 1930 there were many brave words coming out of Washington, D.C., about how the feared recession was over and business would soon be back to normal. It was this kind of inaccurate thinking that gave Franklin Roosevelt his presidential victory in November of 1932 (although he did not take office until March of 1933 because of the traditions of the time).

Thus, the housing industry (as were many others) was completely flat on its back when President Roosevelt began his famous 100 days of furious legislative activity in March of 1933. Things began to improve immediately over the next few years, but there still is debate over whether government action dragged the country out of recession or whether the initial stirrings of activity in the late 1930s in preparation for World War II was the biggest factor. But as far a housing recovery is concerned, there is no doubt that governmental activity, especially the creation of the Federal Housing Administration (FHA) in 1934 (see listings for June 13, 1933, and June 27, 1934), was responsible for the recovery of the housing industry.

1933 *Middletown* — Quotes from the 1933 version of *Middletown* by sociologists Robert and Helen Lynd (first version published in 1925) showed how deeply the automobile had become imbedded in life in America in spite of the Depression. One working-class housewife said, "We'd rather give up clothes than give up the car." Another said, "I'll go without food before I'll see us give up the car." Little wonder that what home-building there was in the Depression still focused on homes in the suburbs that required automobiles for transportation.

May 18, 1933 — President Franklin Roosevelt signed the Tennessee Valley Authority (TVA) Act. As was the case with many New Deal programs, the primary goal of the TVA was to get unemployed people back to work, especially in the construction industry. However, the stated goals of the TVA were to improve navigability on the Tennessee River, provide flood control, and improve marginal farmlands, among other things. There was a specific section 23 mandating the TVA to improve the "economic and social well-being of the people living in said river basin."

The Tennessee River ran through seven states and included some of the most impoverished areas of the south. There were disputes among the members of the board directing the TVA as to how much emphasis to put on helping the marginal farmers in the area keep their farms and how much emphasis to put on other objectives. President Roosevelt in 1938 dismissed the most contentious member of the board, Arthur Morgan, and the remaining board members, David Lilienthal and Harcourt Morgan, subsequently directed the TVA, with Lilienthal becoming the most widely known for his tenure. By 1941 the TVA was the largest producer of electrical power in the United States.

Private power companies led the charge to claim that the TVA was unconstitutional, but the Supreme Court upheld the validity of the TVA in 1939. The TVA was quite successful in putting people back to work in the construction industry, and in building dams that changed the face of the Tennessee River Valley and generated much electricity for the benefit of people within reach of the distribution system of that power (which was to become a key benefit in the building of the atomic bomb during World War II).

But the TVA had mixed results, as did most government programs directly involved in trying to provide better housing and better standards of living for (mostly low-income) people. When multiple dams, especially the Norris Dam, flooded thousands of acres of the valley and put previous home sites and farms under water, the displaced people were not universally happy with their new home sites. Many who found work with the TVA itself (about 20 percent of one key displaced group) were pleased with their new life versus their old lifestyle, but most who stuck to farming found the same old problems with what was marginal land at best, even though the government tried to help with teaching them how to use new planting techniques and fertilizers.

Depending on one's view of what was expected from the TVA, it was either a great success or a marginal failure. But decades later, the most successful features still stand, while the people involved have passed on, as has most of the prior farming life in the valley.

June 13, 1933— President Franklin Roosevelt signed a law creating the Home Owners Loan Corporation (HOLC). The law helped homeowners in urban-suburban settings while the Emergency Farm Mortgage Act (passed a month earlier) was intended to reduce the huge number of farms being foreclosed. These steps were an immense success.

Between July 1933 and June 1935, the HOLC helped one million mortgage holders, or 10 percent of all owner-occupied residences in the United States. Nationally, about 40 percent of all eligible homeowners applied for assistance from the HOLC. In poorer places such as Mississippi, 99 percent of those eligible applied for assistance. This was help on a scale that really made a difference to Americans.

The HOLC established the concept of a self-amortizing mortgage (i.e., when the last payment was made the mortgage holder owned the house). This was a new concept in the nation. Further, mortgages now had terms of 20 years for repayment rather than the 5–10 years that had been common. Added to lower interest rates, many homeowners who were about to lose their homes could hold on. The HOLC also standardized the appraisal process to determine the value of a mortgage that could be granted. This greatly helped the housing market, but it unfortunately also led to circumstances that kept many blacks and minorities out of the housing market for many decades.

January 18, 1934 — The legislature of the State of New York amended the charter of the City of New York to create a combined department of parks for the five boroughs that make up the city. One administrator called the commissioner of parks was designated to head the new combination. Mayor Fiorello La Guardia appointed Robert Moses to be the first New York City commissioner of parks, and Moses held the job for the next 25 years. He became one of the most powerful and controversial figures in the history of New York and the nation in the process. Including his many positions in government, Moses held power at the city level for 34 years, and at the state level for 44 years.

Moses built almost 600 new playgrounds in the city, but as commissioner of parks and a member of other organizations he was appointed to or essentially took over, he also built bridges and expressways and parkways and subways and world-famous beaches and public housing projects and many other related constructions. His prime connections to the history of housing were the credit (or blame) he received for turning New York City (and other cities that followed his model) into a city most accessible by (and finally dependent upon) the automobile, and his building of roads and housing projects that paved over older houses and neighborhoods while (roughly in the opinion of many) displacing many low-income residents. Moses casually replied that one cannot create an omelet without at first breaking some eggs.

Moses was an expert at writing proposals for the Works Progress Administration (WPA) of the Roosevelt administration, a group that was primarily interested in dispensing funds for public works that would put unemployed construction workers back to work. Federal money flowed into New York City for parks and recreational facilities to the tune of $113 million in the first two years of the existence of the WPA, and most fell under the direction of Robert Moses. His achievements became known nationally, and other cities sent representatives to New York to learn from Robert Moses. His influence thus became nationwide.

One measure of the quantity of work done by Moses was that when his leadership ended in the 1960s, there was a total of 5.8 million acres of state parks in the entire nation. Of that total, 2.6 million acres or 45 percent was in the state of New York, nearly all attributable to work directed by Robert Moses. And there was national agreement that not only did Moses build many parks, the quality of his work was surpassed by no one.

One writer stated that Moses did as much to promote the use of the automobile as Henry Ford, through the use of parkways, expressways, and new access roads to beaches and parks. It was claimed that commuters, nature lovers, beach lovers, and passionate drivers are forever in his debt. On the other hand, critics who promote public transportation will never forgive Moses for what they see as his transgressions.

June 27, 1934 — The National Housing Act was adopted. The stated purposes of the act were to stabilize the housing market by establishing sound housing standards and financing arrangements (mortgages), but the real purpose was to reduce unemployment in the construction industry. The Federal Housing Administration (FHA) grew out of this act, and the FHA was the single most important federal government program ever created to help the housing industry in the United States.

Work was started in 1933 on the concept of the FHA. A committee was formed to respond to President Roosevelt's desire to create an agency that would stimulate housing without requiring government spending. He wanted an agency that would achieve the required stimulation but would essentially use private sector funds to achieve its goals. Mariner Eccles, a close friend of the president, led the group at its beginning, but looking back many persons credited Winfield Riefler, an economics and statistics expert, with making the major contribution to the creation of the FHA. The committee had received much information concerning the need for financing help in the housing industry and they concentrated their efforts in that direction. If the government could insure the financing in the proper way, private financing would arise to drive the construction projects.

The final FHA bill increased guaranteed mortgage loans to 93 percent of the appraised value of the property compared with the average of about 58 percent previously required. This reduced the down payment for a house to less than 10 percent compared with a minimum of more than 30 percent previously required. Further, mortgages were made available with repayment terms of 25 to 30 years at a fixed low rate of interest. This greatly reduced the monthly payments required, and protected the mortgage holder against the need to refinance when interest rates might be very high in a period of tight money. As a result, home mortgage foreclosures fell nationally from 250,000 in 1932 to 18,000 by 1951.

The FHA also established construction standards and a series of inspections to be sure the standards were being met. These standards were adopted by the construction industry even where FHA loans were not involved so the builder could advertise that his houses met FHA standards. National housing starts increased rapidly from the level of 93,000 in 1933 to 332,000 in 1937, reaching 619,000 in 1941 just before the start of World War II. After the war, housing starts per year rose to a regular level of between one and two million per year.

By the beginning of the 1970s, the FHA had helped 11 million families to own homes since its start in 1934. But as had the Home Owners Loan Corporation (HOLC) before it (see entry for June 13, 1933), and as would the Veterans Administration (VA) after it (see entry for June 22, 1944), the adoption of certain standards for insuring loans for mortgages for both home building and ownership would block most blacks and certain other minorities from participating in the housing boom of the second half of the twentieth century.

The FHA provided much more assistance to the suburbs than to the inner cities because its data showed that its loans were much more safely made in the suburbs. Houses in mixed neighborhoods did not hold their value nearly as well as those in homogenous (which meant mostly white) neighborhoods. This helped accelerate the movement of whites out of cities and the concentration of blacks and minorities into cities. When questioned about their policies early during its existence, FHA officials stated quite correctly that its charter from Congress was to reduce unemployment by reviving home building, not to necessarily assist cities. The effect, even if unintended, was to help turn the United States into two countries, those who lived in cities (especially older cities), and those who lived in the suburbs.

1935 GE House— The General Electric Company (GE) sponsored an architectural competition for the best design of a small, single-family house. The entrants were required to list the GE appliances used in their design, and of 2,040 entries, one had 76 GE appliances. This event was typical of the aggressive advertising taking place focused on model homes because of the decline of the construction business in the Great Depression. Between 1928 and 1933, the construction of residential property fell by 95 percent, and the home repair business fell by 90 percent.

April 30, 1935— President Franklin Roosevelt issued an executive order establishing the Resettlement Administration function within the United States Department of Agriculture (USDA). This executive order was in response to the Emergency Relief Appropriation Act of 1935 established by Congress. The Resettlement Administration made small loans for multiple purposes to help farmers get though tight times in the Great Depression, and it eventually grew into the Farmers Home Administration (FmHA). The FmHA, with other farm programs including the Rural Electrification Administration (REA — see following paragraph), combined to form the USDA Rural Development function in 1994.

During 1935, the Rural Electrification Administration was also formed as a result of the same basic act by Congress, and many consider the REA and the Resettlement Administration to be among the most significant actions taken in the Great Depression to help farmers stay on their farms. The REA worked with local utilities to bring electrical power to nearly every rural location in the nation. In 1949 a similar program would be established to do the same for telephone service.

June 16, 1937 Harlem River House— Mayor Fiorello LaGuardia dedicated the Harlem River Houses project in New York City. This was a project sponsored by the United States Housing Authority (USHA) which had replaced the Housing Division of the Public Works Authority (PWA), the all-purpose organization created by President Roosevelt in 1933 to get Americans back to work. This particular part of the PWA had used several methods to attempt to replace slum housing in big cities with new housing, partially to help the poor but primarily to increase employment in the construction industry. But initial attempts in this area via private enterprise or via local public authorities had only limited success.

Finally, the new USHA took over the program and tried a brute force approach. It condemned via eminent domain or directly purchased land and started 21,000 units in 49 separate projects totaling about $129 million. The most significant of these projects was a seven-unit complex in Manhattan on the Harlem River that was opened on June 16, 1937. However, even before the opening the law permitting the condemning of land for low cost public housing was found unconstitutional in January of 1935 by Federal Judge Charles I. Dawson of Kentucky. His ruling was upheld on appeal, and the federal government was left only with the option of purchasing land at market prices. This essentially killed the programs, but it finally led to the Wagner-Steagell Act of 1937, which put the federal government firmly in the public housing business (see entry for September 1, 1937).

September 1, 1937 Wagner-Steagell Act— The United States Housing Act (also known as the Wagner-Steagell Act) was signed by President Roosevelt. This act permitted the United States Housing Authority (USHA) to fund duly constituted local agencies to create public housing. The first projects under this act started on March 17, 1938. By the end of 1962, two million people lived in the about 500,000 public housing units built under various public housing programs. But other than in numbers, the program would eventually be a dismal failure as crime would fill the public housing units even faster than the people, and "public housing" would become an epithet for housing for the poorest of the poor. Eventually units would be demolished in recognition of the overall failure of the program to fulfill its goals.

October 1, 1937 Greenbelt— The first families began moving into Greenbelt, Maryland, not far from Washington, D.C. Greenbelt was the first planned community built by the federal government. It was part of the actions taken by Rexford Tugwell of the United States Department of Agriculture (USDA) under the auspices of the Resettlement Administration (see entry for April 30, 1935).

Greenbelt was one of three planned communities built under the Resettlement Administration. The others were Greendale, Wisconsin (near Milwaukee), and Greenhills, Ohio (near Cincinnati). A fourth such community, planned for New Jersey, was never built. These towns were experiments in both layout and arrangement of the town and in social terms in that low-income residents had their own planned housing (but following the trends of the time, only white residents were admitted).

Following the reluctance of Congress to get involved in the housing business in normal times, the greenbelt communities were sold off to private owners in the 1950s. Greenbelt, Maryland, still exists as a historical footnote to the federal government's one attempt at town planning.

1937 House of Tomorrow— The *Ladies' Home Journal* (see entry for 1919) opened a "House of Tomorrow" exhibit as part of the massive advertising effort in the later 1930s (see entry for 1935 regarding the General Electric Company) to stimulate the moribund construction industry. These exhibits featured all the new technology and appliance items being used in new homes. Finally, the World's Fair of 1939 featured 21 single-family homes as the "Town of Tomorrow."

December 22, 1937 Lincoln Tunnel— The Lincoln Tunnel was opened to traffic. The tunnel ran about 100 feet below the Hudson River between Weehawken, New Jersey, and midtown Manhattan. It eventually added two more tubes and is now the busiest vehicular tunnel in the world. When the first tube opened in 1937, the usage was less than expected. But traffic soon built to the point that new tubes were required in 1945 and 1957. The building of the Lincoln Tunnel and the Holland Tunnel (see entry for November 13, 1927) acknowledged that travel by automobile (and truck) was the wave of the future. These modes of transportation would support the move to suburbia throughout the rest of the century.

1937 Williamsburg Restoration— The restoration of Williamsburg, Virginia, that began around 1927, was essentially completed in 1937. Although not a housing project in the conventional sense, many authorities have said that this restoration had a greater influence on home design in the United States than any other program, project, or person. The great publicity that attended the restoration brought the designs, colors, interiors, fireplaces, chimney details, and the fences to the attention of people involved with home design everywhere in the United States.

The beginning of the restoration of Williamsburg came in 1925 when Dr. W. A. R. Goodwin, rector of the local Bruton Parish Church in Williamsburg, gave a lecture to the Phi Beta Kappa Society in New York on his favorite subject, the preservation and restoration of the Colonial architecture of Williamsburg, Virginia, once an important colonial town and the home of William and Mary College, where Thomas Jefferson had been schooled. John D. Rockefeller, Jr., heard the lecture and immediately took an interest in the project.

Rockefeller visited Williamsburg a few months later, and initial work on the restoration was begun by 1927. Originally designed by Christopher Wren, Williamsburg was essentially one of the first planned communities in America. In all, the restoration involved tearing down 440 buildings, moving 18 outside the restoration area, replacing or restoring 66 buildings, and reproducing 84 on Colonial foundations. In addition, all open spaces, walks, streets, and gardens were restored to their Colonial appearance.

1938— Considering the impact of the automobile on society at this point in the twentieth century, noted sociologist William F. Ogburn stated that the "invention of the automobile has had more influence on society than the combined exploits of Napoleon, Genghis Kahn, and Julius Caesar." The automobile was not only supporting the flight to the suburbs, it was causing major cities to decline as it was also supporting a national move towards decentralization.

1939— As the decade ended, housing starts were enjoying a boom. Thanks to federal government action, especially including the birth of the Federal Housing Administration in 1934 (see listing for June 27, 1934), housing starts rose from the record low of 93,000 in 1933 to 336,000 in 1937, 406,000 in 1938, and 515,000 in 1939. This surge would carry over into 603,000 in 1940 and 706,000 in 1941 before the start of World War II returned housing starts to the 200,000 to 300,000 level from 1942 through 1945.

December 9, 1940— The Arroyo Seco Parkway (later named the Pasadena Freeway) opened in California connecting the city of Pasadena to downtown Los Angeles. It was the first section of what would become the largest freeway system in the world. Officially planned to bring shoppers downtown, the freeway raised the value of Pasadena real estate to such an extent that developers and builders urged the building of more such freeways. By 1960 the Pasadena Freeway was carrying 70,000 cars a day compared with a planned capacity of 45,000.

December 1941—As the United States prepared for war after the attack on Pearl Harbor, 3,000 Navy men formed the first regiment of the Navy's fighting Construction Battalions. The initials C. B. became Seabee, and the logo of a feisty cartoon bumblebee about to go out to work in construction became famous around the United States, if not the world. An article published in the *American Builder* magazine in early 1942 urging red-blooded men with building experience to sign up was credited with leading 260,000 men to subsequently sign up.

The Seabees did an amazing job in the conflict in the Pacific Ocean, building crucial bridges and laying airstrips in record time as the United States hop-scotched from island to island. The Seabees often did their work while fighting was still going on for possession of a specific island, landing with first wave of invaders. They were known as a can-do outfit, encompassing adventurous men from all building trades, with ages ranging from 17 to 50. One known saying about them was, "The difficult we do immediately, the impossible takes just a little longer."

Joining this elite force during the peak of the war in the Pacific was Bill Levitt, who with his brother and father revolutionized the building of housing in the United States after the war with Levittown (see entry for October 1947). Levitt later said that his experience with the Seabees, sitting with his teammates at night and planning the next day's work, thinking always of how to do it faster (lives were at stake) and how to best use the materials and men at hand was very helpful. There were no union rules in the Pacific war, and the only issue was how to get the job done well in the minimum amount of time.

Levitt and his family had been involved with building homes for war workers in Norfolk, Virginia, in 1941, and initially it was a disaster in terms of meeting schedule. The Levitts and their managers broke down the building process into 27 separate steps, figuring out how to best assign the men to each step, and how best to pay the men for their productivity on the job. Bill Levitt combined this experience with his work in the Seabees, using the Pacific war zone as a giant laboratory in building quickly and reviewing it with his peers. It was invaluable experience that he would use in building Levittown so successfully.

But Levitt never lost his animosity for unions that he developed on the Norfolk construction task. He was 38 years old when he left the service, and he had packed a lot of experience into those 38 years. He was quoted as saying that Thomas Jefferson made a huge mistake by implying that are men are equal. They might be created equal, but they certainly not equal in he sense of talent and willingness to work hard. In Levitt's view, a union's prime function was to protect the slowest and least efficient worker. Levitt hired only nonunion workers. He paid them top dollar and offered them many incentives that enabled them to earn extra money. Levitt's workers often made twice as much as those on comparable jobs elsewhere, but they made the money on Levitt's terms. This was one of the many uncommon approaches Levitt used to become the top builder in the United States (see Appendix) in his era. Several writers have noted, looking back at the 1940s and 1950s, that if Henry Ford was the first great business figure of the American century, the second was William J. Levitt.

February 1942— President Roosevelt issued an executive order combining under one roof the 16 different agencies trying to get defense housing built for war workers. The new organization was named the National Housing Agency and was headed by John B. Blanford. So-called war housing was the area where large builders after the war such as William Levitt (see listing) and Henry Kaiser (see listing for March 1943) learned to build housing quickly and cheaply, which they did in huge quantities after the war.

March 1943— The inhabitants of Vanport City, Oregon, a city of about 40,000 (nicknamed Kaiserville after Henry J. Kaiser, the shipbuilder whose shipyards on the Columbia River the city was built to serve), took up their tools to build ships at a record pace with "Rosie the Riveter" leading the way. The shipyards operated 24 hours a day, seven days a week, and the city was uniquely built in about ten months for the Federal Public Housing Authority to serve the unique needs of the workers.

Families, single parents, or other households had houses to serve their particular needs. Whites, blacks, Asians, and Hispanics were integrated in the shipyards and the city. There were seven child-care centers built in a straight line with job sites so no one had to travel far out of their way to reach a child-care center. The centers themselves operated 24 hours a day to fit the schedule of the shipyards. The child-care centers included infirmaries, child-size tubs to save their mothers time needed to give baths at home, and food services so mothers could take hot food home with their children. The cost of all of this was seventy-five cents a day for the first child and fifty cents a day for additional children. Public transportation buses connected everything.

There were nursery schools, kindergartens, five grade schools, and seventeen well-supervised playgrounds. In the eyes of many, it was the perfect town of the future. But it existed only because it was needed to win the war for the United States. Its citizens, men and women of all kinds and colors, could produce munitions of all kinds in huge numbers because they were well housed and their children were well cared for. The prime problem they had to focus on was outproducing the enemy.

But after the war Vanport City was dismantled in spite of the great housing shortage in the United States. Direct government subsidies were no longer available for such housing projects, and the plain houses of Vanport City were of little interest to returning servicemen and their families. The returnees flocked to developments like Levittown (see listing for October 1947), and Henry J. Kaiser, who had built the very successful shipyards using Vanport City as his prime source of shipbuilding labor, turned to building housing much like a West Coast version of Levittown. Kaiser was familiar with the intricacies of government subsidies, and he turned this expertise to use in gaining FHA (Federal Housing Administration) and VA (Veterans Administration) financing for his new housing projects, as had the Levitt brothers on the East Coast.

July 1, 1943— A merger of competing groups produced the National Association of Home Builders (NAHB). This was essentially a trade organization for the housing industry, and it would evolve into one of the most powerful trade organizations in the country, reaching a membership of over 125,000 by 1980. It would, of course, offer help and information to its members, but it would become one of the most influential organizations walking the halls of Congress pushing for what it considered favorable legislation.

June 22, 1944— The Serviceman's Readjustment Act, otherwise known as the GI Bill of Rights (or simply the GI Bill), was signed into law by President Franklin Roosevelt. Among many other things, the bill created a Veterans Administration (VA) mortgage program similar to that of the Federal Housing Administration (FHA), but the VA was generally more liberal in the terms it offered veterans for obtaining mortgages.

Housing was desperately needed for the returning veterans. In total there were an estimated 3.6 million (some estimates ran up to 5 million) families lacking homes by late 1945, and veterans were living in trailers, Quonset huts, used trolley cars, converted feed grain bins, and various and sundry converted buildings, in addition to doubling and tripling up with friends and relatives.

In concert with the GI Bill, housing programs were rushed through the government, causing much confusion in some cases where the release of materials previously restricted to military use had to be untangled. Several bills were hurriedly passed, but many contained defects that did not become apparent until it was attempted to put them into effect. The one constant was that each attempt to liberalize financing via the FHA or the VA had strongly positive results. Many entries in this chronology, especially since the 1930s, will show how more liberal financing was always successful in creating a housing boom. Even the massive housing booms of the early 21st century were primarily a result of creative financing, even though the prime agent of change was private rather than federal financing.

A quotation in nearly every book dealing with the history of housing in this era when World War II was winding down and the veterans were beginning to return en masse was credited to writer John Keats, who captured the sense of the chaotic rush to create housing and identified the one approach that actually worked. As a bill rushed through Congress with very little in the way of controls and very much in the way of federal mortgage guarantees to protect builders, Keats commented: "The real estate boys read the bill, looked at one another in happy amazement, and the dry rasping noise they made rubbing their hands together could be heard as far as [the other side of the world]." Other commentators noted that perhaps it should not be surprising that in a capitalistic society the tool that worked best was the appropriate application of capital.

Because of the combination of the Great Depression and the contingencies of the war years, new home starts in the United States had averaged less than 100,000 a year for the past 16 years. The new VA and FHA rules helped create a massive building boom as servicemen and women returned home. Housing starts jumped from about 125,000 in 1944 to just over one million in 1946, to 1.4 million in 1948, and to a then record of nearly two million in 1950. In addition, large construction firms were building large numbers of homes compared to the previous tradition in the United States that most homes were built in relatively small numbers by a large array of small contractors. Before World War II, one-third of all homes were built by their owners. Small contractors who built about five homes per year on average built another third. By the late 1950s, however, about two-thirds of all homes were built by large contractors using FHA and VA loans in various creative ways. The contractors who built on the largest scale during this time were the Levitts, whose crowning achievement was Levittown (see listing for October 1947).

1945 TEW Bill—A housing bill known as the Taft-Ellender-Wagner Act (TEW) was introduced in the Senate. A key assumption of TEW was that there was a need for government-built rental housing at the lowest level of rentals. It was felt that this was an area private industry could not afford to serve and which local government was not fully capable of serving. Among other things, the bill proposed building 500,000 public-housing units over the next 14 years.

What happened to this bill and the bitter debates about the bill over the next few years are worth noting because the results can serve as a template for the basic fate of public housing issues in the United States, even up to the present time. Starting with the Puritans and their practice of warning off what they saw as undesirable visitors to their towns (see entry for 1637), the general population of the United States has long been ambivalent about how to provide for people who will not, or can not, provide for housing and other necessities on their own. This is especially true of people seen as foreign to the general population, whether it be European immigrants in the 19th century, blacks migrating north after the Civil War and before, during, and after World War II, and Hispanics (legal and illegal) coming north in the 20th and early 21st centuries. Public housing has long been difficult to sell to the general population, and the dismal results of many projects that ended in crime-ridden disrepair further turned the public against public housing. The debate is also complicated by politics as a Democratic Congress is more favorable to public housing, and a Republican Congress is more favorable to construction handled by the private sector.

The Democratic-controlled Senate of 1945 easily passed the TEW bill, but by the time the bill reached the house in 1946, the chairman of the House Banking and Currency Committee, Jesse P. Wolcott, a Republican and a foe of public housing, declared it dead on arrival. Wolcott was emboldened by the congressional elections in the fall of 1946 in which the Republicans had regained control of Congress for the first time since the elections of 1932, when Franklin Roosevelt first came to power.

The results of the 1946 election were a public backlash to the many strikes that unions had rained down upon the American public since the end of World War II. The public got to see for the first time how unions would use the power they had gained under the Roosevelt administration, and the public did not like what it saw. Veterans returning home from a war where they had risked their lives were not pleased to see strikers marching in the streets demanding increases in wages that were already far above anything the GIs had received. And men like labor leader John L. Lewis appeared to act like the dictators the soldiers had worked so hard to depose overseas. The Republicans ran under a theme of "Had enough?" and the American people voted as if they definitely had "had enough." Republicans gained 15 seats in the Senate to take the lead 51–45, and they gained 56 seats in the house to lead 246–188. The unions got rewarded with the dreaded Taft-Hartley bill in 1947, when Republicans and Democrats alike voted to override President Truman's veto of the bill. The unions never regained the power they had had in 1945-46, in spite of Truman's surprise win in 1948 when the Democrats regained control of Congress.

In the meantime, the Republicans led committee hearings in 1947-48 that became known as the McCarthy Hearings on Housing (see listing). Senator Joseph McCarthy dominated these hearings before he gained notoriety as a communist hunter. The hearings were meant to try to determine how best to provide the mass housing the nation required at the time.

1947-48 McCarthy Hearings on Housing— The results of the 1946 election in terms of housing was that nearly any housing bill that involved private builders using FHA and VA help was passed, but public housing was looked on much more unfavorably than before. Still, the public hearings held in 1947-48 were intended to discover how the mass need for housing could best be met, be it by mass production of prefabricated housing, lowered cost of conventional housing so it was affordable for most Americans, or public housing (which the Republicans were predisposed to oppose).

In spite of the mostly negative reviews written by various historians about the hearings and their domination by Senator Joseph McCarthy, much useful material was gathered by the hearings that helped to lower the cost of conventional housing. Conventional low cost housing was demonstrated by Levittown (see listing), whose construction was started while the hearings were going on and whose builder, William Levitt, became a star witness for the committee. Regardless of the emotions involved in the hearings, it is worthwhile to examine in detail some of the witness material because it shows well how the home construction industry had to be revolutionized in the late 1940s and early 1950s to meet the need for housing on a mass basis.

Senator Joseph McCarthy of Wisconsin in essence presided over the public hearings during 1947 and 1948 (see also listing for October 1948) held by the Senate Joint Committee Study and Investigation of Housing. McCarthy was an avowed foe of public housing and the TEW bill (see listing for 1945) and was the lightning rod for much partisan criticism. He got himself elected vice-chairman of the committee, after helping another foe of public housing and the TEW bill, Ralph Gamble of the House, get elected chairman. The notoriety Senator McCarthy later gained for his avowed search for communists in the government in the 1950s later clouded the fact that the hearings actually were a search for methods to build much-needed housing on a mass basis, and to determine what actions were hindering the building of such housing. The TEW bills presented public housing as one option, but, as noted, McCarthy was pre-disposed to oppose public housing, and the hearings were mainly remembered for that fact. Unfortunately, the hearings were not well remembered for uncovering a number of items that were hindering the transition to mass housing projects. But the hearings were a vital link in the transition of housing in the United States from essentially a craft business before World War II to a mass production business after World War II. Thus, some details from the hearings are worth noting in understanding this transition.

The committee held formal hearings in 33 cities across the United States amid much publicity. As noted, the prime issue was whether housing should be built by private or public (government) concerns, and how private concerns could best be helped to build housing for the masses. For all his blus-ter, Senator McCarthy became an expert in how the existing jumble of hous-ing codes (set both locally and by national union rules) was hindering mass production costs and efficiency. At one point in the hearings he explained:

"I had a gentleman who is in the automotive industry in the other day, and he was talking about the consideration his company was giving to the mass production of homes, and he made a comparison which I thought was rather good. He said the situation today, as far as the mass production of homes is concerned, is pretty much as if it would have been twenty years ago [in the automotive business] if in one town you had to have automo-biles with rubber fenders and in another town you had to have a wheel base of five feet and in another town you had to have a wheel base of four feet, eight inches. In another town a certain size tire and in another town a cer-tain type horn.... It was his position [that] the [building] codes more than anything else act as an absolute bar against any intelligent low cost of mass production."

In this case the discussion was about mass production of prefabricated homes, which really never caught on in the United States in a big way. But the committee found that building codes, which originally were developed to set a minimum standard of safety and quality, were now very much out of date, and were politically motivated in some areas to force the use of prod-ucts made in the area. For example, heavily wooded areas mandated wood frame construction while brick-making Denver required the use of bricks and banned wood frames while glass-making Newark encouraged the use of glass blocks, etc, etc. There were over 2,000 local codes essentially block-ing the use of modern materials and construction methods. This pushed up the cost of even conventionally built houses.

A *Collier's* magazine article of the era noted that "to catch up with the inventions and discoveries of recent years in both materials and building practices, most of the existing codes require review and revision." One irony was that some communities claimed changes needed to be reviewed to be sure they were safe, while many proposed new materials and techniques came directly out of World War II where they had saved the lives of countless GIs (see entry for December 1941 and the Seabees).

In addition to the building code issues, there were traditional proce-dures that served simply to enrich parasitic middlemen and keep material prices high. A popular witness was William Levitt of Levittown fame (see entry for October, 1947 et al). Levitt testified that many traditional hous-ing building procedures and codes, such as the use of union labor and work rules and the need to buy materials from middlemen rather than directly from manufacturers, simply increased prices while providing no benefits to the consumer. Levitt testified that some building material suppliers, who were used to receiving high prices for low unit quantities for expensive homes, did not want to supply materials at lower prices for mass orders. Further, a local web of middlemen served as order takers for the materials. Levitt testified that these middlemen caused mark-ups ranging from 20 percent to 55 percent for doing nothing but issuing invoices and buying lots of "stationary and a three cent stamp." Building manufacturers were happy to let this practice continue as it helped keep prices generally higher than if they had to deal directly with builders who wanted to negotiate lower prices for large buys. McCarthy engaged in a shouting match with one such middleman who defended his work, but when McCarthy turned committee material over to the local district attorney, the man was convicted of grand larceny, and the general gray-marketing practice begin to decline. The bad publicity other traditional practices received from the hearings also helped start the change to a more competitive and thus lower price market.

A final example from the testimony before the committee helps explain why so many Republicans were opposed to public housing. In Pittsburgh, John Nickalus, Jr., associated with Pittsburgh Real Estate dealers, testified that he had witnesses prepared to "swear that government housing in Pittsburgh is rented, not only to the worthy poor, but also to city employees earning good salaries and to people of various professions. Government housing is nothing more than a political football. About 85 percent of the tenants are Democrats."

Some Democrats defended this in the name of diversity, but that begged the question of how such practices matched the goals of the TEW program to build public housing at the "lowest level of rentals" which "private industry can not afford to serve" (see entry for 1945). It was hard for most Republicans to determine any basis for renting such housing to professionals while millions of poor people were still looking for affordable housing. In the view of these Republicans, such public housing was simply another New Deal boondoggle.

Also, considering the costs involved with building public housing under union work rules, especially in such areas as the number of bricks to be laid daily and the efficiency of spray paining versus painting with a brush, many old union work rules were under attack by various magazines and the media. The union defense was usually on the traditional grounds of health and safety, but it seemed more than coincidental that the union rules always preferred the slowest and most labor-intensive methods. Bill Levitt's high-speed construction of Levittown without union labor or rules with good safety records seemed to settle the argument for good. But Republicans felt that government housing would never follow such anti-union techniques and would be much more costly than necessary. This was another dagger in the heart of public housing. Thus, the hearings would end without any public housing being authorized.

But, as noted before, the battle over public housing would obscure much good information uncovered by the hearings, and public housing would win other battles when the Democrats regained control of Congress.

October 1947—The first 300 houses were occupied in Levittown, New York, a community on Long Island that was only 25 miles east of Manhattan. The Levitts, father Abraham and sons William and Alfred, had learned to build houses on a large scale for the federal government when they built 2,350 homes for war workers in 1941 in Norfolk, Virginia. They had also built federal housing in Portsmouth, Virginia, and Pearl Harbor, with William Levitt gaining much useful experience on duty with the Navy Seabees during the war. The Levitts had previously built homes in more modest amounts from 1929 through the 1930s on Long Island in New York, the place they would launch their biggest project in 1946 by acquiring 4,000 acres of potato farms in the town of Hempstead, Long Island.

Levittown was initially for veterans only (it was originally called "Island Trees"), and the houses were for rent only with an option to buy after a residence of one year. The Levitts created a building machine of such efficiency that nearly everyone finally bought their homes because the total monthly payment for principal, interest, and taxes was less than the rent for a home that included built-in appliances such as television and laundry appliances. After 1949, all houses were for sale only.

Buyers stood in line for hours in the summer of 1947 to rent houses that would not be available until October. Eventually Levittown would have more than 17,400 houses and 82,000 residents. It was the biggest housing development ever constructed by an individual builder, and it also represented about the lowest-cost housing that any builder could attain. The 750 square foot Cape Cod was the standard house, but it was easily expandable upstairs in the unfinished attic or into the yard. In a basic way the Levittown house was similar to Henry Ford's Model T in that it met a fundamental need with good design and a mass-produced rock bottom price that was easily in reach of the middle class.

The standard Cape Cod was priced at $7,990 and was available with no down payment and no closing costs plus a VA-FHA 30-year mortgage. The entire buying and financing process could be completed in two half-hour steps. Architects complained about the lack of originality in the massive development, but it was a huge success. A peak was reached in March of 1949 when 1,400 sales contracts were closed in one day. The Levitts went on to build more Levittowns near Philadelphia, Pennsylvania, and in New Jersey. They were not quite as large as the original, but they featured the same low prices and sold very well. William Levitt became the prime mover in the family as he pushed his father into retirement.

The appendix contains more detail on the fundamental techniques the Levitts used to build their houses in mass production. They truly produced a revolution in the construction industry, and major builders across the United States followed their lead, both in construction techniques and financing, throughout the rest of the century and into the twenty-first century. Millions of homes have been built using the Levitts as a guide.

One notable point about Levittown and its descendants was that, as noted earlier in this book about the restrictions of government mortgages, no one wanted to loan money to build houses in mixed neighborhoods which people felt would not hold their real estate values. As did many others, the Levitts refused to sell to blacks for two decades after the war, and resellers of the original homes did the same. In 1960, Levittown had 82,000 residents and not a single black. William Levitt was quoted as saying, "We can solve a housing problem, or we can try to solve a racial problem. But we cannot combine the two." FHA officials in the late 1930s said much the same thing about trying to solve an unemployment problem or a social problem. In their view they could not do both.

Some observers of American history have said that the two most important persons in the nation in the first half of the twentieth century in terms of shaping American culture were Henry Ford and Bill Levitt. Both did in essence the same thing. They brought what was initially reserved for the well off into the reach of the common man. They did it by inventing mass-production techniques for a product that was initially hand-crafted (and thus expensive), and they set the stage for changing an entire industry as all others in the field paid Ford and Levitt the ultimate compliment by copying their techniques. The whole nation changed as a result.

Levitt gave Ford the credit for developing techniques that Levitt copied. Ford had the car move along an assembly line where workers did specific tasks to finish the product. Levitt made the house stationary and moved groups of workers from house to house to do specific tasks to finish the product. Both Ford and Levitt created or adapted special tools for the task and carefully planned the steps needed to assemble the finished product in the most efficient way. Each made use of the special materials available in his time. The result was a quality product that was far less expensive than the competition, and each was rewarded for his efforts by immense demand for his product by consumers, and each set the tone for the massive growth in his industry that followed.

To demonstrate the problems that Levitt encountered primarily because he used new techniques, Levitt had designed his houses to be built on a concrete slab rather than digging a basement for each house as was then standard practice. This saved the homebuyer a considerable sum for something that was basically obsolete (Levitt used to point out that the ancient Romans never used basements). But the local building inspector denied Levitt a permit on general principles. Levitt was infuriated, but when the *New York Herald Tribune* heard of the denial, they ran a devastating editorial and the local bureaucrats withdrew their objection.

Levitt similarly made new and inventive use of FHA and VA mortgage insurance rules. This raised some eyebrows, but everything he did was perfectly legal. The builders of Lakewood, California (see listing for 1949), an essential carbon copy of Levittown, took the financing approach a few steps further, and ended up facing a congressional investigation. The sense of the investigation was that no one had done before what the Lakewood developers had done, so there must be something illegal about it. The conclusion was that it was devious, but not illegal. It was another example that the initial visionaries who first try something new are often thought of as possible villains of some sort, until their new approach becomes standard.

Late October 1947—As the initial surge of residents moved into Levittown on the East Coast, construction was started on a housing development in Lake Forest, Illinois, a community of about 3,000 acres 30 miles south of Chicago. The development was planned to be a GI town, meaning that it would have mixed housing areas, commercial areas, and industrial areas. It would include multi-family housing and would be a true village, rather than just a suburb, and it would be built with union labor.

There were a number of other idealistic items in the original plans, but many of these gave way to bottom-line pressures as the development grew and faced economic problems. They originally planned about 4,000 homes at prices ranging from $12,500 to $14,000, higher than Levittown (see October 1947) or Lakewood (see entry for 1949). But local tract developers became very competitive, so Park Forest mover to a lower cost mix of houses and cut other costs in many areas. These cuts tended to eliminate many of the features that the developers thought would make Park Forest unique.

Finally, in the 1950s, Park Forest attained a population of about 30,000. It was deemed a success, especially by those who had hoped it would present quite a different picture of suburban development than Levittown and Lakewood. But the bottom line was that many of the planned differences were ultimately scrapped to keep sales moving. Some observers commented that in many ways Park Forest was another example of the fact that most of the critics of suburbia don't live in suburbia, and the occupants of suburbia are too busy and content with their lifestyles to pay much attention to those who feel the constant need to criticize. It was observed by some that the critics feel the need to tell suburbanites that they should dislike certain aspects of suburbia that the critics dislike, and the inhabitants of suburbia in essence don't care what the critics have to say; they simply go on enjoying their chosen lifestyle.

1948— Richard and Maurice McDonald, two brothers originally from New Hampshire, developed a plan for mass producing hamburgers based on their experience of operating drive-in restaurants in Pasadena and San Bernardino in Southern California since 1937. They called it the Speedee Service System, the cheapest lunch around, and made a great success of it in San Bernardino, a somewhat distant suburb of Los Angeles.

Ray Kroc, a salesman who sold milk-shake machines, noticed the huge volume done by the McDonalds in their San Bernardino restaurant with the golden arches, and arranged to franchise the concept in suburban locations across the United States. The rest, as they say, is history. Many other fast-food franchises copied the McDonalds' approach, and the suburbs had another business entry that would grow over the years and help eliminate the need to go downtown for anything. Suburbs would become known as edge cities in many places, where they would grow from suburb to suburb rather than around some central core. The old definitions would not necessarily apply, but the growth of the nation would continue in the suburbs rather than in the core of the old established cities.

October 1948— FHA offices were inundated with applications for so-called Section 608 mortgages, which were for building rental housing. Legislation had been passed earlier in the year to extended mortgage loans for such purposes to 27 years at 4 percent interest. The new legislation came as the Taft-Ellender-Wagner bill supporting more public housing died in committee. The TEW bill had been struggling through Congress since it was introduced in 1945 (see entry), and had been the subject of bitter debate ever since. Opposition came from several housing organizations and members of Congress (led by Senator Joseph McCarthy), which saw it as socialized housing. The new FHA legislation for improved Section 608 loans was considered a much more favorable approach by Congress.

Early 1949— The Federal National Mortgage Association (FNMA), which had been authorized by legislation in the fall of 1948, began to operate. FNMA (which soon became affectionately known as Fannie Mae in the mortgage industry) created a strong secondary market for VA and FHA mortgages, giving long-term stability to the housing industry, and providing an easy way for investors to participate in the mortgage market. This greatly increased the funds ultimately available for mortgages in the United States.

1949 TEW Bill— After years of intensive argument, the Taft-Ellender-Wagner housing bill that had been introduced in Congress in 1945 (see listing) was finally passed. This was a public housing bill, and it had drawn strenuous objection from Senator Joseph McCarthy and a number of real estate industry organizations. Even after the bill was passed, subsequent nego-tiations constantly reduced the number of units authorized under the legis-lation. Other provisions initiated slum clearance efforts that did not work out well, even when done under the name of urban renewal. Public hous-ing in the United States could never be called a success.

1949 Lakewood— Three real estate developers in Southern California bought 10 square miles of land near Long Beach, California, and started building a $250 million planned community that became the city of Lake-wood. It grew to contain about 17,500 houses and 80,000 people. The houses were built on lots of about 50 feet by 100 feet, the smallest size permitted in Los Angeles County. The standard house averaged about 1,100 square feet in size, and it was possible to add several kinds of appliances at a typical cost of nine dollars per month.

By 1952 a huge (and very profitable) shopping mall had been completed, and in 1954, the Lakewood system of contracting for services from Los Ange-les County rather than creating police, firefighting, and similar services on its own had been established. This technique became very popular in South-ern California, and many small municipalities were created inexpensively following the Lakewood system. There were many so-called snobbish crit-ics who turned up their noses at Lakewood because of its homogeneity in housing and inhabitants (most were white at the beginning), but many of its early inhabitants were quoted in various sources as saying they loved the city and the comfortable life they found there.

Some analysts point out this is a common story in the development of the suburbs in the United States. Many critics decry the homogeneity of the suburbs and insist that the proper development of the nation should have featured high-density housing with a mix of racial inhabitants, and it pos-sibly would have if not for the many direct and indirect subsidies provided to suburban development by federal and state government. But the suburbs are clearly a case where people voted with their feet and found the type of housing environment they wished for themselves and their families, regard-less of "unfair" subsidies (of which most people were unaware) and what the critics thought best.

In 1954, when Lakewood was essentially completed, an investigation was held under the aegis of Senator Homer Capehart of Indiana into irreg-ularities in the federally backed mortgages and construction loans used to build Lakewood. After much discussion, the investigation concluded that the men who built Lakewood had used what were called devious methods of using housing legislation to obtain their goals, but they had done noth-ing illegal. Observers commented that in a sense this was the American way. The massive suburbs in the United States were built by men who saw new opportunities in the many pieces of housing legislation that had been passed to do things on a grander (and more profitable) scale than had been previously imagined. Those who were used to the old ways did not have such vision, and they often found the amazing things done via the new ways suspicious. The new ways were by definition new, but they were not illegal. Soon, the suspicious new ways become the standard way. William Levitt, the prime pathfinder in the housing industry, whose techniques the developers of Lakewood had basically copied, had the same sort of problem back on the East Coast (see listing for October 1947).

1950— As 1950 opened, a definite housing boom was well underway. Housing starts reached 1.95 million in 1950, the highest on record to that date, and a pace that would not be equaled for 21 years. Veterans who had returned from World War II and their families were still making up the bulk of the buyers, but people who had survived the Great Depression were also looking for a better situation in their personal lives, and a new home (and a new car) topped the dream list for most of them.

Favorable FHA (Federal Housing Administration) and VA (Veterans Administration) financing helped fuel the demand for new homes, and in the decade of the 1950s houses would be better built, better laid-out, and better equipped than ever before. A total of 15.1 million homes would be built in the decade, a new record, and a record of 29 million people would be added to the population of the nation, increasing the need for new housing. The Korean War broke out in June of 1950, and the demands of the war dampened the production of new houses afterwards, but decade records were eventually set in spite of yet another war. In addition, metropolitan suburban population grew by 50 percent in the 1950s.

The 1950s began a massive migration of people within the United States. From 1950 through the next three decades, 18 of the top 25 cities in terms of population in the United States suffered a decline of population. In the same period, the suburbs grew by 60 million people, meaning that 83 percent of the nation's growth took place in the suburbs. By 1970, more people lived in the suburbs than in the cities (by 2000 more people would live in the suburbs than in the cities and rural areas of the nation combined). This massive shift of population produced great social and political changes in the nation, just as would be expected following a national revolution of this type.

One additional point needs to be made about housing construction as the 1950s opened. There was a clear revolution going on in housing in terms of construction methods, materials used, and financing. William J. Levitt and his several Levittowns (see listings) were leading the way, together with the Lakewood development near Los Angeles (see listing for 1949) and many developments similar to those of Levitt and Lakewood. If the 1930s were about a revolution in federal government financing, and the 1940s were about learning how to build housing quickly and cheaply on a large scale using new materials and techniques, the 1950s were about learning to use the techniques derived from the 1930s and 1940s on an ongoing basis to build in large volumes and to change nearly everything that was standard in the housing industry in the United States. Once the shock of using federal government financing and building houses without cellars on slabs of cement had worn off, the developments in housing after the 1950s were basically simply incremental improvements of the truly revolutionary elements of the 1930s through the 1950s. Only the many new financing techniques developed to support the high-cost housing boom of the early 21st century could be considered truly revolutionary in the same way as the developments of the 1930s through the 1950s.

1951—The magazine *The Bulletin of the Atomic Scientists* devoted an entire issue to the theme of "Defense Through Decentralization." Their recommendation for avoiding national destruction in a nuclear attack was to disperse existing large cities into smaller communities. Ideally, urban cores should be depopulated and surrounded by satellite cities and low-density suburbs. It was a vote for suburbs over cities from an unexpected source. No direct action came from the proposal, but it added to the pressure that was building for some sort of national road system that would permit rapid evacuation of populated areas in case of an attack.

Mid-1952—President Truman signed a version of the Veteran's Readjustment Assistance Act or the GI Bill of Rights (see listing for 1944) that extended its benefits to veterans of the Korean War. In some ways the bill was not as generous as the original 1944 bill, but it gave a boost to the already boiling housing construction industry by providing, among other things, financial assistance to veterans and builders of their homes by making it easier for veterans to qualify for mortgages and for builders to obtain funds with which to build.

October 1952—An article in *Fortune* magazine praised the Levitt brothers (see listing for June 1947) for offering "The Most House for the Money." Levitt, in addition to sophisticated assembly-line building techniques, also pioneered the idea of including brand-name washers, stoves, and televisions with his homes and creating a common advertising program with the manufacturers. By this date, Levitt was still the biggest private homebuilder in the United States.

1953— The American Road Builders Association sponsored a national essay contest on the need for better roads. The winner of the $25,000 first prize was Robert Moses, by then a 65-year-old senior citizen who at the time was the greatest individual builder the world had ever known. This was a result of his long career (which had another decade to run) as a park commissioner (among other posts) in New York City since the 1930s (see entry for January 1934).

Together with his work in creating parks, Moses believed passionately in urban expressways, and the title of his winning essay was "How to Plan and Pay For Better Highways." Moses knew whereof he spoke, and he was noted more than any other individual for creating major road-building efforts in cities. Moses saw the expressway (or parkway) as a means for pleasure driving through his parks, and he shrugged off criticism that he should spend more for mass transit by saying mass transit was not his job. Similarly, he ignored criticism that his projects eliminated many slums without properly considering the people involved. Moses noted that one cannot eliminate slums without moving people just as one cannot create an omelet without first breaking the egg.

Moses actually left a great legacy in building parks, but he was most known by his critics for making the city ever more dependent on the automobile, just as suburbs were also, even if at a different level.

Mid-1953— Congress passed the Housing Act of 1953. This act gave the president power to adjust FHA (Federal Housing Administration) and VA (Veterans Administration) interest rates on the mortgages they guaranteed. It added $1.5 billion for FHA mortgage coverage, and lowered the down payment on FHA loans. The act also gave the Federal National Mortgage Administration (FNMA) power to make advanced commitments, and raised its ceiling $500 million.

Housing bills were the subject of much debate in 1951, 1952, 1953, 1954, 1956, 1957, and 1959. The debates often focused on the extent to which the government should be involved in public housing versus the extent to which it should concentrate on providing assistance to private builders. The Congress generally sided with the private sector in terms of expanding FHA, VA, and FNMA services together with supporting other private mortgage agencies. The result was lower down payments and longer mortgage payment periods (up to 40 years) that greatly supported the housing boom in the 1950s.

The most notable of these housing bills after 1953 are discussed in the following entries for the years in which they were passed.

May 17, 1954— In a landmark decision, the United States Supreme Court announced that the "separate but equal" doctrine used to establish segregated schools was unconstitutional, and that all public schools (schools established by local or state governments) must be desegregated. This ruling was considered to be one of the most important rulings ever made in the field of education, but it had a major corollary effect on housing as well. The decision accelerated the movement of whites from areas with substantial black populations (such as inner cities) to areas with mostly white populations (such as the suburbs).

There was a substantial migration of poor blacks from the rural south during the 1950s and 1960s to the major cities of the north where, for one thing, they felt more job opportunities were available. The result of the Supreme Court decision and this migration was an ever-increasing population of poor blacks in cities, especially in the old cities of the northeast and Midwest, just at the time the mass exodus of whites was reducing the resources in those cities, making it more difficult to provide the black arrivals with decent housing and good schools. In addition, there was considerable conflict between the mostly white governmental structure (including policemen) that had been put into place in these cities in the previous decades when the cities were mostly white, with only about 15 percent of the population being black.

The awkward implementation of the 1954 Supreme Court decision made the situation even worse. The court took a full year to determine how best to implement the decision, which seemed prudent, but after that year the best they could do in May of 1955 was to state that the local entities involved should proceed with integration "with all deliberate speed." The vagueness of that statement permitted those school boards opposed to integration to decide that a time of perhaps five decades would meet the requirement of "all deliberate speed." The battle to integrate schools in Little Rock, Arkansas, for example, required the sending of federal troops to Little Rock in 1957. The governor of the state subsequently closed the schools, and while all the issues wound through the courts, an even partially integrated school system did not begin in Little Rock until the fall of 1959 (it would take until 1972 to get fully integrated schools in Little Rock). Most attention was paid to Little Rock, but similar stories took place elsewhere.

Adding to the confusion, a Supreme Court decision in 1971 permitted busing between neighborhoods to achieve integration within a city school district. Local judges used that decision to initiate busing even across county lines to get integrated schools when it became clear that in many cases schools in large cities were de facto segregated as much or even more than before as "white flight" moved white students to the suburbs. While these cases were being appealed to the Supreme Court, chaos and bitterness on both sides further separated persons in inner cities and suburbs.

Finally, in 1974, the Supreme Court ruled that such busing was "wholly impermissible" and was not justified by the 1954 ruling. It further stated that achieving integration did not require "any particular racial balance in each school, grade, or classroom." The court emphasized the importance of recognizing local control over the operation of schools. Some observers commented that it took twenty years after the 1954 desegregation decision for the court to give very specific, clear guidance as to how the decision should be implemented. The lack of such guidance in the prior twenty years contributed greatly to the chaos that ensued after the decision was issued. Such chaos included the Watts riot of 1965 (see listing) and the Newark and Detroit riots of 1967 (see listing). It can also be noted that the chaos contributed mightily to the mindset that inner cities are dangerous places with bad schools that can best be escaped by moving to the suburbs. This mindset has continued to the present time, effectively dividing the nation into those who can afford to live (well) in the suburbs, while (mostly poor) minorities have been collected into the central cores of cities.

1954 IRS — The Internal Revenue Code was rewritten to permit "accelerated depreciation" of new income-producing property. The straight-line depreciation of such property over 40 years was changed to seven years. The change was intended to encourage the building of such property to help overcome a small recession, but as often happens, builders and developers discovered ways to reap a bonanza from it, and even if not the intent of the change, it gave another federal boost to the suburbs.

The code change essentially permitted the original builder to write off the cost of the original property in seven years and then sell it to a new owner who could depreciate it all over again at slightly less favorable terms. There was a boom in building malls, fast-food restaurants, office parks, industrial parks (for light industry), motels, and other commercial strips in the suburbs where land was cheaper and new construction of this type generally welcomed.

Such franchised operations as Holiday Inn and McDonald's benefited greatly from the tax code change. It was reported that the number of motel rooms jumped 50 percent in four years, and the new interstate highway program that started in 1956 (see listing) was lined with motels and fast-food restaurants at nearly every significant interchange. A person could stay on the interstates, sleep and eat at any convenient stop, and never go downtown at all except to drive rapidly through on the way to the next stop.

Harry J. Sonneborn, the partner of Ray Kroc (see listing) in franchising McDonald's, was quoted as saying that his company actually was not in the fast-food business; it was in the real estate business. "The only reason we sell 15-cent hamburgers is because they are the greatest producer of revenue from which our tenants can pay us our rent."

The new tax code write-off produced much development on the out-side edge of existing suburbs and beyond, where land was cheapest, and sub-urbs continued to grow without regard to what was once the central core city they once encircled. The Tax Reform Act of 1986 ended this particular tax bonus bonanza, but the preceding three decades saw a lot of construc-tion that continued to exist into the new century.

Fall 1954 Housing Act— Congress passed the Housing Act of 1954. It included 30-year, no down payment loans for veterans, and 5 percent down for others. The bill also reorganized the Federal National Mortgage Admin-istration (FNMA) to expand its secondary market and special assistance pro-grams. This further stimulated the flow of private capital into housing construction.

The 1954 act also adopted the term "urban renewal" to replace the con-cept of "slum clearance." Under the bill, the FHA created new sections (220 and 221) to encourage private builders to undertake both renewal and hous-ing for families displaced by government action. This in essence described public housing, but it was public housing involving the private sector, which was more likely to get a favorable response in Congress.

1956 Housing Act— The 1956 Housing Act again liberalized FHA and VA terms and conditions, and raised the ceiling on Section 207 Rental Hous-ing mortgages to 90 percent. A severe restriction against windfall profits or mortgaging out was included. Public housing was again cut back in reaction to widespread voter disapproval.

June 29, 1956— While in his hospital bed, where he was recovering from surgery, President Eisenhower signed the Federal Aid Highway Act of 1956. This innocuous-sounding piece of legislation was one of the most impor-tant acts of the federal government in the 20th century. The bill authorized $25 billion to be spent over the next 12 years to begin construction of a "National System of Interstate and Defense Highways." It also created a Highway Trust Fund that would receive income from a tax on gasoline and diesel fuel.

An attractive part of the bill for the states was that it set the federal portion of highway construction at 90 percent and the state portion at only 10 percent. In addition, there were considerations for advance acquisitions of rights-of-way, and a number of standards for highway construction and route marking. Although it was intended that the interstate highway system be completed by 1972, it actually took until the end of the century, and the costs went up accordingly. There was little complaint about the late com-pletion because the roads were being installed on a regular basis every year.

The only sour notes came later in the century when people began to complain that the country was becoming clogged with highways.

The act was the final step in committing the nation to a transportation system featuring cars and trucks. As such, it was also a stamp of approval on the national housing flight to the suburbs and away from cities. Essentially, every part of the nation was now connected to every other part by a network of excellent roads, and the best way to move about on the country's surface was by car or truck. Railroads appeared finally officially doomed, but by switching their focus to freight traffic and trying to ignore passenger traffic, some railroads managed to survive and even prosper.

The Highway Act was one of those rare pieces of legislation of which everyone approved — at least initially. In 1956, 72 percent of American families owned an automobile. By 1970, the number would rise to 82 percent, with 28 percent of the families owning two or more. As a result, personal purchases of gasoline and automobiles more than doubled over the same period. The automobile was now a basic part of the lifestyle of almost every family, and these new interstate highways would allow people to move about as they wished to an extent never before possible. Housing locations could similarly be chosen almost without respect to work locations or the locations of the family home in which people had grown up.

By 1976, 20 years after the project had begun, 38,000 miles of road had been opened at a cost of $62 billion. Yet even as the project was nearing completion, tax increases for the highway trust fund were required to maintain the roads already built. National motel and fast-food chains clustered around the interstate highways, and local malls and shopping centers were built as close to an interstate exit as possible. This further accelerated the exit of such facilities from the center of downtown, whether that meant a large or small town. This gave the residents of suburbia even less reason to be involved with the cities they originally surrounded. Movement from suburb to suburb became more important than movement from suburb to city.

By design or indifference, the nation had committed itself to transportation primarily by car or truck (or bus). Controversies arose over pollution, overcrowded roadways, and dependence on foreign oil, but in 1956 the American people chose the car as the key to their lifestyles, and by the end of the century there was no turning back. Similarly, there was no turning back from suburbia either.

1957 Housing Act— A mild recession resulted in the Anti-Recession Housing Act of 1957 being rushed through Congress in three weeks. It cut FHA (Federal Housing Administration) down payments to 3 percent, extended VA (Veterans Administration) mortgages and adjusted their rates, and gave FNMA (Federal National Mortgage Association) an additional authorization of $1.5 billion. It was claimed that this act resulted in 200,000 homes being built and 500,000 jobs being created.

1957 MGIC— Max Karl created his Milwaukee-based Mortgage Guarantee Insurance Corporation (MGIC) that was the first private mortgage insurance corporation to compete with the FHA (Federal Housing Administration). Other private insurers would follow his lead, and eventually MGIC would surpass FHA in the volume of insurance written. The fact that relatively few homeowners default on their mortgage, and the fact that the vibrant United States housing market makes it possible to often recover mortgage costs even if a buyer does default, has brought many competitors into the mortgage business over the last several decades, including foreign investors anxious to invest in the United States housing market. This massive flow of money has much to do with the nationwide housing boom of the early 21st century.

1958 Frank Lloyd Wright— Famous architect Frank Lloyd Wright wrote a book titled *The Living City* in which he predicted the end of large cities. He felt cities had been built to a scale much better suited to the Middle Ages than the automotive age. He felt congested urban cores would evolve into essentially what we now call edge cities (see entry for 1991) where population density would be much reduced and transportation by car much easier. Wright stated that "decentralization ... is an innate necessity," and he insisted that his "new city" was "inevitable."

October 1958— The Federal Home Loan Bank Board advised all Federal Savings and Loan Associations that they could make 90 percent loans on homes up to a value of $18,000. This put the savings and loans on an almost equal footing with the FHA (Federal Housing Administration) and brought some sharp competition between the two loan sources. As would be expected, this gave a boost to the volume of houses being built (it also later caused a crisis in the Savings and Loan Industry when many firms carelessly made loans that could not eventually be repaid, requiring a massive financial rescue by the federal government).

Summer 1959— The so-called kitchen debate between Vice President Richard Nixon and the leader of the Soviet Union, Nikita Khrushchev, took place in Moscow at an American exhibit displaying a model house (nicknamed "Splitnik"). The house had many modern amenities for the time, and Nixon boasted that the house proved the superiority of the American way of life because an ordinary American worker could own it. The postwar housing boom had moved into the political arena of the cold war.

1959 FHA— The Federal Housing Administration (FHA) celebrated its 25th anniversary. President Eisenhower commented on the "miraculous financial record" of the FHA at a ceremony marking the occasion. In 25 years, the FHA had insured five million home mortgages and 22 million home-improvement loans. It had returned $65 million to the United States Treasury, had built reserves of $719 million, and had operated at a profit every year after 1940. It was noted that no other governmental agency had done so much for so many at such a low cost to the taxpayer.

The FHA also chose its 25th anniversary year to issue its new construction bible titled *Minimum Property Standards* (MPS) for one- and two-family homes. The MPS was a volume of some 300 pages, and it defined in detail the requirements that property must meet to be eligible for FHA financing.

It was pointed out once again that the FHA is a financing service for the construction industry, not a social program. Thus, one unintended but powerful side effect of the FHA is that it actually hinders any development planned for mixed race or even mixed class communities. The FHA recognizes the many-times demonstrated fact that homes in such communities tend not to maintain their value as well as those in more homogenous communities. As a result the FHA does not readily guarantee loans in such communities, and this greatly hinders their development.

September 1959 Housing Act— The Housing Act of 1959 was passed after several months of debate and several revisions. Democratic control of Congress had been increasing since 1954, and in President Eisenhower's view this housing bill was "unfair and unwise," and it generally was considered inflationary. The sticking point once again was the extent of urban renewal and public housing. This part of the bill had to be watered down extensively before the bill managed to pass. The bill also lowered some FHA (Federal Housing Administration) down payments and added more funds for FNMA (Federal National Mortgage Association). The bill also contained assistance to cooperative and rental housing and the elderly.

1960— The 1960 Census, as analyzed by author G. Scott Thomas, showed that for the first time in the nation's history, a higher percentage of the nation's population lived in the suburbs than in the cities (or in any other classification). This suburban edge would grow until by the census of 2000, with areas as defined by the census, more than half of the nation's population would live in the suburbs, i.e., more people would live in the suburbs than in all other defined areas combined.

1961 Mumford— In his book *The City in History*, famous historian and author Lewis Mumford decried the growth of the suburbs and the decline of the city. It was a sentiment he had been making for four decades, but he felt the situation had grown much worse with the event of Levittown and its imitators (see entry for October 1947).

Like most critics of the suburbs, Mumford believed them to be of numbing similarity and their (mostly white) residents to demonstrate an overwhelming conformity. But other critics pointed out that Mumford and others like him were missing the point. Because the homes in a community were nearly identical at the start did not mean that the people in those homes were identical. Further, people moving into the new suburbs were not trying to make a social comment or to take sides in the city-suburb debate. If they thought about people like Mumford at all, they dismissed them as social snobs. And in terms of voting patterns, the 2000 presidential election (see listing) would emphasize a trend that had been developing for decades: inner-city residents were far more homogenous than the residents of the much-maligned suburbs in determining how they would vote and who they would vote for.

People moving to the suburbs, these other analysts commented, were, in effect, voting with their feet. They wanted personal safety for themselves and their families, they wanted privacy of a sort unavailable in big cities, they wanted good schools (and safe schools), they wanted air free of big city pollutants, and they wanted all of these things and many more, right now, not in some ambiguous future. The suburbs offered these things at a price they could afford. No one held a gun at their backs and insisted they move to the suburbs. They went there freely — and joyously.

The suburb-city argument has been going on since 1800 (or earlier) in the United States, and what many so-called sophisticated commentators seem to miss is that the suburbs continue to win out because people want to move there for what they consider good reasons. As the decades progress and the world continues to be an even more dangerous place in the view of many, they respond by moving to what they see as a safe haven in the suburbs.

1961 White— Theodore White, who wrote a popular series of books on successive presidential elections in the United States, wrote in 1961 about his travels in 1960 covering the campaign between Jack Kennedy and Richard Nixon. White, who had spent much time in China as a correspondent in the 1940s, felt compelled to comment on the changes he saw developing in housing in the United States during his travels. He wrote:

"From the census, one had the impression of a strange new society being formed, a series of metropolitan centers growing and swelling in their suburban girdles until the girdles touched one another, border on border, stretching in giant population belts hundred of miles long while wilderness rose again on the outside of the girdle (we now count more deer in the United States than when the settlers came) and rot blighted the inner urban core."

White was actually seeing what Frank Lloyd Wright had forecast in 1958 (see listing) and what would become the edge cities written about by Garreau in 1991 (see listing). What White could not foretell, even though he was a master of politics, was that the "inner urban" cores "blighted" by "rot" would become politically much more homogenous than the suburbs that surrounded them even though the suburbs would often be criticized for their alleged homogeneity (see listing for the election of 2000).

March 5, 1962—Chicago mayor Richard J. Daley personally welcomed the first tenant, James Weston, to the Chicago project known as the Robert Taylor homes. The project did not officially open until November of 1962, but tenants began to move in as soon as suitable facilities became available. The high-rise towers of the project rose above a cement desert, and as happened to most government projects for low-income residents (nearly all black), the projects became a center for drugs and crime in all its aspects, including murder.

The projects were a big step up in living conditions for their residents when they opened in the cities where they were built (such as New York, Boston, Philadelphia, Chicago, and St. Louis), but nearly all seriously decayed in living conditions during their lifetime and many ended up being finally torn down. Ironically, during the heyday of projects, the number of housing units in the United States lacking some or all plumbing declined from 55.4 percent in 1940 to 2.6 percent in 1980. Further, the percentage of housing units with more than one person per room (the definition of overcrowding) declined from 20 percent to 5 percent. But on an overall basis, the concept of projects was a complete failure.

August 11, 1965—A riot began in Watts, a mostly black suburb of Los Angeles. The immediate cause of the riot was the arrest of three members of the black Fyre family who lived in the area. Two brothers were in a car stopped by police on suspicion of drunken driving, and a crowd gathered as the brothers in the car argued with police. When the mother of the boys arrived on the scene, tensions rose and finally all three members of the family were arrested and driven away. The crowd left at the scene soon became a mob, looting and arson followed, and the riot was underway.

But as is usually the case, there were many other problems that led to the riot beyond the immediate events that sparked it. Watts was a poor slum area where it was estimated at the time that 30 percent of the adult males were unemployed. There was also simmering resentment over a fair housing law passed in California in 1963 barring discrimination in housing that was overturned by a ballot initiative in 1964 (which in turn was subsequently overturned by the United States Supreme Court in 1967). The poor housing available to blacks in Watts had been a festering problem, and the initiative was seen as a last straw. All of this helped trigger the riot in 1965. The riot lasted for six days, 34 people were killed, 1,000 wounded, 4,000 arrested, and a great deal of Watts was burned to the ground, accounting for about $50 million to $100 million in property damage.

Race riots had occurred previously in the United States, but what was unique about the Watts riot was that it was seen nationally on television. Analysts identified the Watts riots as greatly increasing the chasm between mostly white suburbs and mostly black inner cities across the United States, especially as the 1954 Supreme Court decision ordering integration in schools (see listing) and its awkward implementation afterwards was causing "white flight" everywhere. Watts was considered a causative effect for subsequent riots in July of 1967 in Newark and Detroit (see listing).

In many ways a vicious circle was operating. As more whites moved out of the inner cities, the cities were left with a higher percentage of poor black residents and fewer resources to help provide them with many necessities, including affordable decent housing and better schools. The governmental structures in the cities were manned by mostly white officials (including policemen) as they had been built up over several decades previously when the inner cities were still mostly white. The rapid change in demographics in most cities left many blacks feeling that they were being harassed by the police, who felt in turn they were simply doing their job. The subsequent unrest led to more "white flight" and the cycle continued.

Gallup polls showed that before Watts, a majority of respondents felt that race-related problems between blacks and whites would ultimately be worked out. But the optimism faded after Watts and the subsequent riots. This feeling was a major factor in the 1968 and 1972 presidential elections, and people continued to flee to the suburbs as before, for a variety of reasons, but now personal safety for themselves and their families became a much stronger incentive.

In Los Angeles, the feeling did not change as the percentage of blacks in the inner cities declined over the next several decades, while Hispanics grew to have a much higher percentage of the population. Today (2006), over 73 percent of the Los Angeles school district is Hispanic and 6 percent Asian. Blacks account for only 12 percent and whites 9 percent. The prior black-white issue has been overtaken by events. Most analysts feel that the perception of safety in the suburbs versus chaos in inner cities will not change in the foreseeable future regardless of which minority group predominates in the inner city. Thus, continuing growth of the suburbs is assured regardless of how many sociologists say such growth is undesirable. Considerations of sprawl and architectural niceties carry very little weight compared to a sense of personal safety.

In Los Angeles, even the Hispanics (and Asians) who can afford it choose to flee the inner city. As of the 1990 census, for example, the distribution by race in the city was 39 percent white, 13 percent black, 10 percent Asian, and 38 percent Hispanic. In the suburbs it was 54 percent white, 6 percent black, 9 percent Asian, and 31 percent Hispanic. The suburbs in Los Angeles tend to sprawl over great distances rather than just surround a specific central city core, and the major difference in the distribution of minorities in the suburbs versus the inner city is that the distribution of blacks in the suburbs is 54 percent lower than in the city, while the distribution of Hispanics and Asians is only 17 percent lower in the suburbs than in the city. The composition of the racial issue is now much different than it was in 1965 when Watts was seen in primarily black versus white terms. But it is still seen as a very dangerous place to live.

September 9, 1965— The United States Department of Housing and Urban Development (HUD) was established on this date, although it was not activated until January 13, 1966. HUD is a Cabinet level department of the federal government, and is charged with the responsibility of developing and executing policies on housing and cities. HUD has largely reduced its urban development function and now focuses primarily on housing issues. The secretary of Housing and Urban Development manages HUD, and in 2004 had a budget of $46.2 billion and 10,600 employees.

Historically, until the administration of Franklin Roosevelt in the 1930s, the federal government had avoided any direct role in the area of housing. But it jumped in then with both feet, so to speak, in an effort to stimulate the construction industry and thus ease unemployment. Many acts and programs established by the Roosevelt Administration were highly successful in getting the housing industry back on its feet. Many of these programs extended well past the 1930s, and in 1965, thanks to huge majorities in Congress, President Lyndon Johnson assembled these housing programs into HUD, which was part of his Great Society.

Included in HUD are the nation's prime mortgage insurance functions: the Government National Mortgage Association (Ginnie Mae), the Federal National Mortgage Association (Fannie Mae), and the Federal Home Loan Mortgage Corporation (Freddie Mac). A major difference to investors in the financial products of these insurers in that Ginnie Mae is backed by the full faith and credit of the United States Treasury. The others are stockholder corporations that it is unlikely the government would permit to fail, but there is no absolute guarantee as there is with Ginnie Maes.

The basic Federal Housing Administration (FHA), started in 1934 (see listing for June 27, 1934), is now part of HUD. The FHA mortgage insurance program is the single most important step taken by the federal government in the area of housing in the 20th century. It is now the largest insurer of mortgages in the world, and it has insured nearly 33 million properties since its inception in 1934.

Another notable present HUD feature is its Office of Public and Indian Housing, of which the so-called Section 8 programs are probably the best known. These programs offer rent subsidies to low-income people, paying a share of the market price of the rent so that low-income families can move into already existing housing stock. The programs are very popular with the public and long waiting lists exist in nearly every area where they are active, but landlords tend to give the programs mixed grades because of the normal red tape existing with any government program. However, programs of this type have largely replaced attempts at building public housing, which has largely fallen out of favor.

July 1967 — On July 12 and July 23, respectively, race-based riots broke out in Newark and Detroit. Many analysts felt these riots had partly been triggered by the Watts riots of 1965 (see listing), but each event had causes unique to its area, although many other basic causes were similar. The results were also similar — increased "white flight" from the inner cities to the suburbs across the United States.

In Newark, the specific cause of the riot was the arrest of a black cabdriver for a traffic violation. He was taken to a precinct station around which a mob gathered as news of the arrest spread. In the tenor of the times, civil rights leaders soon arrived (and pleaded for calm). As false rumors of the death of the cabdriver spread, bottles and bricks rained down on the precinct station, and in a short time a full-blown riot was underway. After six days of rioting, 23 people were dead, 725 were injured, and 1500 had been arrested.

A basic cause of the Newark riot was the dramatic change in demographics when whites and industry began leaving the city for the suburbs after 1950. At the same time, blacks, many from the poor rural south, began to move to the city. Newark dropped dramatically in total population after 1950, falling from nearly 440,000 in 1950 to 380,000 in 1970 (and to about 280,000 today). But the black population increased from 70,000 in 1950 (about 16 percent of the total) to 220,000 in 1967 (about 58 percent of the total). City resources declined as the total population shrank (the more affluent white population fell from 363,000 to 158,000 between 1950 and 1967, a drop of 56 percent), and most of the newer blacks were poor and in need of city services, especially decent affordable housing.

Further, as was typical in such a situation of rapid demographic change, the city government structure, including policemen, was mostly white because it was put in place over the past three decades when the city was also mostly white. The result by 1960 was cries of police brutality whenever policemen and blacks came into ever-increasing contact.

Unavailability of decent housing, made worse by urban renewal programs that removed mostly black slums, and a sense of isolation from city government made the Newark riots almost inevitable. It was the era of Black Power, and national civil unrest had followed the poor implementation of the 1954 integration decision by the United States Supreme Court (see listing).

Nearly the same analysis applies to the Detroit riots, which took place only a few days later. The immediate cause was a police raid on an illegal drinking club in a black neighborhood. As soon as the police left the area, looting of nearby stores began and so did the riot. After 5 days, 43 people were dead, 1,189 injured, and 7,000 arrested with 1,300 buildings destroyed and about $250 million in damages recorded.

A rapid change in demographics had taken place in Detroit as in Newark (and other cities of the northeast). Total Detroit population (and available city resources) fell sharply as whites left the city after 1950. The total population fell by 9 percent by 1960, 18 percent by 1970, and 50 percent by 1990. The white population fell by 23 percent by 1960, 42 percent by 1970, and 83 percent by 1990. Blacks continued to flock to the city, many from the poor rural south as in Newark, but even their dramatic increase could not prevent the losses in the total population. The black population was 303,000 in 1950 (16 percent of the total), 487,000 in 1960 (29 percent of the total), and 606,000 in 1970 (about 40 percent of the total) near the time of the riots. It presently stands at about 685,000 (about 72 percent of the total), as Detroit, the fifth largest city in the United States in 1950, continues to shrink as it falls off the top 10 list (it is now in 11th place).

Neighborhood changes in demographics were even greater than the overall changes. For example, the area in which the riot of 1967 started had changed from 99 percent white to 96 percent black in about 13 years between 1947 and 1960. Such rapid changes in demographics produced the highly flammable situation where a white government structure (including policemen) put in place when the city was 85 percent white was now seen as oppressive and exclusionary by the much large percentage of blacks it now governed. Cries of police brutality mingled with outrage over urban renewal programs that seemed to destroy black slums only, were the fuel for riots that could be (and were in 1967) triggered by almost any confrontational event.

The result in housing was an accelerated white flight to the suburbs (the suburbs around Detroit are now 91 percent white), which left the cities unable to provide such things as decent affordable housing to its remaining residents. Detroit may be an extreme case, but it serves as a model for what happened to the older cities of the northeast and Midwest after 1950 in the United States.

1969 — Kaufman & Broad Builders raised $30 million in capital funds through a $16 million public offering of 250,000 common shares, 500,000 warrants, and a $15 million private offering of 5 percent, 25-year convertible debentures. This was just one of many large home building firms to go public in the 1960s. Not all succeeded, of course (although Kaufman & Broad was still a leading home builder in 2006), but the point to be made was that home building in the United States by the 1960s was no longer the complete province of many small firms building a few homes per year, as it was before World War II. Home building was now big business and it required a company large enough to realize the economies of scale to be competitive.

However, some companies proved to be too large as in the case of the acquisition of the now large company of Levitt & Sons by the multi-billion International Telephone and Telegraph conglomerate (ITT). Bill Levitt could never adjust to big corporation ways, and eventually left. The housing part of ITT declined, and was ultimately sold off in parts and pieces. Sometimes bigger is not always better, and it was the turn of the housing industry to go through the growing pains of the transition from one-man shows to major corporations.

But in spite of these tales of big business taking over the housing industry, when considering the United States as a whole with all its nooks and crannies, the majority of homes in the United States were still being built by thousands of small volume builders (except in the rental housing market).

1970s — The decade of the 1970s was a then-record decade for housing, in spite of many tumultuous events both nationally and internationally in the period. There were 17.8 million housing units built in the 1970s, of which 12.4 million (70 percent) were single-family homes. All of these numbers were record highs at the time.

Housing starts topped two million units a year for the first time in 1971, and they reached that level in three other years in the decade. The population movement from the older cities of the east and Midwest that had started in the 1950s continued, fueling the flight to the suburbs all over the country, but the outflow was mainly to the west and southeast (the Sun Belt).

1970 Home Loan Mortgage Corp — In 1970 Congress chartered the Federal Home Loan Mortgage Corporation as a privately operated, government-supervised entity. Its purpose was to increase the availability of residential mortgage financing by developing and supporting an active secondary market in conventional residential mortgages. Near the end of the decade it would be turning a profit of $25 million buying residential mortgages and selling mortgage-backed securities.

1971— The Environmental Protection Act (EPA) of 1971 was the most far-reaching of the about two dozen laws Congress passed in the 1970s following Earth Day on April 22, 1970. It started a far-reaching debate that goes on even today, with environmentalists on one side and individual proprietors and general business concerns on the other side. The question is basically one of the extent of costs that are necessary in the pursuit of a better environment, as well as how many programs actually improve the environment as claimed or simply reflect the personal wishes of special interests that cloaked their desires under the magic words "the environment." It appears to be a debate without end, and a cost-benefit analysis of the environmental movement is far beyond the scope of this book.

But as far as the housing construction business was concerned, the EPA of 1971, the Water Pollution Control Act of 1972, and the Coastal Zone Management (or Wetlands) Act, and the Flood Disaster Act of 1973 all were seen as simply new problems to overcome, however well meaning the legislation may have been. From the view of housing, the environmental movement was a source of dramatically higher costs and delays in building houses and rental units. Perhaps the delays were the most aggravating because environmentalists and no-growth advocates soon discovered that it was not necessary to win a specific battle, but simply to pull out every possible law and interpretation thereof to delay a proposed project to the point where it was no longer economically feasible for the builder. This kind of struggle is still going on today.

Within the (perhaps biased) view of the housing industry, two items emerged that expressed their opinion of the battle in a humorous way. The first was the sarcastic question and answer session:

QUESTION: How many environmentalists does it take to change a light bulb?

ANSWER: Eleven — one to change the bulb and ten to prepare the environmental impact report.

Also in this vein was a proposed bumper sticker: "Have you ever met an unemployed environmentalist?"

Later in the decade, a study by the Urban Policy Research section of Rutgers University concluded that the costs of government regulation added $9,844 (almost 20 percent) to the cost of a three-bedroom home priced at $50,000.

1975— In his book *The Car Culture*, James J. Fink surveyed the relatively brief history of the automobile in the United States and concluded that Henry Ford's major contributions — the Model T, the moveable assembly line, and the five-dollar day — had affected America more in the twentieth century than the Progressive Era and the New Deal combined.

However, it still seemed to be a paradox that America's love affair with the car persisted in spite of the damage to the environment that appears when a society takes to the road and arranges its housing preferences accordingly.

1977— The Bank of America (BOA) pioneered a move into mortgage-backed securities with pass-through type securities backed by pooled conventional mortgages. Other financial organizations quickly followed the lead of BOA, giving yet more flexibility in the mortgage business in terms of raising cash for mortgages.

June 6, 1978— The voters of California passed an initiative by a winning margin of 65 percent that many analysts felt was the beginning of a tax revolution across the United States. The California initiative, known as Proposition 13, primarily limited property taxes to 1 percent of the assessed value of the property, while at the same time limiting annual increases in the assessed value. There were cries of gloom and doom from many cities which depended on the property tax to directly or indirectly fund many programs, but Governor Jerry Brown, a staunch opponent of Proposition 13, declared after it was passed that he would accept the will of the people, and he led a transfer of funding from local governments to state government. In essence, much of the property tax funding was ultimately replaced by funds from the state income tax.

Ironically, most analysts felt Proposition 13 was an unintended consequence of an attempt by a very liberal California Supreme Court to equalize funding to schools between wealthy districts and poor districts. Most schools were funded in California (as in most states) by local property taxes, and wealthy districts naturally had more funds at their disposal than poorer districts. The United States Supreme Court found nothing unconstitutional about this procedure in a March 21, 1973, decision. The justices noted that there is no basic right to education in the Constitution, and Justice Powell added that, in respect to the question of the level of wealth and education, the equal protection clause of the Constitution "does not require absolute equity or precisely equal advantages."

The California Supreme Court decided it knew better, and if funding of education by property taxes did not violate the equal protection clause of the Constitution of the United States, the California Supreme Court felt it violated the equal protection clause of the constitution of California. The result was a highly complicated series of actions that were undertaken in 1977 which were meant to equalize school funding in California, including capping expenditures in some districts and transferring funds to other districts. The details of the decisions and their consequences are beyond the scope of this book, but they are perhaps best summarized in a book titled *First to Worst* by John Mockler. It describes how California fell from among the top states in per-pupil educational funding to among the worse.

It was the late 1990s before any real equalization of funding was achieved, and great differences still remained between poor inner-city school districts and those in wealthy suburbs. As any educator will tell you, there's much more to achieving good schools than funding.

Proposition 13 was triggered by the realization that wealthy districts would not necessarily gain better schools from their high property taxes, and that California in total had more than enough funds to finance social engineering programs (especially those that didn't work as intended). Further, senior citizens who were threatened with being driven out of their long-time homes by steadily increasing property taxes, rising in response to growing property wealth around them, could keep their property taxes nearly constant as long as they stayed in their homes.

Proposition 13 was a boon to the housing market, reducing real-estate taxes by an average of 57 percent. It eventually produced situations where neighbors paid greatly different property taxes on the same homes, depending when the homes were bought and sold. But overall Proposition 13 was a huge hit with oncoming waves of homebuyers. Nearly 30 years later, local communities were receiving much higher tax revenues than anticipated. This was because of the huge run-up of home prices and basic assessed values in California in the late 1990s continuing into the early twenty-first century. Several attempts have been made to change Proposition 13 since its inception, but none have succeeded at the ballot box or in the courts. Descendents of the Howard Jarvis Tax Foundation, the organization named after the person who carried the battle to pass Proposition 13 in 1978, are quick to mobilize against any proposed change that would result in higher taxes, and they continue to carry the day.

1979 Private Mortgage Insurance— By 1979, the Private Mortgage Insurance business started by Max Karl in 1957 (see listing) now consisted of 13 firms that in total did $85 billion in business, exceeding the total issued by the Federal Housing Administration (FHA) for the first time. In spite of the essential reverence with which the FHA is generally regarded, the Private Mortgage Industry had grown rapidly because there was a demand for mortgage insurance with much less red tape than the federal FHA could offer.

1979— As the decade of the 1970s ended, there was a definite trend towards more large building operations building large numbers of houses. As recently as 1975, the typical builder in the United States produced less than 20 units per year, and large builders of 1,000 or more units accounted for only about 5 percent of total production.

However, by 1978-79, so-called construction giants who had revenues of more than $10 million yearly were pushing their share of the market towards 20 percent. There were less than 500 such giants among an estimated 127,000 active residential builders. Housing was still primarily an individualistic trade, but ever-larger firms were gaining a larger share of the business. This hopefully meant lower prices for new houses in the future.

1987— Author Robert Fishman declared the end of suburbia in his book *Bourgeois Utopia*. This was primarily because the old definitions of a suburb surrounding a central core city no longer fit the development of new suburbs in the United States. He saw Los Angeles as the ultimate end of the standard suburb with its massive decentralization that it developed mostly before the 1950s. He suggests the new word "Technoburg" to describe the new suburbanization in the United States, where massive suburbs in the old sense now merged together without any apparent core city.

But this new definition did not catch on, and by any name the majority of people in the United States still continued to prefer the detached (and decentralized) single-family house to any form of higher density housing. So strong is this preference that new forms of financing continue to arise to enable persons to buy houses in spite of their ever-increasing median prices.

October 1989— The respected Gallup Poll reported that big cities were enjoying a temporary surge in popularity when people were asked which of four types of places they would prefer to live in. Cities still ranked last as they had in the 1960s and 1970s, but their percentages had gone up somewhat. The overall poll gave "small town" 34 percent; "suburban area" 24 percent; "farm" 22 percent; and "city" 19 percent. Professional critics could continue to complain about suburbs as much as they wished, but people still preferred them as a place to live.

1990— Historian John Teaford published a book called *The Rough Road to Renaissance* in which he analyzed development trends in cities during the years of the Carter (1976) and Reagan administrations (1980 and 1984). Teaford found that politicians and the press joined in "an era of unprecedented urban hype" to improve the images of major cities regardless of whether such positive publicity was warranted. Teaford stated: "During and the late 1970s and 1980s, Cleveland had to be proclaimed a comeback city even if it was not, and Baltimore had to be painted pink by image makers even though much of it was dull gray."

Teaford's complaints had much to do with the fact that the cities were being celebrated for the building of various new facilities downtown, but the cities were still filled with declining infrastructure and growing numbers of the poor.

1991— Journalist Joel Garreau wrote a book called *Edge City: Life on the New Frontier.* Garreau described the new kind of suburb that had evolved, which he called edge cities. He defined such cities as having "five million square feet or more of leaseable office space — the workplace of the Information Age," plus "600,000 square feet or more of leaseable retail space," i.e., "the equivalent of a fair-sized mall." Garreau said he had identified more than 100 such cities in the United States.

One of the most notable examples he included was Tyson's Corner in Fairfax County, Virginia, not far from Dulles Airport in Washington, D.C. In the 1930s Tyson's Corner was exactly that, an intersection at which one could get a cold drink at a general store also featuring a couple of gasoline pumps. Today, Tyson's Corner marks the place where Route 66 intersects the Capital Beltway, and the old corner now has more commercial space than downtown Miami.

Garreau noted that an edge city has more jobs than bedrooms, and is perceived by the public as one place. As Tyson's Corner does, it has high-rise and low-rise buildings, houses, apartments, garages, shopping malls, fast-food franchises, and a conglomeration of corporate headquarters. Writer Robert Lang used the term "edgeless cities" to describe such places, which he expanded to include smaller growth "nodes," but the term "edge city" has generally been used to describe this new types of metropolitan growth.

Edge cities represent an evolutionary type of suburban growth in the United States, but others dismiss them as just another version of suburban sprawl (see 1995 listing). However, as usual in the story of suburban growth in the United States, dismissed or not by some critics, edge cities are here and thriving and are a fact of life, choosing in a way to dismiss their critics who choose to dismiss them. They were essentially predicted by Frank Lloyd Wright in his *The Living City* in 1958 (see listing), which stressed the need for decentralization of cities.

April 29, 1992— Four members of the Los Angeles Police Department (three white and one Hispanic) were acquitted of using excessive force when arresting Rodney King, a black motorist who had led them on a high speed chase about a year earlier. King had refused to stop when flagged down for a traffic violation (he was on parole from prison on a robbery conviction and later said he fled to avoid being returned to jail). The trial was held in Simi Valley, a mostly white city in Ventura County, where a new courthouse was available to handle the media crush surrounding the trial (the jury was impaneled from within Los Angeles County and held no residents from Simi Valley, but was drawn mainly from the nearby San Fernando Valley which was predominately white and Latino).

An unseen observer had made a videotape of the end of the chase in 1991, and the subsequent beating of King with police batons by the policemen involved. They claimed he resisted arrest and had lunged for an officer's weapon soon after exiting his car (that part of the arrest was missed by the videotape). The videotape ran on national television for some time, and was the key piece of evidence at the trial. However, the lawyers for the policemen used the grainy videotape in slow motion to show how each blow was justified in the view of the police by King's behavior. King was a very large man who had a history of drunken driving and was believed to be on PCP. Hence the jury found the officers not guilty of using excessive force.

Riots erupted in Los Angeles when the verdict was announced, and fires and looting followed. A white truck driver, stopped at a red light while driving at the time through Los Angeles, was pulled from his truck and savagely beaten, including being bashed in the head with a piece of concrete (he eventually recovered and some of his attackers were arrested and taken to trial). Two of the officers who arrested King were found guilty of violating King's civil rights at a trial held in Los Angeles at the urging of the federal government nearly a year after the Simi Valley trial. Thus, the events surrounding Rodney King went on for almost exactly two years, one year each before and after the riot.

The result of the Rodney King riots from a housing standpoint was once more an accelerated movement of people from inner cities to the suburbs. In Los Angeles the people moving out included Asians and Hispanics as well as whites. The dynamics of racial issues in Los Angeles are much different than in many other places due to the ever-increasing presence of Hispanic and Asian immigrants in the area, and this affects the suburbs as well as the inner city. As noted in the entry discussing the Watts riot of 1965, the racial composition of Los Angeles according to the 1990 census, near the time of l'affaire King, showed the inner city to contain 39 percent whites, 38 percent Hispanics, 13 percent blacks, and 10 percent Asians. The suburbs held 54 percent whites, 31 percent Hispanics, 10 percent Asians, and 6 percent blacks. Thus, the inner city issues were much more than just black versus white, and the unfolding of the riot showed this very clearly.

The results of the riot were very serious, with an estimated 50–60 persons killed, 2,000 injured, and 10,000 arrested, with 3,600 fires destroying

1,100 buildings. Between $800 million to $1 billion in damages resulted from the fires and looting. At one point firemen did not respond to fire calls because they were being shot at when they arrived. Policemen were sometimes held off the site of stores being looted so as not to inflame the situation. The National Guard and federal troops were eventually needed to quell the riot after six days.

Analysts said the riot was nominally a race riot, but there were several other factors involved. In the decade before the riot, the Hispanic population had increased by 119 percent, and many black janitors in the downtown area had lost their jobs to Hispanic immigrants willing to work for half as much. Blacks and Korean immigrants were at odds as the Koreans began to take over stores in the black areas, especially greengrocer and liquor stores, and blacks felt that they were mistreated as customers and possible employees. The acrimony peaked just a year before the King verdict, when on March 16, 1991, a frail Korean woman shot and killed a fifteen-year-old black girl who towered over the Korean woman and beat her savagely in a dispute over an apparently stolen bottle of orange juice. Blacks were outraged over what they saw as a lenient sentence given the Korean woman. At the same time, the largest Los Angeles street gangs, the Bloods and the Crips, had declared a truce and had decided to concentrate on making political demands on the police and what they saw as the Los Angeles political establishment.

The result was a riot that was described by some observers as involving thousands of black, Hispanic, and even white young males, who embarked on a spree of lawlessness. Stores were looted and burned (especially those owned by Koreans), bystanders were beaten, and street gangs settled scores both with each other and with the police while other criminals used the chaos to benefit themselves. Reporters who interviewed looters to determine if they felt the looting was an appropriate response to the King verdict were greeted with answers saying they had no idea who Rodney King was (one answered that he didn't follow sports and thus didn't know King). The looters were mainly there because they heard on the street that the store was available for looting.

Los Angeles had had a black mayor, Tom Bradley, a prior police lieutenant, from 1973 to 1993, and would have a black chief of police, Bernard Parks, in 1997. But this made little difference in the cries of "police brutality" that would arise from the inner city. What most residents of the inner city had in common was poverty, not race, and the outs are often resentful of the ins.

The prime lesson to be drawn from the Rodney King riots in terms of housing is that race is not so much the issue now in the national movement to the suburbs as is poverty. Inner cities now collect the poor of all races, and inadequate employment, housing, schools, and healthcare lead to young adults, mostly male, who turn easily to crime. Inner cities are filled with drive-by shootings and murders, lawless gangs, and males who don't finish even high school. Few people of any race choose to live in such an environment, and most people pick the suburbs if they can afford them. Whatever social defects so-called experts find in life in the suburbs, people find them safe and full of good schools. These are the issues that carried the greatest weight.

July 1992 — William Schneider, a known television political commentator (especially on CNN) and an expert in determining trends, wrote an article in the *Atlantic Monthly* titled "The Suburban Century Begins." In his view the argument about whether suburban living was the wave of the future in spite of the complaints of critics was already determined. Suburban living was here to stay for some time, and it would not easily be replaced by other modes, regardless of the wishes of professional critics.

Schneider has commented that "to move to the suburbs is to express a preference for the private over the public.... Suburbanites' preference for the private applies to government as well." The converse of this thought is that those left behind in the inner cities will express a growing preference for the public in government as was shown so starkly in the presidential election of 2000 (see listing).

1992 Mall — Following decades of shopping mall construction in the United States, with each new mall seeming to boast of being the biggest yet, the Mall of America (MOA) was opened in Bloomington, Minnesota, a suburb in the Minneapolis area. This mall set out to be the biggest superregional mall of them all, and by 2002 it had met its goal. MOA included 4 anchor large department stores, more than 520 other stores, 51 restaurants, 8 nightclubs, 14 theater screens, and various theme park attractions. Camp Snoopy had 28 rides, a speedway, a bowling alley, and an aquarium with a 1.2 million gallon capacity and 3,000 marine animals.

The mall had a building area of 4.2 million square feet, and leaseable space of 2.5 million square feet. With its many demonstrations and special attractions, the mall drew between 600,000 and 900,000 visitors ever week, or about 42.5 million yearly. The MOA claimed to top Disney World, Graceland (and Elvis), and the Grand Canyon as the top tourist destinations in the United States.

People everywhere (especially women) love to shop in retail surroundings, and in 2000 the United States had about twice as much retail shopping space per citizen (1900 square feet) than any other country in the world. Most of it was in the malls in the suburbs. For example, even though not as big as the MOA, the South Coast Plaza/Mall in suburban Orange County,

California, claimed to do more retail business every day than all of downtown San Francisco. There were over 43,000 malls of all types in the United States around 2000, and most were quite easily accessible by car in the suburbs. In fact, some critics complained that some mall planners deliberately made access by public transportation difficult to restrict the attendance at the malls to a more upper class clientele. True or not, malls were generally a suburban phenomenon and supported the movement of people to the suburbs and away from the cities.

May 15, 1995— Peter Gordon, an economics professor at the University of Southern California, commented on what he saw as elitism in those who derided the suburbs. He said, "There is this strange conceit among architects that people ought to live in what they design. If you look at how people really want to live in this country, suburbanization is not the problem, it is the solution."

1995— The Bank of America issued what became a famous report on sprawl in California. The report was titled "Beyond Sprawl: New Patterns of Growth to Fit the New California." The report stated, "Urban job centers have decentralized to the suburbs. New housing tracts have moved even deeper into agriculturally and environmentally sensitive areas." The report then decried certain costs associated with such sprawl, and stated that it was time to stop these costs for the general good.

But even a decade later sprawl continued in California, driven as usual by people who want to live in the suburbs and contractors who build homes to support their desires. Analysts comment that once again, the move to suburbia continues to feature persons on one side wringing their hands about what they see as undesirable consequences of the move, and persons on the other who are moving to what they see as a preferable (i.e., safe) area to live.

January 21, 1996— James DeFrancia, a housing developer in suburban Washington, D.C., said that critics who claimed suburban sprawl was not an efficient use of land were missing the point. He commented, "Sprawl is what you do on Sunday afternoons on the couch. It's comfortable and it's got some room. Efficiency is when you get the middle seat on USAir with the crying baby next to you." There was no question in his mind which choice most people would prefer.

July 29, 1996— Writer G. Scott Thomas (see entry for 1998) published an article in the journal *Business First* titled "What Downtown Workers Think About Downtown." A survey of 400 business leaders in Buffalo, New York, two-thirds of whom lived in the suburbs, commented on the reasons outside work they were attracted back to the core of the city. The top five reasons included the performing arts, sports, festivals and special events, bars and restaurants, and music at clubs and concerts. But almost none mentioned such things as shopping or housing. These latter items were now seen as the province of the suburbs. Even among people who worked downtown, the only reason to visit the core of the city was to attend some form of entertainment. Otherwise, it was a place to avoid.

November 1996— The election for mayor of metropolitan Miami was used as a model by writer G. Scott Thomas (see entry for 1998) to try to forecast how whites, blacks, and Hispanics would cooperate politically as they gained nearly equal shares of the populations of inner cities. As the movement to the suburbs by whites continued to reduce their presence in the inner cities, other races would gain higher percentages of the total. Thomas had developed a model for the United States using what he called "mother cities" essentially to represent the large cities that had dominated the country around 1940, and then lost their control in the next half-century as the result of the massive movement to the suburbs.

As of the 1990 census, mother cities in the United States were 51 percent white, 28 percent black, 16 percent Hispanic, and 5 percent Asian. By 2020, the mix was expected to be 30 percent white, 31 percent black, 29 percent Hispanic, and 10 percent Asian. The question Thomas was trying to answer was whether the once-minority mix of blacks and Hispanics would tend to work together politically if they held equality with whites or whether race would tend to predominate in the new arrangement within the cities as whites continued to move to the suburbs.

The Miami election for mayor seemed to be a good test case. The candidates were a black Republican, Arthur Teele, and a Hispanic Democrat, Alex Penelas. Because blacks tend to vote Democratic everywhere, and Miami Hispanics tend to vote Republican, it would be a good test of party versus race. It was no contest. Whites divided their votes almost equally between the two candidates, blacks voted 95 percent for the black candidate even if he was a Republican, and Hispanics voted 92 percent for the Hispanic candidate even if he was a Democrat. The clear winner was race.

The Hispanic Democrat Penelas was elected mayor. In a famous picture he was embraced at his victory party by Congresswoman Ilena Ros-Lehtinen, who was a Republican, but more importantly in her mind, a Hispanic. The lesson Thomas drew from the election was that in the inner cities, race topped party. In a national election, inner city voters in large cities cast their votes for Democrats by more than 80 percent because they are bound by similarities of being mostly poor and in favor of "Big Government" support (see listing for the presidential election of 2000), but within a given city, local government elections are usually won on the basis of race.

This process is the result of the movement to the suburbs during the second half of the 20th century, leaving the nation essentially split into those who live in the suburbs and those who do not. In the 1990 census, the suburbs were 81 percent white, 7 percent black, 8 percent Hispanic, and 4 percent Asian. By 2020 they are forecast to be 67 percent white, 9 percent black, 16 percent Hispanic, and 7 percent Asian. This change is not due to fewer whites leaving the inner cities for the suburbs, but due to the fact that the Hispanic percentage of the total population in the United States will grow substantially by 2020. But some experts feel that the political vote in the future, at least in the suburbs, will divide more along suburban-urban lines than along racial lines. Whether you reside in or out of the suburbs will still be the great dividing line. Some analysts comment that the United States has always had ethnic differences in voting, but now they have been collected into two regions, the suburbs and the inner cities.

January 19, 1997—The *Denver Rocky Mountain News* reported that the Smithsonian Institute in Washington had decided to include an original home from Levittown (see listing for October 1947) in the collection as the most notable element of modern suburbia's early days. But after some months of searching, the Smithsonian was unable to find such a home. Levittown's over 17,000 original homes had all been modified since 1947. Most of the modifications included expansion, especially in the addition of garages and bedrooms. In a few the modifications were less dramatic, but not a single original home appeared to exist as it was built some 50 years ago. The Smithsonian still concluded that Levittown was the most notable "souvenir" from the initiation of the mass-produced suburb, but finding an original house was not to be. Some other approach would have to be taken.

March 23, 1997—The *Washington Post* reported that Fairfax County, Virginia (see listing for edge cities and Garreau, 1991), had lost 40 percent of its tree cover, mostly since the mid–1970s with the arrival of Tyson's Corner and several other edge cities. In a clear demonstration of both sides of this issue, newspaper reporters Glenn Frankel and Steven Fehr interviewed Til Hazel, the key developer of Tyson's Corner, and told him that twenty acres a day were disappearing because of new construction. Hazel's response illuminated the gap between the two sides:

"So what?" Hazel was quoted as saying. "The land is a resource for people to use and the issue is whether you use it well.... Is the goal to save green space so the other guy can look at it?" When asked about his decades of legal wrangling in this area, Hazel replied, "It's a war. How else would you describe it?"

May 4, 1997 — Writing in the *Detroit News*, reporter Jon Pepper noted that in 1996, a total of 23,338 building permits were issued in the seven counties of southeastern Michigan, but only 86 were for the city of Detroit. Economist David Littman of Comerica Bank noted that even where construction was taking place in Detroit, it was offset by demolition and the reduction of values elsewhere. Such offsets did not occur in the suburbs of Troy and Bloomfield Hills, for example. The result was continued growth in the suburbs and continued decline in the core city of Detroit.

1998 — Writer G. Scott Thomas, in his book *The United States of Suburbia*, published in 1998 (see Bibliography), points out that as predicted by famous landscape architect and historian Frederick Law Olmsted as early as 1860, the older suburbs in the United States have already entered the phase of decay that caused their original inhabitants to leave the city and move to the now decaying suburbs years earlier. At that time those suburbs offered a respite from city life. It would appear that the market and environmental pressures that began the march to the suburbs have already begun to consume the older suburbs.

Olmsted was a pioneer landscape architect who built Central Park in New York City and did much work on the capitol grounds in Washington, D.C., among other notable places in the late 1800s. Olmsted was a great believer in the attractiveness of green space and wooded areas, and he foresaw that affluent city dwellers would be attracted to the suburbs around city areas. In a letter written in 1860, relative to the villas being built in suburbs around New York City which were then overrun as the city continued moving outwards, Olmsted said the suburbs would not produce what the builders wanted "if they failed to offer some assurance to those who wish to build [new] villas that these districts shall not be bye and bye invaded by the desolation which thus far has invariably advanced before the progress of the town."

A little over 100 years later, in the 1970s, the inner suburbs of Boston, Cleveland, Pittsburgh, and St. Louis lost over 10 percent of their residents. In the Detroit area, the poster child for such losses, the 21 first ring suburban communities adjoining the city lost 19 percent of their population between 1970 and 1990, a net decline of almost 170,000 people. The city lost 486,000 of its population during the same time (about a third of its total). Even such previously elegant suburbs as Dearborn and Warren were now showing clear signs of urban decay.

Thomas stated that such decay is inevitable. However, the outer rings of such suburban areas can continue to thrive for some time because they essentially lose contact with their prior core city and its first-ring suburbs. For example, in Detroit, the city and its first-ring suburbs accounted for 45 percent of the metro area's population in 1970. But by 1990, their share dropped below 34 percent. Further, the city and its inner rings accounted for $21 billion in aggregate income while the outer rings totaled $59 billion. Thomas sees such decay eventually spreading across the nation.

An example of his forecast coming true is the note from Fairfax County, Virginia, in June 2002 (see listing) that local government was forced to ban the paving over of front yards where local immigrants had gathered in large numbers in what were considered suburban homes. They came together to share the rent or mortgage, and began paving over their front lawns to provide parking for everyone jammed in the house. Analysts noted that this is one way the decay from inner cities invades the suburbs and lowers property values accordingly, giving credence to the basic FHA (Federal Home Administration) rationale to limit mortgage guarantees in areas having mixed residents.

June 1999— Architect Douglas Kelbaugh, in an article in *Urban Land*, noted archly "suburbia may be paved with good intentions, but mainly it is paved." It was yet another professional complaint against the way suburban malls and office parks continued to expand in a way designed to serve the automobile instead of any form of public transportation. But most of the complaints continued to be from professionals in the field of housing. "Regular" people continued to move to the suburbs and patronize their malls and office parks.

1999 Wal-Mart— Wal-Mart passed a total of 900,000 employees, making it the largest private employer in the United States, surpassing General Motors. Wal-Mart has since extended its lead. Wal-Mart is by far the biggest of the big-box stores, carrying literally everything (including groceries) in its huge stores ranging from 50 thousand to over 250 thousand square feet. Wal-Mart claims to serve 93 million American shoppers weekly.

With its relentless drive to improve efficiency and cut costs, Wal-Mart (and smaller specialty stores like it) have driven many local stores out of business in both old downtowns and older suburbs. The State of Iowa estimated that in the ten years between 1993 and 1983, a total of 7,326 retail stores went out of business within its borders. As the businesses failed, fewer and fewer people remained in downtown areas and more and more people moved to the suburbs, where both the best shopping and jobs existed.

1999— One problem that was driving the need for more suburbs in this era was the fact that the average new house being built at this time contained 2,250 square feet on a 12,910 square foot lot. In the 1950s, even though households were generally larger than now, the average new house held 800 square feet on a 5,000 square foot lot. As a result, the amount of land needed to house Americans grew much faster than simple population growth would have suggested.

In addition, in 1999, garages were needed to house the cars required by the family, and these garages could exceed the 750 square feet for a standard Levittown house in the late 1940s (see listing for 1947) if children in the house had reached the car ownership stage. This drive towards ever-larger houses with extra space created a period of tear-downs where older (and smaller) homes were torn down to build larger houses (dubbed "McMansions") in the same neighborhoods. Such homes were often out of scale and style with their neighbors.

2000 Census— The census of 2000 counted 72.3 million children under age 18 in the United States. It was pointed out that the Bureau of Transportation counted 131.8 million passenger vehicles registered in the United States as of 1998. Thus, one measure of the extent to which Americans treasured their cars and light trucks was that there were almost twice as many cars and trucks in the country as there were children under age 18 (some of which already owned their own cars and trucks).

It was this ownership level that easily supported the movement of people and businesses to the suburbs, where personal transportation was mandatory and public transportation almost non-existent.

October 2000— Data taken from the Census of 2000 showed that 80 percent of the total housing stock existing in the United States had been built since 1940. Also, of the just over 100 million occupied housing units, nearly two-thirds were single-family detached homes. These houses have been getting larger and larger in each decade since World War II, but households have been getting smaller. For example, the standard married-couple family with children under 18 made up less than 25 percent of all households in 2000, and most of these families had two wage earners where the wife worked outside the home. Perhaps most surprising was the fact that about a third of all households consisted of one person living alone.

An additional point about a sometimes-contentious issue was the fact that in the United States only 2 percent of the population resides in so-called public housing. In most industrial countries, the percentage is usually at least 10 times as high. This reflects the continuing debate in the United States as how best to provide housing for the poor. It is a debate that has been ongoing for about 350 years.

October 24, 2000— *The New York Times* carried an article by Tamar Lewin titled "Now a Majority: Families with 2 Parents Who Work." The article pointed out that nearly 60 percent of mothers with children under the age of one were in the paid labor force. The need to have two incomes was often a requirement for affording the mortgages and other costs of the new and larger houses in the suburbs.

November 7, 2000— The presidential election of 2000 was held, but it took until December 13, 2006, nearly six weeks later, to get a final result. George W. Bush was then declared the winner over incumbent Vice President Albert Gore. It was a very contentious election, and one special factor was that for the first time since 1888, a presidential candidate (Gore) received more popular votes than the electoral winner, Bush. In 1888, Democrat Grover Cleveland lost to Republican Benjamin Harrison in a near carbon copy of the 2000 election in terms of percentage of the vote received.

Another notable factor was the 2000 presidential vote demonstrated the degree to which voters in the inner cities, especially those of both East and West Coasts and the Mid-West, had become a homogenous voting block. Al Gore gained his overall total vote margin in the 2000 election in just nine heavily Democratic enclaves focused on inner cities that together accounted for only 9 percent of the total vote.

These Democratic enclaves voted for Gore by a margin of 73.3 percent and gave him an edge of 4.3 million popular votes. The rest of the country, including the suburbs where the majority of the people lived, represented 91 percent of the total vote, and gave Bush a winning margin of 52 percent, which amounted to a popular vote margin of just over 3.7 million votes. The result was that Gore won the national popular vote by a margin of 0.6 million popular votes, primarily because the inner cities voted homogenously for Gore, while the supposedly homogenous suburbs split their vote almost evenly.

The nine Democratic enclaves were downtown New York City (the Bronx, Brooklyn, Manhattan, and Queens), Los Angeles County and accompanying Alameda County, Cook County (Chicago), Wayne County (Detroit), Philadelphia County, and Cuyahoga County (Cleveland), and the cities of Washington, D.C., and San Francisco. Downtown New York City voted for Gore by 83 percent, San Francisco by 82.6 percent, and Philadelphia by 81.6 percent, and Washington, D.C., by an astounding 90.5 percent.

These results would seem to conflict with the complaint by many critics that the suburbs are much too homogenous. Politically, at least, the vote in the suburbs (which are most of the rest of the nation) was close to 50–50. But in the large cities the vote is as unanimous as such things ever get. In a world in which one is fortunate to get a vote margin of 60 percent when the question is as simple as where to have lunch, the Democrats get vote margins well over 80 percent in the coastal big cities and the old cities of the

Midwest. If one is looking for almost complete homogeneity in terms of voting patterns, these big cities are the place to look, not the suburbs.

And this reverse-homogeneity is the point. Decades of movement to the suburbs have left the coastal big cities and the old cities of the Midwest listed above almost identical in demographics (as well as economics and related issues). These cities now primarily consist of poor minorities and poor whites, and the proportion that is made up of minorities continues to grow. Minorities and poor whites are the biggest users of governmental welfare systems, and their prime employer in these enclaves is often the government as well, in teaching and running healthcare and welfare systems to serve their demographic group. Such persons are strongly in favor of what used to be called "big government," and this explains their overwhelming tendency to vote Democratic.

The nation is essentially divided economically by housing status (within inner cities and outside inner cities), and these left in the inner city enclaves listed above are far more homogenous in terms of their voting patterns than those who have escaped to the suburbs and elsewhere. The appendix shows how such voting homogeneity in the Democratic enclaves gives them an influence far outweighing their total numbers because of their tendency to vote absolutely alike.

June 2002— Fairfax County in Virginia, not far from Washington, D.C., passed a controversial regulation forbidding homeowners to pave over their front yards. The issue arose as a result of immigrants of all types forming households of many people all joining together to pay the rent or mortgage. They are coming together in suburban homes because these turn out to be close to the jobs they are able to find only in the suburbs, rather than the cities. Many people in the house means many cars competing for limited parking space, so the house owners began to pave over their front yards for parking. Their neighbors complained to the city, and the city fathers responded with the new regulation.

November 2002— The most recent revision of the American Housing Survey issued by the Census Bureau showed 106.3 million occupied housing units in the United States, of which 31.7 million (29.8 percent) are in central cities, 53.6 million (50.4 percent) in suburbs within metropolitan areas, and 21 million (19.8 percent) in rural areas (some of which are also suburbs). This means that as of this date, more housing units were in the suburbs (well over 50 percent) than in the central cities and rural areas combined. This margin will continue to grow because most of the average of 1.5 million housing units built in the United States between 1994 and 2002 were built in the suburbs.

2003 Setha Low—A book written by anthropologist Setha Low titled *Behind the Gates: The New American Dream*, estimated that about 16 million American people as of 2002 were living in gated communities for the extra sense of security they perceived they gained. A sense of a safer living place (and safer schools) has always been a strong factor in attracting people to the suburbs.

2003 Dolores Hayden—In her comprehensive book *Building Suburbia* (see Bibliography), noted author Dolores Hayden ends the book with a chapter which is an impassioned plea to preserve older suburbs as one way to achieve the lower cost housing she envisions will be needed in the 21st century to house the "people of color" and related groups who have not had an equal opportunity in the past to share in the nearly permanent housing boom in the United States in the prior century. Some critics of this kind of upbeat ending have said that such books often conclude in essence that if only everyone in the housing business, buyer and seller, will act differently than they have done in the past, things will be better in the future. Hayden, who is no fan of the suburbs as they have developed in the United States, and as is usual for writers taking this hopeful approach, does not describe how the long-standing patterns of housing development that got us to this point will change their dynamics.

November 2, 2004—The presidential election of 2004 was very similar to that of 2000 (see listing for November 7, 2000) except that incumbent President Bush and the Republicans did a little better in all areas and beat Democrat John Kerry in both the electoral vote and the popular vote. From a housing standpoint, the Democratic big-city enclaves on both coasts and the upper Midwest (see November 7, 2000) still voted overwhelmingly Democratic, showing that the nation continued to be divided into two voting groups: those who lived in the inner cities and those who live outside the inner cities. Further, in terms of voting patterns, the big cities continued to be much more homogenous than the suburbs, contrary to the claims of many critics of excessive homogeneity in the suburbs.

September 13, 2005—DataQuick Information Systems, a real estate research firm, released data showing that the median home price in the six-county Southern California area rose 17 percent to $476,000 in August of 2005 compared to August of 2004 (the six counties included in the Southern California designation are San Bernardino, Los Angeles, Riverside, Ventura, Orange, and San Diego in order of highest percent change). This increase was a bit of a surprise because similar increases in June and July had been 16.7 percent in July and 15 percent in June respectively, making it appear the average increases of over 20 percent for the years 2003 and 2004 were finally slowing down (the increase in May of 2004 was a huge 26.9 percent). It was felt these increases were not sustainable, and the result of a continuation of such increases would be the popping of a real estate bubble similar to what happened in the stock market crash of 2000 after the dot-com bubble of the 1990s finally popped.

The August data suggested that the real estate market had not yet begun to cool down substantially in Southern California, one of the nation's hottest markets. However, the increases in San Diego County were only 2.1 percent. Prices have been relatively flat in San Diego County since last December, and total sales have been declining for the last 13 months. San Diego County has been a bellwether for the area during the five-year boom, so it may be a leading indicator for the decline as well. The declining sales usually portend falling prices, but in most of the region the supply of houses remains far lower than the demand, and this effect keeps the prices of the houses that do get sold going higher.

The biggest factor in pushing house prices continually higher is the availability of easy financing with low interest rates. Mortgages are available even for those with poor credit with low (in some cases no) down payments. People continue to buy affordable monthly payments without much concern for the prices of the houses. Easier underwriting standards can be tolerated because with constantly rising housing prices those who default can still sell out for a profit. The housing industry has become one of where many people are looking for potential capital gains rather than a place to live per se. How long such circumstances can continue remains to be seen.

September 18, 2005— Two reports were made in the past week that raised questions about mortgage practices that are typical of those that arise during — or near the end of— housing booms. The first report was from the Federal Reserve that questioned whether factors other than economics were at work in causing more blacks and Hispanics to have higher cost (subprime) mortgages than whites and Asians.

Generally, about 33 percent of blacks and 20 percent of Hispanics had such loans compared to 9 percent of whites and 6 percent of Asians. Mortgage industry spokesmen pointed out that is exactly what should be expected in an industry where loans are made primarily on the basis of income levels and credit histories. Activists claimed racial factors were at work, even if the data did not clearly indicate such was the case.

Analysts pointed out that this type of data is often seized upon by those looking for evidence of racial discrimination who tend to find what they are looking for, even though objectively the data are simply another indicator that because of many factors, blacks and Hispanics unfortunately tend to have lower incomes and poorer credit histories than whites and Asians. A second report seemed to confirm that racial factors are not at work because many observers are concerned that lenders seem to have greatly lowered their underwriting standards in an effort to keep loan volumes high.

The prime objects of the complaints are the adjustable-rate loans, some with introductory rates as low as 1 percent, that permit people to buy homes with mortgages they will not be able to pay when the rates rise as scheduled. Some estimate that by 2007 as much as $1 trillion in rate increases could be due compared to $83 billion in 2005. These increases are the result of the fact that an unprecedented 63 percent of all loans written in 2004 were of the adjustable-rate mortgage (ARM) type.

Analysts point out that many companies want to write a high volume of loans to keep the income from fees associated with writing the loans at a high level. Such companies often sell their mortgages at a discount to other companies who deal in such mortgages. The basic mortgage writer wants nothing to do with future payment risk. They only want the fee income. To some extent they are like the real estate brokers who encourage homeowners to list their homes for sale at inflated prices. These brokers are only interested in the commission they receive for listing a house. They don't care if the house ever sells, they only are interested in listing commissions.

Such things are not new in the housing industry, but they tend to accelerate when a boom is nearing its end and everyone wants one additional piece of the pie. The definitions and potential problems associated with such loans are discussed in the appendix.

October 7, 2005—A report in the *Los Angeles Times* described how the housing frenzy in the United States has spread to Mexico. The Mexican government is helping workers get mortgages with payments as low as $75 a month. This permits them to finance houses with a size of only 328 square feet, smaller than a typical American two-car garage. The houses sell for prices in the $16,000 range. Proponents of the plan say the houses are better than the typical slums that ring big cities in Mexico, and in addition building the houses create jobs in the construction industry. Buyers of the houses see them as a legacy they can leave to their children instead of wasting their money on rent payments.

Mexican critics contend that in thirty years when the mortgages are paid off the generally poorly built houses will not be worth much as a legacy, even if anyone wanted to continue living in what will almost certainly be the slums of tomorrow. But the urge to own a house and share in the possible future appreciation they see ahead is almost overwhelming in light of the housing boom they see taking place in the United States.

October 11, 2005—A presidential commission took up the question of eliminating or reducing some "sacred" income tax deductions homeowners presently receive, such as mortgage interest and real estate taxes. These deductions have existed for many years, and capital gains taxes were eliminated in 1997 on most home sales. This has given impetus to the housing boom that has existed for nearly the same period.

Huge forces are at work in this issue. It is estimated that the capital gains exemption drained nearly $30 billion from tax receipts in the United States last year alone (about 60 times as much as originally estimated). In all its forms, the tax break to homeowners exceed $100 billion yearly. The argument is that these incentives fuel the demand for home ownership which fuels construction jobs, and sales of such things as home furnishings and appliances. Further, it is anticipated that the selling price of homes would drop significantly if some of the tax breaks were reduced. So any moves in the direction of reducing tax incentives for home ownership would have to be made very carefully.

Few meaningful changes were made in 2005, especially since 2006 was an election year. However, pressure is building for action in this area because the home ownership rate has barely budged in the last four years (moving from 68.1 percent to 68.6 percent), and if the goal of higher home ownership is not being met (the rate has actually changed very little for decades), the tax breaks may not be worth the cost to the nation's budget. There is also a view that the tax breaks favor the wealthy. It seems clear some changes will be made, but when and how much are still very much undefined.

October 26, 2005— Los Angeles mayor Antonio Villaraigosa announced that he was planning to try to put a $1 billion bond measure before voters to address the low end of the housing market to provide housing for the poor and homeless.

More money would be spent on building apartments for the poor and to provide more subsidies for first-time homebuyers. But critics pointed out that low-income housing has a stigma attached and voters often did not approve such bond issues. There is also the issue of placement of such housing projects. Even those who might be inclined to help want to be sure such projects are built somewhere else, not next door.

The mayor's announcement came just one day after he promised to assign $50 million to offer more services and housing for the homeless. He promised to make this money available by shifting funds from agencies within the city's purview and thus no voter approval would be needed. But Orlando Ward, a spokesman for the Midnight Mission that helps the homeless on skid row, said the money would be useful only if it were part of a larger overall plan to combat the entire issue of homelessness. This issue requires much more than assistance in providing housing of some sort. Many of the home-less are mentally disabled, ill with AIDS/HIV, or addicted to drugs. As such, many refuse well-intended help. According to Ward, there are about 91,000 homeless people in Los Angeles County, and about 35,000 (almost 40 per-cent) are chronically homeless individuals whose needs are more medical than simply a question of shelter. Simply providing shelter is not enough. Pro-viding some sort of what's known as supportive housing has worked out much better in small trials and studies, but long-term commitments are needed to assure success. In Ward's view (he is an ex-homeless drug addict), incentives are needed to get most homeless off the street and shelter is just one piece of the puzzle.

October 27, 2005 — After falling almost constantly from the middle of 1995, mortgage default notices rose slightly (3.5 percent) compared to a year earlier during the July–September quarter of 2005 in California, according to a report from DataQuick Information Services, a real estate research ser-vice. Combined with a separate report issued by the Commerce Department in Washington, D.C., that the inventory of unsold homes nationwide rose to a new record, the data seemed to indicate that the housing boom may be slowing to a "tiny" extent. Neither report was very significant on its own, but real estate market watchers are looking very carefully at all relevant data to be sure to be among the first ones out if the market shows any signs of faltering. One DataQuick analyst said, "It's hard to call it a cooling market. What's cooling is the rate of hotness."

October 31, 2005 — A report in the *Los Angeles Times* described how crit-ics have complained that Ameriquest Capital Corporation, a large supplier of refinancing mortgages in Southern California and in the nation, is con-ducting an advertising campaign appearing to offer attractive mortgages for which most of its ultimate customers will not be able to qualify. Ameriquest specializes in so-called sub-prime loans for homeowners who have poor credit histories and thus must pay higher costs and fees to obtain mortgages with higher interest rates than well-qualified customers. Critics contend that even well qualified customers who happen to apply to Ameriquest are steered into higher cost loans.

Ameriquest is trying to settle inquiries into its lending practices by attorney generals and regulators of 30 states. The company has set aside $325 million toward a resolution of the issues. Ameriquest claims that its advertising campaigns are not misleading per se, but are simply part of an effort to raise awareness of its name so that its direct mail advertisements are more likely to be opened rather than simply thrown in the trash. The issue again is a sign of the almost frenzied efforts that loan companies take to keep up their market share of mortgages written at what appears to be the peak of a housing boom.

December 13, 2005— Writer Joel Kotkin, author of *The City: A Global History*, replied in the opinion section of the *Los Angeles Times* that Mayor Antonio Villaraigosa was mistaken in pronouncing that Los Angeles needed to mimic the large cities of the East Coast and Europe in terms of developing more high-density apartment buildings that are transit-dependent. The mayor stated that living in a three-bedroom home with front and back yards was a concept of the past.

Kotkin stated that to the contrary, it was the mayor's vision that was a concept of the past, and the city of Los Angeles has constantly pursued the concept of dispersion and living in single-family homes. Trying to make the city more densely populated would simply create a third-world city of high congestion like Tehran or Mexico City. Zoning laws passed just after the beginning of the twentieth century encouraged the development of sub-centers, single-family homes, and widely dispersed industrial centers. Subsequent development encouraged the use of the automobile to connect its widely dispersed regions, and in 1923 the city planner stated that Los Angeles had avoided "the mistakes which have happened in the growth of metropolitan areas of the East."

One editor of the time stated that Los Angeles residents could enjoy their flowers, orchards, lawns, and plenty of elbowroom. In the 1930s, single-family residences accounted for 93 percent of the city's residential buildings compared to almost half that percentage in Chicago. Voters in 1986 passed a growth-limitation issue by nearly 70 percent to protect residential neighborhoods. In 2003, a poll showed that 86 percent of residents preferred to live in a single family home. So much for dense high rise development.

Kotkin pointed out that in most places in the advanced industrial world, from Tokyo to Toronto to Paris to Buenos Aires, the bulk of metropolitan job and population growth was occurring in places that look more like Manhattan Beach, California, than Manhattan, New York. Meanwhile, the congested centers of noted cities like Chicago, Boston, San Francisco, Paris, Frankfurt, Hamburg, and Tokyo are losing population. The reason is that people prefer privacy and space to density.

Los Angeles needs to concentrate on building a better version of what it is, a city that has created a new model of urbanism, rather than trying to become something it is not and most of its residents do not wish to be.

December 14, 2005— The *Los Angeles Times* carried a report from the Housing and Urban Development Department that in 2003, the year for which the most recent data were available, 5.18 million low-income households

(4.89 percent of U.S. families) experienced critical housing needs because of low incomes, high rents, or substandard conditions. This compared with an almost identical number of 5.2 million in 1995 in spite of the great housing boom since 1995.

Of the households with worst case needs, 2.76 million (57 percent) were white, 1.04 million were black, and 1.04 million were Hispanic (meaning blacks and Hispanics evenly divided the other 43 percent).

January 9, 2006—In the last two years, over 160 dairies, nearly 80 percent of those previously in operation, have been sold to real estate developers in what is known as the Inland Empire in the Los Angeles region. A report by the Milk Producers Council, a California industry trade association, said that in five years what was a $500 million dairy industry in the area could be gone entirely.

Real estate developers are offering $400,000 to $500,000 an acre or more for land that farmers bought for as low as $50,000 to $100,000 per acre just five years ago, and at a fraction of that price decades ago. The milk production lost in the Inland Empire is being easily replaced by other milk producing areas of California. In 1947, the Levitt brothers bought out the potato farmers in Long Island to start Levittown (see listing), and today dairy farmers about 100 miles from the ocean are being bought out to start housing tracts in Southern California to meet the demand for new homes. Homeowners in the Inland Empire are willing to drive several hours to commute to their jobs near Los Angeles and the ocean because the only houses they can afford to buy are being built on the relatively cheap land that used to be populated by Holstein cows.

January 17, 2006—The National Association of Realtors issued a report showing that 43 percent of first-time homebuyers in the nation put no money down on their purchase, financing 100 percent of their home. An additional 50 percent financed 71 percent to 99 percent of their purchase. This means that less than 7 percent put down the 20 percent to 30 percent of the cost that used to be traditional in the real estate industry.

This trend helps to explain the nationwide housing boom that has been taking place over the last five years or so. Financing a house is being made easier and easier as nontraditional mortgage lenders seek to find ways to keep the volume of mortgages they are writing as high as possible. Whether this will contribute to the eventual busting of a housing bubble remains to be seen.

January 18, 2006—Statistics released by DataQuick Information Systems, a real estate research firm, showed that the median price of a home in

Southern California rose by "only" 13 percent in December of 2005 compared to a year earlier, the lowest such increase in nearly four years. Although 13 percent is objectively a large increase, this number is being watched closely by real estate personnel to see if they can catch the beginning of a cooling trend in the housing market before others do.

Data also showed that the inventory of unsold houses on the market has grown to 19 weeks, compared to 14 weeks a year ago. This is another indication that the housing market may be cooling somewhat. Essentially, the real estate market in Southern California, which has been one of the hottest in the nation for the last five years, has moved into a cat-and-mouse game of watching whether prices are gaining or losing. This determines what kind of exotic mortgages are needed to match to selling prices. The fundamental questions of what kind of house is needed for the size and lifestyle of the family doing the buying has slipped into the background.

January 25, 2006 — The National Association of Realtors issued a report showing that sales of existing homes in the nation fell by 5.7 percent in December 2005, reaching their lowest level since March of 2004. But for the year of 2005 in total, sales were 7.1 million units, meaning that 2005 was the fifth year in a row to set a new record.

Housing statistics have recently begun to take on this double-edge nature. New records continue to be set, while the most recent data indicates some cooling of what has been a red-hot market. Everyone seems to anticipate a decline in the housing boom, but how big it will be and when it will happen is unknown. In the meantime the disparity in the market in terms of location was shown by the fact that the nationwide median sales price for a house was $211,000 in December of 2005, while in Southern California it was $479,000.

January 26, 2006 — The California Building Industry Association reported that the number of building permits issued in the residential market in the state in 2005 dropped for the first time in ten years. The statistic was similar to most statistics issued recently in the housing industry. The headline was that the number declined from the previous year (by 3 percent), but the bulk of the story revealed that the absolute number itself was still a record high. Then much discussion was spent on whether this might mean a slowdown in the red-hot California housing market and what the implications might be in several areas. The only statistic many people are involved in at the moment is whether housing prices are going to continue to go up or may start going down.

January 29, 2006— An article in the *Los Angeles Times* said that a new type of suburb was being developed in Southern California. Rather than continuing the trend towards suburban sprawl, suburban towns are being built much more like small communities with smaller house lot sizes and mixed-use arrangements encouraging moving around the community by foot. Joel Kotkin, a senior fellow with the Washington, D.C.-based New America Foundation, a non-profit public policy institute, discussed the new approach in a book.

Kotkin's book is *The New Suburbanism: A Realist's Guide to the American Future.* The city of Fullerton in Orange County, California, is considered a stellar example of Kotkin's suggestions in the way it built new residential areas such as Amerige Heights after Hughes Aircraft Company left its 2 million square-foot plant and a 340-acre site in the early 1990s. Pasadena is another city following the approach.

But critics say the new approach is simply a stealth technique to make suburbs denser, a kind of social engineering that will actually cause the suburbs to lose their small-town character by having mixed-use projects forced upon them. This conflict appears to be yet another battle between those who say suburbs must eventually become more dense, and those who resist the idea saying suburbs are doing very nicely as they are.

February 27, 2006— The Commerce Department reported that nationwide sales of new single-family homes dropped 5 percent in January 2006 to a seasonally adjusted annual rate of 1.23 million units, the slowest rate since January of 2005. This was despite a warmer-than-usual January which analysts though would produce a small sales increase rather than a decline.

The reduced sales rate left the backlog of unsold homes at a record high, but this must be considered against the background of five straight years of record sales. Almost by definition the backlog must peak if sales slip somewhere in such a run. As usual, the prime question about the data was whether it reflected a normal variation or whether it indicated the start of a decline in the national housing market.

March 8, 2006— A poll conducted by the *Los Angeles Times* and Bloomberg Associates showed that most homeowners nationwide were optimistic that their home prices would keep on rising, although many were worried about keeping up with their adjustable mortgage payments if interest rates kept rising. Only 5 percent of respondents predicted no increase in the next three years. However, 26 percent expressed discomfort with the status of their adjustable-rate mortgages.

Analysts pointed out that most investors are usually optimistic about continual increases in the value of their assets just before any bubble bursts.

For a short time it can be a self-fulfilling prophecy because if sellers refuse to sell because they expect prices to continue to go up, prices will not fall immediately. But if a bubble is indeed ready to pop, it will do so with an even louder bang than if sellers had not resisted to the bitter end.

The poll results differed in different regions of the country, and other analysts said that such polls might result in self-fulfilling prophecies of a different kind. Bubble or not, if questions keep being asked about the expectations of homeowners for continually rising prices, some homeowners may worry too much that some unfavorable event is coming and plan to sell out before it arrives. Then prices may indeed fall. These analysts agree that the bottom line is that no one knows what is going to happen. However, those who believe the housing boom was built artificially on financing reflecting the actions of the Federal Reserve in continually lowering interest rates feel some retribution is due as rates return to higher levels.

March 14, 2006 — DataQuick Information Systems reported that the median housing price in Southern California rose to a record $480,000 in February 2005, while the number of houses sold dropped to 19,500, the lowest such number in five years. The cat-and-mouse game between buyers and sellers continues, while mortgage brokers have upped the ante by introducing 40-year mortgages in an attempt to generate ever-increasing mortgage loan volumes.

March 18, 2006 — Ted Steinberg, an environmental historian at Case Western Reserve University and author of *American Green: The Obsessive Quest for the Perfect Lawn*, pointed out in an article in the *Los Angeles Times* that in the United States, with its 50 million households and 16,000 golf courses, lawn care amounts to a $40 billion-a-year industry. That is equal to the gross national product of Vietnam. The United States is overwhelmingly the world's leader in cultivating "perfect, weed-free, ultra-trim, supergreen grass."

Some claim this need for green open spaces is genetic, because mankind developed in evolution on the open savannas of Africa. But the United States desires these green areas much more strongly than other nations, whose people evolved under the same circumstances. Steinberg claims the real reason lies with the development in the United States after World War II of the mass production of suburban homes such as Levittown (see listing). Every one of the nearly 18,000 homes in Levittown had perfect mass-produced lawns. Other large real estate developments that copied Levittown also copied their green grass ethic.

Lawn care companies then emerged in the 1950s with a mixture of products to serve the newly arising market for the perfect lawn as any company would rush to serve any new market in its purview. Stressing a higher and higher approach to perfection, lawn care companies did very well selling consumers products they didn't know they needed until they entered the race for the perfect lawn. As often happens in our capitalistically competitive society, our need for the perfect lawn is no more genetic than our need for many other products clever marketing convinces us are a requirement for our fundamental happiness.

March 25, 2006—The vagaries of the housing market in California (and elsewhere) were clearly shown by an article in the *Los Angeles Times* highlighting the sudden drop in sales of homes in a place called Merced, a town in Central California, southeast of San Francisco, that is perhaps best known as the turnoff campers take from State Route 99 to head for Yosemite Park. In 2005, Merced shared in the housing boom that made the Central Valley one of California's best real estate markets. However, in 2006, houses brought 20 percent less than they did last summer, if a buyer can be found at all.

In 2005, houses appreciated by 31 percent in Merced, making it first for appreciation in California, and ninth in the nation. Then in September of 2005, when the new university scheduled to be built there opened its first section, housing sales suddenly stopped for no apparent reason. Merced housing had been appreciating for years on what economists call the "greater fool" theory (the asset in question is not intrinsically worth what is being paid but maybe a greater fool will come along and pay more), and the greater fools had seemed to disappear. Housing sales plunged and prices did as well. In Merced, at least, the bubble had popped.

The day before the Merced article appeared in the *Times*, the Commerce Department in Washington, D.C., announced that sales of new homes nationwide had fallen 10.5 percent in February, about five times more than had been expected. This was the biggest drop in new home sales in nearly nine years. In the Western region, which includes California, sales were down 29.4 percent. In spite of all this gloomy news, sales in Southern California for the month of February were at their strongest level since February of 1988.

All of this seems highly contradictory, but it was noted that many factors are being considered in housing sales that make headlines. First, much data is collected including sales of new homes and sales of existing homes. Then the backlog of each category being offered for sale is computed, and then all of this data is compared to data for the previous month and the previous year, and periods in between. Then this pile of statistics is compiled on a nationwide basis and on a regional basis.

It is very easy to select a statistic from this mass of data to write a headline that will grab attention. For example, sales that are up from the previous month may sound optimistic until further examination shows that sales for the previous month were at the lowest level for that month in several years. And vice-versa. The bottom line is that in previously booming Merced, California, buyers have disappeared, and regardless of good news or bad news from other regions, the bubble has burst. To what extent this will happen in other regions, and when (or if), remains to be seen.

April 2, 2006— A report in the *Chicago Tribune* noted that one feature of the present housing boom is the growing number of people who own more than one home. "Snowbirds" often own more than one home in hot and cold regions for obvious seasonal reasons, but more and more people are doing it for investment purposes. The National Association of Realtors estimates that there are about 44 million second homes in the United States, 7 million for private vacation use and 37 million for investment. A survey sample showed 20 percent of homeowners own a second home, and 9 percent owned two or more "second" homes. As with the general housing market, consistently low mortgage rates are credited with the boom in second homes. It also helps that the tax laws permit two mortgages to be deducted for income tax purposes (up to certain maximums). It is another example of the how the tax laws in the country, directly or indirectly, support the growth of the single-family house as the favorite type of residence in the nation.

April 12, 2006— Data released by DataQuick Information Systems showed that, for the first time, the median price for a home in Los Angeles County exceeded $500,000 last month. The median price was $506,000, up 15 percent from a year earlier, up about 100 percent from 2002, and up more than three times from 1988. It's good news for homeowners, but on the other hand it has landed Los Angeles County on many lists of the nation's most overpriced homes markets.

There are the normal conversations about a housing bubble, but so far sellers are simply pulling their homes off the market if they don't get the price they want, and overall prices stay high. How long that situation can continue is anyone's guess. With the local economy in good shape, a mini-recession that could push people to sell to go where the jobs are is not in sight.

May 2, 2006— The parent company of Ameriquest Mortgage announced that it was planning to cut 3,800 jobs. This would amount to about one-third of its national work force. In addition, the company announced it would close all 229 of its retail branches and rely on Internet marketing instead. This is a result of a general slowdown in the housing market, and a specific slowdown in the subprime market in which Ameriquest has specialized. There have been inquires by 40 states into the manner in which Ameriquest has handled its mortgage business (mostly refinancings for subprime or poor-risk borrowers), and in January of this year Ameriquest agreed to pay $325 million to settle the cases and agreed to change its way of doing business.

Ameriquest executives said that its industry was undergoing fundamental changes that required it to cut costs. The parent of Ameriquest, ACC Capital Holdings, said it would centralize loan production in four regional offices in California, Arizona, Illinois, and Connecticut. Customers would fill out loan applications on the Internet, and then be contacted by someone from one of the regional offices.

Some analysts said the move to close all the regional offices may have been prompted by a desire by ACC Capital Holdings to gain more control of its loan operations. When all loan officers are concentrating in the four regional offices, rogue officers trying to make extra profits are more easily spotted. Among other things, claims have been made that Ameriquest has been making loan-to-own loans. In this process, loans are made to customers whose financial situation and history are so poor that they are highly likely to default. The lender collects the very profitable fees from making the subprime loan, then when the customer does default, the lender forecloses, and in an environment of rising home prices is able to make additional profit on the house even after paying selling costs.

ACC Capital Holdings stated that the change was triggered by competitive changes in its market that make the maintenance of 229 retail branches too expensive. But they also said that the move was consistent with their agreement in January with the 40 states to settle various outstanding claims. However, ACC Capital Holdings denied any wrongdoing when the claims were settled.

The economic background to the changes is that declining home sales (even if prices continue to rise) and rising interest rates have combined to cut refinancing applications by 50 percent since mid–June of 2005. A number of mortgage lenders have recently cut staffs, and subprime lender Acoustic Home Loans, based in Orange County, California, closed its doors last month. The subprime market is generally in worse shape than the overall mortgage market analyst Mike McMahon of Sandler, O'Neill and Partners in San Francisco, said. The subprime market is an undisciplined market characterized by cutthroat pricing in an attempt to gain market share, McMahon added, and he claimed the subprime market is going through the pains of transitioning to a more orderly market from both a price and regulatory standpoint. In such an environment, other analysts pointed out, more changes among subprime lenders can be expected, especially if the housing market keeps softening.

Announcements on the same day that overall mortgage defaults had risen in California by 29 percent (33 percent in Southern California) to the highest level in two years were not encouraging. Then, on May 6, it was announced that Ameriquest loan volume had dropped by 46 percent in the first quarter of 2006, possibly causing the loss of 3,800 jobs announced on May 2. This announcement also triggered rumors that Ameriquest was being put up for sale. At this point analysts said the future looks clouded for Ameriquest because its reputation is so poor that buyers would be reluctant to acquire it, and the continuing decline in mortgages being written, especially in the subprime area, will make it hard for the revenues of the company to bounce back to previous levels.

May 16, 2006— Data released by DataQuick Information Systems of La Jolla, California, showed that the median prices of homes in the Southern California region in April had increased to $485,000, an increase of 9 percent since April of 2005, but actually a decline from the March 2006 value of $486,000. This was the first year-over-year increase in single digits since 2001. Further, sales for April declined by 21 percent from last year, the biggest percentage drop in 11 years.

Taking into account the fact that price increases in the last six months in the region have risen only 2.5 percent, the overall data indicates that there is a definite slowdown taking place in the five-year housing boom in Southern California. Analysts point out that price increases are being artificially sustained to some extent because homeowners who do not feel an urgent need to sell are refusing to accept lower prices or are pulling their homes off the market. Thus, although the prices buyers are generally willing to pay have declined, this effect has not shown up yet in the average price of completed transactions as the number of actual sales continues to decline.

There is still some debate over whether prices will eventually decline or simply level off at a new plateau (a soft landing). Prices in the Southern California region have increased by an average of 7.2 percent over the past 18 years, including declines in the early 1990s. Thus, it is hard to forecast price declines immediately ahead in such a market.

May 24, 2006— The Commerce Department announced that nationwide sales of new homes were up a surprising 4.9 percent in April, hitting the highest rate (1.2 million annually) of the year. But experts in the field greeted the announcement with many caveats. They said that the rates were somewhat skewed by the fact that the government had recently revised rates downward for previous months. They also noted that the inventory of unsold homes hit a historical high in the month, and that the sales of new homes following aggressive sales campaigns were made at the expense of existing homes.

The median price of a new home nationwide in April was $238,500, up only 0.9 percent from a year earlier, much lower than the double-digit gains that had prevailed previously. Once again, experts in the field predicted softening of prices in the coming months as homeowners realized that they would have to begin to lower their asking prices to make sales. Thus the good news that sales were higher in April was loaded with so many "buts" that it began to look like bad news. The result was once more that no one really knows what will happen nationwide in the housing market, but most present forecasts are negative.

June 4, 2006—A bill was introduced in the House of Representatives in Washington. D.C., which would authorize the Federal Housing Administration (FHA) to expand the limits on the mortgages it insures to be more consistent with median home prices in especially expensive housing areas such as the Southern California region. The bill was just beginning its progress through the long legislative process, but it had bipartisan support.

June 13, 2006—Harvard University released a report showing that the record housing prices in the United States had driven housing affordability, the measure that calculates what percentage of the public can afford the standard mortgage on a median priced house, to a two-decade low. The average mortgage payment rose to 24 percent of the median income after taxes, the highest it has been since 1984 when it was 25 percent in an era when interest rates were as high as 15 percent. This affordability problem explains why so many buyers are using exotic mortgage loans such as risky interest only mortgages. These accounted for a third of all mortgages in 2005.

June 16, 2006—KB Homes, one of the largest homebuilders in the United States (it builds homes in 15 states and is one of the largest builders in France), cut its sales forecast for the year as home sales forecasts continued to soften across the nation. KB's reduced forecast followed a reduced forecast by Puite Homes, the nation's second biggest homebuilder, about two weeks ago, and a reduced forecast by Toll Brothers, the nation's largest builder of luxury homes, which was made on May 20. The outlook for new home building nationally is still officially unclear, but the largest builders have decided it is clear to them. In their view, sales are going to decline for at least 18 months.

June 20, 2006—DataQuick Information Systems reported that home sales in the Southern California region fell to their lowest level in seven years in May of 2006. Prices continued to stay relatively high, although prices in May of 2006 were "only" 6.4 percent above their level of a year earlier, the smallest such increase since July of 2000.

The highly regarded UCLA Anderson forecast said that it expects prices to level off for about five years, but "absent a recession" there should be no dramatic drop in prices because other parts of the region's economy are still doing well in spite of the cooling housing market.

The Anderson forecast has been pointing out for some time that home prices are much too high in the Southern California area, but a dramatic drop in prices could be avoided if the economy remains strong and homeowners are not forced to sell to find jobs elsewhere. But the forecast warned that there could be "some consequences" from the end of the long housing boom.

Realtors point out that as speculators withdraw from the cooling market and new buyers make commitments more slowly, realizing prices are stabilizing, sales will inevitably slow. But as sellers simply withdraw their homes from the market rather than accept a lower price, the overall median price of homes will decline very slowly.

June 26, 2006— In yet another report from the Commerce Department in Washington, D.C., regarding the housing market that had mixed interpretations by analysts, the department announced that sales of new single-family homes in the United States rose by 4.6 percent in May of 2006, confounding expectations of a slowdown in the housing market.

However, this increased rate was still down 5.9 percent from that of a year earlier, and it benefited from a downward revision of housing data from April of 2006. Reactions ranged from that of Mark Vitner, senior economist of Wachovia Securities in Charlotte, who said: "On the surface it looks like a strong number, but beneath the surface the housing market is cooling substantially," to that of Richard DeKaiser of National City Research Corporation in Cleveland who said: "On the whole, this is a comforting report to those worried about the housing market. There is no sign of a precipitous decline in demand. This is more consistent with a moderation than a steep loss." The median sales price for new single-family homes fell 4.3 percent from April to $235,300 in May 2006, a decline that left the price still 3.1 percent higher than a year earlier. There was something for everyone in the report, regardless of his individual predictions concerning the future of the housing market.

July 12, 2006— DataQuick Information Systems, a real estate information firm based in La Jolla, California, reported that housing prices in San Diego County had reached a milestone of sorts. For the first time since July of 1996, the median price of a home in San Diego County in June of 2006 fell from the median price reported a year earlier. The median price in June 2006, was 1 percent lower ($488,000) than the median price reported in June 2005 ($493,000). At the same time, the median price in Los Angeles County rose by its smallest margin since 2001.

The decline in San Diego County got the most attention because the county is generally credited with being the county where sharply appreciating housing prices kicked off a national housing boom in 2001 that resulted in home prices generally doubling in the next five years. The key questions are whether the decline will spread to other areas, and if so, how severe the decline may become. A number of areas, including Miami, New York, and Las Vegas, have shown dramatic reductions in the rate of increase recently, but San Diego County is the first major market to show an actual decline.

Reports later in the week showed that although home sales are down on the order of 20 percent in the Southern California region, median prices continue to hold up due to the more or less standard practice by now of homeowners simply refusing to sell if they can't get the price they want. The backlog of unsold homes continues to rise, but the median price of deals actually done doesn't show any declines as they did in San Diego County. Whether this can continue remains to be seen.

July 21, 2006 — The chief economist of the California Association of Realtors, Lois Appelton-Young, said she was no longer forecasting a soft landing for home prices, i.e., a gradual decline in prices as the market adjusts to declining sales. Appelton-Young said she now expects "a fairly significant shake-out." In a way, considering the old bromide that activity peaks just before a crash, the number of real estate agents in the state passed 500,000 for the first time. This confirmed Appelton-Young's forecast. One real estate agent now existed for every 55 adults in the state of California.

August 9, 2006 — The National Association of Realtors reported that the median price nationally for existing homes will increase in 2006 to $229,000 from $219,600 last year. That would represent a growth rate of 4.3 percent, below the 5 percent average of the past 50 years according to Freddie Mac, the number two mortgage buyer in the United States. Even at that, the National Trade Group for Realtors was more optimistic than many observers of the national real estate market.

September 1, 2006 — Nearly every day between the middle of August 2006, and the beginning of September of 2006, the newspapers carried at least one article reflecting negatively on the real estate market in the United States. The level of housing sales kept dropping everywhere in the nation, with 30 percent declines in such places as Southern California, where decade lows were being approached. Housing construction companies and mortgage issuing companies were reporting present and anticipated lows in activity, and the stock market values of such companies were falling. Further, there was great concern over the fact that holders of existing exotic mortgages would be unable to keep up with the new payments as the initial liberal terms of such mortgages began to expire.

The only news with a positive slant was that housing prices had not yet begun a general decline, although the present rate of increase was typically much less than anytime in the previous five years. Many industry observers commented that house prices had not yet declined only because homeowners refused to admit that the present boom was over. They simply refused to sell at prices below their expectations. This kept the inventory of unsold homes at record levels, but that was only delaying the inevitable in the view of many observers. When homeowners reached the point where they had to sell for whatever reason, prices would tumble.

The question in the air was how big would be the explosion when the housing bubble finally popped. Even the most optimistic observers felt that housing prices would remain flat for several years. The more pessimistic foresaw a decline of perhaps severe proportions.

APPENDIX 1.
PUBLIC HOUSING
IN THE UNITED STATES

Discussions of public housing in the United States go on in many ways and venues, but such housing has had a relatively small impact in the overall history of housing in this country compared to other countries. This appendix is meant to summarize the key items involved in public housing in the United States, and to show the steps that led to its becoming a relatively minor part of the housing built in the nation up to the present day.

From the time the Puritans in New England in the 1600s warned off people they saw as undesirables in their midst who might became wards of the public, through the present day of 2007, Americans have had ambiguous feelings toward those who could not, or would not, provide for themselves in the area of housing. Up until the Great Depression of the 1930s, the federal government left everything involved with housing to the individual states (except for a brief period in the 1917-1918 era when the federal government got involved in building housing for war workers).

As in so many other areas in American life, the New Deal of President Franklin Roosevelt's administration gave a major impetus to public housing with his signature of the Wagner-Steagall bill on September 1, 1937. This bill was in response to the elimination of prior federal government attempts at funding public housing that either failed to elicit the needed actions from the private sector or the states, or that finally were declared unconstitutional in January of 1935 by federal judge Charles I. Dawson (upheld on appeal) when the government tried to use the principle of eminent domain to build such housing.

The Wagner-Stegall Act (formally known as the United States Housing

Act of 1937) gave the government authority to build low-cost public housing by having the United States Housing Authority (USHA) fund designated
municipal authorities to build public housing. It was seen as the final answer
by most in the Roosevelt administration to providing housing for the poor.

However, the promise of replacing slums with government provided
public housing was never fully realized. The good news was that a quarter of
a century later, as of the end of 1962, more than two million people lived in
the about 500,000 units built under various public housing programs. But
Congress was often reluctant to fully fund such programs, especially during
the building of the many private housing projects needed to house the returning veterans from World War II, and public housing often took a back seat.
The bad news was that by 1980, about 1 percent of the United States housing market was represented by public housing, compared to 46 percent in
England and 37 percent in France.

Even where public housing was supported initially in large cities in the
United States, it finally fell out of favor as the projects became crime-ridden
and overrun by lawless gangs of black youths. This was in part because the
projects were nearly always located in existing slum areas, and the projects
eventually accepted as tenants nearly anyone on welfare rather than the
"deserving poor" who needed some temporary help as had been the original
intent. The Wagner-Steagall bill required "local initiative and responsibility" that was a "voluntary" action. This brought local politics into play, and
resulted in most public housing being built in already segregated cities and
not in suburbs. The result was many poor blacks being attracted to already
poor cities such as Newark, and some projects that were built with such high
hopes in various parts of the nation were ultimately demolished as being
hopelessly crime-ridden. Public housing came to be seen as the housing of
last resort, and the home of already segregated poor blacks (who in some
cases said slum removal was more accurately defined as black removal).

The key issues in public housing were played out in the so-called Senate Joint Committee Study and Investigation of Housing that took place in
1947-1948. These hearings became notorious because Senator Joseph
McCarthy, who later gained notoriety himself for the controversial methods
he used to pursue real or imagined communists of all types in the federal
government, essentially ran them. This was unfortunate because a great deal
of useful information was uncovered by the hearings, which were held in 33
cities across the United States.

The basic purpose of the hearings was to decide how best to meet the
massive housing needs of the veterans returning from World War II. Housing had never been built on a mass production basis in the United States
(outside of mass "plain vanilla" housing projects built for the defense workers during World War II). The question for the committee was to decide

whether to try to build such housing on a commercial scale (as the Levitt brothers were then attempting to build) and to discover what was preventing the low-cost construction of such housing, to try to see if the development of the mass production of prefabricated housing was feasible, and whether to implement a massive public housing program.

Politics, of course, was a major issue. The Republicans had scored a major victory in the 1946 congressional elections, primarily as a result of the massive strikes rained down on the American public after the end of World War II by the labor unions that flexed in the most arrogant way the power they had gained during the Roosevelt administration (President Roosevelt had died in 1945). This gave the Republicans control of Congress for 1947 and 1948, the first time they had been in control since the elections of 1931 brought Roosevelt to power. They were basically opposed to the concept of public housing, and many facts brought to light in the so-called McCarthy hearings in 1947-48 supported that view.

One housing bill that was already on the table when the hearings began was the Taft-Ellender-Wagner Act (TEW) of 1945 that proposed, among other things, to build 500,000 public housing units over the next 14 years. That bill never made it through Congress because of the results of the 1946 elections, and it was being considered as part of the study being conducted by McCarty in 1947-48.

Regardless of his blustery manner, Senator McCarthy became an expert in the existing jumble of building codes that existed across the United States. Once established to assure safety and consistent building methods, they now served a political purpose, especially with the help of unionized codes that were meant to increase the labor content of the building process and create jobs than for any other reason. Even national magazines such as *Collier's* ran articles stating that national building codes needed substantial revision to permit the efficiencies of building methods and materials discovered during World War II to be applied to the mass production of housing in the United States.

An automotive industry executive considering the entry of his company into the mass prefabricated housing business told McCarthy that the codes, if applied to his business, would require cars of different tire sizes and different fender materials and different wheel bases in different towns. No one could apply the techniques of mass production in such a situation.

Politically, heavily wooded areas mandated wood frame construction while brick-making Denver required the use of bricks and banned wood frames while glass-making Newark encouraged the use of glass blocks. In addition, union construction codes always seemed to favor the most labor-intensive approach in the name of safety and tradition. The fact that the Levitts were building Levittown with a good safety record while achieving very low costs and high rates of production while refusing to use union labor and traditional middlemen seemed to settle in the committee's mind that Levitt's approach was the one to take to achieve mass production of housing in the United States (William Levitt was a regular witness before the committee).

As far as public housing was concerned, the leaders of the committee doubted that any housing construction led by the government would dare to refuse to use union labor and traditions in the way Levitt was doing. Almost by definition, the leaders of the committee felt government-sponsored housing efforts would be far from efficient. Further, a witness from Pittsburgh had witnesses prepared to testify that government public housing in Pittsburgh was rented not to only the worthy poor as intended, but also to city employees earning good salaries, and to people of various professions. The witnesses claimed public housing was nothing but a political football in Pittsburgh, with 85 percent of all tenants being Democrats.

The proponents of the TEW bill had said it was needed to build rental housing at the lowest level of rentals for the very poor. That hardly matched the results in Pittsburgh, and in the eyes of the Republicans on the committee, such public housing was just another New Deal boondoggle. Thus, the hearings would end without any public housing being authorized.

However, the Democrats regained control of Congress in the famous upset pulled off by Harry Truman in the fall of 1948. As a result, the TEW bill would be passed in 1949. But constant renegotiations would reduce the number of public housing units actually built well below the number authorized. That would be the future history of public housing in the Congress. Actual units built would generally fall far short of units authorized.

Another problem with the public housing bill was that one unit of slums had to be eliminated for every unit of public housing built. With local leaders in charge, efforts were focused on maintaining local real estate values rather than providing good housing for the poor. This again pushed public housing into high-density units in the center city rather than into decentralized units in the suburbs. This increased "white flight" from areas into which prior slum dwellers were pushed as public housing was constructed.

In the late 1960s, public housing had failed in the area of public opinion. Most people felt that the failures were due mainly to the characteristics (or lack of good character) of the mostly poor blacks who occupied such housing. In the view of many, providing low-cost housing did not provide the solution needed to bring the people occupying such housing out of the cycle of poverty and crime, so the problem must lie with the people themselves. Others pointed out that public housing was a successful part of the welfare program in other countries, so the policies and governance of the public housing program here must be at fault.

Probably the most vibrant image many had in the late 1960s of public housing was the study of the Pruitt-Igoe housing project built in St. Louis. The project typified all that was wrong with such high-rise projects. Riddled by crime and vandalism, the project had such a bad reputation even among the poor it was intended to serve that it could not fill vacancies when they became available. The project was torn down in 1976.

A book written in 1964 by Martin Anderson, a Columbia Business School professor at the time and later a key advisor in the Nixon and Reagan administrations, outlined the failings of public housing in the United States from 1949 through 1962, and probably had much to do with the further decline of public housing under the Nixon and Reagan administrations.

The book was titled *The Federal Bulldozer*, and its theme was that Washington had actually destroyed more low-income housing than it had created, and that government could best serve the housing needs of the poor by abandoning urban renewal and public housing. In essence that is what the Department of Housing and Urban Development (HUD) decided finally to do. Created as a cabinet-level department during the heyday of the administration of President Lyndon Johnson in 1965-66, HUD was charged with the responsibility of developing and executing policies on housing and cities. HUD was not any more successful with urban renewal and public housing than had been the agencies before it. It reduced its urban development (public housing) activities and focused on existing housing issues.

HUD's so-called Section 8 activities, in which HUD pays a substantial portion of the market-value rent for existing rental housing for qualified low-income applicants, is very popular. Long waiting lists exist everywhere the program is active, and the tenants end up living in what could be described as normal low-rent housing rather than isolated and stigmatized projects. Landlords give the program mixed reviews in that they don't like the red tape associated with any government program, but they are happy in many cases to accept the rent subsidies for property that might go otherwise unrented.

Such programs really represent the public housing of today in the United States. As in so many areas of housing, they exist in the United States as in other countries, but in a way and a form quite different from that of other countries. Probably New York City, once the home of most tenements in the nation, has the most reasonably successful public housing programs in the classical sense. Some buildings have waiting lists of potential new tenants, and old buildings are being torn down and replaced because of age rather than simply crime issues. There are plenty of crime issues still to be dealt with, but there are tenants who have lived there for decades, and who plan to eventually occupy the replacement buildings.

APPENDIX 2.
THE HOMOGENOUS
VOTING PROCESS OF
INNER CITY RESIDENTS

The greatly changed demographics of large cities in the United States, primarily due to the movement to the suburbs by whites and the movement to the large cities by blacks and immigrant minorities of all types, have greatly changed political voting patterns in the United States. The suburbs have the majority of the voters in that more people live in the suburbs than in the cities and rural areas combined. But these votes tend to be rather closely split between Democrats and Republicans. However, in a political sense, the cities are much more homogenous than the suburbs, the reverse of the usual charge by critics which heap scorn on the suburbs for their perceived homogeneity. This city voting homogeneity gives cities an important position in determining the total vote winner in presidential elections. Specific big city enclaves typically vote for Democrats by a margin of over 80 percent. The much more non-homogenous suburbs in this view vote for the Republicans by margins just a few points above 50 percent. This appendix shows how that difference gives big cities an influence far beyond their relative size in presidential elections.

By the presidential elections of 2000, the big cities of the northeast, mid-west, and California costal area of the United States had become steadily more concentrated with (poor) minority populations. Blacks predominated in some areas, Hispanics in others, and poor whites in some. Where elections were held within a given city of this type, the results were nearly always dominated by racial factors. But in an election on a much larger basis, such as a presidential election, the different ethnic groups came together and voted on the basis of the one thing that united them — their relative poverty.

Poor voters have come to expect the "womb-to-tomb" benefits of the type that once were typical of big government as espoused by the Democratic Party. Further, many inhabitants of the core city and even its nearby suburbs work for local, state, or federal government in order to administer the welfare plans needed by the inhabitants of the city, or in the schools providing such education as the city dwellers can hope to get. In mass transit programs, most of the workers are union members who routinely vote Democratic. So cities, especially large cities, often vote Democratic by margins exceeding 80 percent. This overwhelming margin (traditionally any winning margin exceeding 55 percent is considered a landslide in the United States) turns many entire states into so-called blue states even where most of the state on a county-by-county basis is red rather than blue.

This red-blue designation is named after the presidential election eve practice of the television networks of showing states won (or forecasted to be won) by Republicans in a red color and those won by Democrats in a blue color. If voting on a county-by-county basis were used, the United States would appear almost entirely red because about 85 percent of all counties vote Republican. However, a county in Montana may contain a few thousand voters, while the County of Philadelphia contains all 1.5 million inhabitants of that city. This effect will be discussed in greater detail later to show that in many ways present presidential elections are simply the big cities versus the rest of the country, following in many respects the distribution of preferred housing in the country.

The election of 2000 pitting George W. Bush versus Al Gore was an extreme example of the tendency of certain large cities to vote overwhelmingly for Democrats and thus give the nation one winner on a total vote basis (Gore) and one winner on an electoral vote basis (Bush) for the first time since 1888. Overall, Gore won 73.3 percent of the vote in just nine Democratic enclaves, many of which included a core city vote exceeding 80 percent for the Democrats. This gave Gore a margin of just under 4.3 million popular votes in combined parts of the country that represented only 9 percent of the total vote in the nation. In the remaining 91 percent of the country, Bush won by a margin of 52 percent, giving him a narrow electoral victory, but a popular vote margin of only 3.7 million votes. The combined results gave Gore a popular vote margin of 0.5 million votes, all earned as noted, in regions representing less than 9 percent of the total votes in the nation.

Specifically, downtown New York City (the Bronx, Brooklyn, Manhattan, and Queens) voted for Gore by 83 percent (giving him a popular vote margin of 1.3 million votes from this area alone); the city of San Francisco gave Gore 82.6 percent; Philadelphia gave Gore 81.6 percent; and Washington, D.C., gave Gore an astounding 90.5 percent. In areas combined with other local areas beyond the core city but still within the applicable voting County, Cook County (Chicago) voted 70.5 percent for Gore, Wayne County (Detroit) 70.4 percent, Cuyahoga County (Cleveland) 65.2 percent, and Los Angeles and neighboring Alameda County combined with San Francisco, 68.6 percent (giving Gore another 1.3 million vote margin in this selected area as well). It is easy to see that the core cities of those mixed areas easily exceeded 80 percent when considered alone.

Further, in terms of the popular vote, it could be said that not only was it a case of the big cities versus the rest of the country, it was actually nearly a case of downtown New York City and the coastal California cities of Los Angeles and San Francisco versus the rest of the country.

With such a great difference between voting margins in the old cities of the United States and the rest of the country, events such as a split in electoral victories and popular votes victories could readily happen again. Although the evolution of voting blocs in the extremely diverse United States is a very complicated issue, a simple example will demonstrate the power of a smaller bloc that votes a certain way by high margins to affect a total vote outcome.

Suppose there are 30 percent of the voters in inner cities, with 50 percent in suburbs and 20 percent in rural areas (a situation close to that actually existing in the United States). If the city voters vote for Party A by a margin of 80 percent, this gives Party A 24 percent and Party B 6 percent of the total vote. If the other 70 percent of the voters vote for Party B by the reasonably large margin of 60 percent, Part B will get 42 percent of the total vote and Party A will get 28 percent. The result is that Party A will win 52 percent (24 plus 28) of the total vote, and Party B will win only 48 percent (6 percent plus 42 percent), even though Party B had a landslide victory among 70 percent of the voters. In this case it can be fairly said that the inner city voters determined the popular vote outcome even though they represented only 30 percent of the voters. This is the kind of effect that the difference in housing has had on the outcome of the last two elections in the United States, and that it will have in future elections.

In the 2004 presidential election, the Republican Party did a better job of getting out the vote among their key followers, and they won the popular vote election as well as the electoral vote election. The Democrats had their typical edge in the big cities, but the Republicans simply worked harder at getting out their key voters, as even the Democrats agreed, and the Republicans had an easier victory in 2004 than in 2000. But the electoral vote was much the same in both elections (although a little better for the Republicans in 2004).

The issue of the red states versus the blue states is mostly media hype. The real story is the Democratic big cities (especially Los Angeles and New York City) versus the rest of the country. A look at the housing distribution in the country tells you most of what you need to know in analyzing national election returns.

The only truly blue state in the nation is Massachusetts, where the basic political sub-division has been named and defined as a central city for centuries. In the rest of the nation, the basic political sub-division is a county. In Massachusetts, as elsewhere, the cities vote predominately for Democrats, (in highly liberal Massachusetts 100 percent of the "cities" vote Democratic), and the color of the state is completely blue. In the rest of the country, if the map is shown by county, most of the nation appears to be colored red. This is because, as noted earlier, about 85 percent of all counties in the nation vote Republican. However, as also noted, a county of thousands of people in the mid-west is just as significant on this map as is the county of Philadelphia, which happens to include all 1.5 million residents of Philadelphia. While counties across the nation may vote more or less strongly for Republicans, the county and city of Philadelphia regularly votes for Democrats by margins exceeding 80 percent. Thus, Philadelphia will counterbalance many less populated counties in Pennsylvania in the total vote count. In the last two elections, although Pennsylvania on a county-by-county basis was clearly quite red, the state was considered a blue state because the more than 50 red counties were outvoted in total by the relatively few blue counties such as Philadelphia and Allegheny (Pittsburgh) counties. Large blue states such as New York and California demonstrate the same effect.

Thus, relatively close popular vote contests can be expected in future elections due to the effect noted above. As the population of the nation slowly grows more rapidly in the west and the south than in other areas, the electoral vote favors the Republicans. Still, various immigrant groups continue to at least maintain the populations of Los Angeles and New York City (and other cities in the west and south), so the inner-city vote by high margins in favor of Democrats will continue to keep the popular vote reasonably close.

One final footnote to the election of 2000 was the hue and cry that the election was stolen from Gore by a single vote on the United States Supreme Court. The reality, as usual, is much less dramatic than the hype. The United States Supreme Court, by a vote of 7–2, overturned the 4–3 vote of the Florida Supreme Court to continue a seemingly endless string of recounts. The basis for the reversal was that there was no standard recount process being employed as various counties were applying different recount standards as they went by that time. Then the United States Supreme Court voted by a margin of 5–4 that there was not enough time (it was already more than a month after the election) to return the case to the Florida Supreme Court to see if a new standard recount method could be devised for yet another recount process within the statutory time remaining. The result was that Bush, who had won all prescribed recounts to date, was officially the final winner.

Most people also forget that in 1991, a consortium of newspapers, led by the *Los Angeles Times* and the *New York Times*, two of the most liberal newspapers in the country, and certainly papers more than inclined to find some paper-selling results to further fuel the controversy, funded a series of recounts to see what would have happened if the recounts requested by Gore and agreed to by the California Supreme Court by that single vote had in fact continued in 2000. After trying several versions of the "pregnant chads" and the "hanging chads" and so forth, the papers concluded reluctantly (from a sensational story standpoint) that Bush would have still been the winner.

The real story about Gore in 2000 was that he failed to carry his home state of Tennessee. Previously elected senator and then vice president as a candidate in Tennessee, the people who knew Gore best rejected him as a presidential candidate in 2000. If Gore had won his home state in 2000, he would have been elected president regardless of the outcome in Florida.

APPENDIX 3.
LEVITTOWN—THE MODEL T
OF THE HOUSING INDUSTRY

Aside from the development of new housing financing methods by the Roosevelt administration during the Great Depression of the 1930s (which are essentially discussed in modern dress in Appendix 5), the most important single housing development in the nation's history was the building of Levittown in 1947 (and after). The mass-production building techniques developed by the Levitt brothers were widely copied at the time, and became the prime basis for housing developments across the country for the remainder of the 20th century. It was said accurately that Henry Ford (and his Model T) was the first great business figure of the American Century, and William J. Levitt was the second.

The Levitt family consisted of father Abraham and his two sons, Alfred and William. The youngest son was William (Bill), but after World War II he was the prime mover of the family business of building houses. The Levitts built relatively upscale houses in the Long Island, New York, area starting in 1929, and learned as they went. In 1941 the Levitts received a government contract to build what became 2,350 houses in the Norfolk, Virginia, area for war workers. The effort soon became a "disaster," in the words of Bill Levitt, in terms of getting houses done on schedule and making any sort of profit.

The Levitts met with their managers and broke the building process down into twenty-seven separate steps. They trained twenty-seven separate teams, each of whom would concentrate on one step. This enabled them to get around the shortage of skilled workers because less-experienced workers could work under a skilled team leader, and the Levitts changed the payment process, determining the time needed for each step and paying the teams extra for extra performance instead of just extra time. The Levitts soon learned how to build houses efficiently on a mass-production basis, and received additional defense worker housing contracts in the Portsmouth, Virginia, area and contracts for barracks for shipyards at Pearl Harbor. They became one of the largest builders in the nation as World War II came to an end.

Bill Levitt became a member of the Navy Seabees at the age of 36, serving in the Pacific from 1943–45. His job was to build instant airfields and supporting facilities as the Navy island-hopped across the Pacific. The Seabees often landed with the attacking forces and did their construction work under fire. Levitt later said that his work with the Seabees was a key to his future career. He would sit with his teammates at night, plan the next day's work, and think about how to do it faster (lives were at stake) and how best to use the men and material at hand. There were no union rules in the Pacific, and the only issue was how to get the job done in the minimum amount of time.

Bill Levitt never lost the animosity for unions he had developed on the Norfolk construction task. He was quoted as saying that Thomas Jefferson was in error by inferring that all men were equal always. They might indeed be born equal, but they were not equal in the sense of talent and willingness to work hard. In Levitt's view, the prime purpose of the union was to protect the slowest and least efficient worker. In the future, Levitt would hire only nonunion workers. He would pay them for work produced, and many would make twice what other construction workers normally made, but they earned their higher pay on Levitt's terms.

After the war, many of Bill Levitt's Seabee friends joined his company. They all wanted the same thing — a home of their own. Before the war Bill Levitt had already taken an option on a thousand acres of potato farms near Hempstead, Long Island, not far from New York City, where the family had built houses before. His brother and father saw only a few acres of land being cleared for some houses, and kept up the option reluctantly under the pressure of Bill Levitt, who had a vision of a huge community that would serve the veterans returning from the war and finding a daunting shortage of housing in the United States. Increasing his holdings to 4,000 acres and fighting tradition-bound obstacles against the construction of mass-housing (see Appendix 1 regarding Bill Levitt's testimony before the Senate Committee researching the housing problem in 1947-48), Bill Levitt set out to make his vision a reality.

Levitt later said that he owed much to Henry Ford. Instead of moving a car along an assembly line and having workers focus on just a few steps in its construction, Levitt made the house stationary and moved teams of work-

ers from house to house, efficiently performing just a few steps in its construction. Both Ford and Levitt created or adapted special tools for the task,
both made use of special materials available in his time, and the result for
both was the conversion of a hand-crafted, relatively expensive product to a
mass produced product made cheaply (and made well with many engineering advances) so as to be affordable to the common man. Both were rewarded
with huge customer demand and profits, and they were also rewarded with
the compliment of slavish imitators who went on to greatly expand the new
industry they had created with their new construction techniques.

Levitt applied all the techniques he had learned on his earlier projects
and in the Seabees. After bulldozers prepared the lot, trucks came in to off-
load a pile of building materials at intervals of 60 feet. A concrete slab was
put in place (no cellar was deemed necessary because, as Levitt was fond of
saying, if the ancient Romans did without who was he to question them?),
and floors of asphalt and walls of composition Sheetrock were added. New
power tools helped the workers get the walls up and the roof on, while freight
cars full of lumber were sent to a cutting yard where a single man cut parts
for ten houses in one day.

The 27 steps Levitt had developed on his Norfolk project were brought
into play again. The first step was laying out the foundation, and the last was
a cleaning sweep of the finished house. The crews were trained to do one
repetitive job for each house. There were floor men and men for the side-
walls and tile men, as well as painters who did red paint and white paint as
the job progressed. All difficult parts and subassemblies were built in central
shops rather than on site. The Levitts defied unions and union work rules,
and insisted all subcontractors work only for them. The Levitts made their
own concrete, made their own nails, grew their own trees, and cut their own
lumber. Part of the vertical integration was to keep the necessary building
materials flowing, and part was because traditional suppliers were not anxious to sell materials in large volumes at lower prices. They were used to
selling in small quantities at high prices to large numbers of individual small
builders. The Levitts changed all that. By the middle of 1948 they were
building 180 houses a week, essentially finishing 36 houses a day (the first
Levittown houses were occupied in October of 1947).

To demonstrate the traditional obstacles Levitt had to overcome, a local
bureaucrat initially denied Levitt a building permit on general principles
because he had never seen houses built without a cellar. But the *New York
Herald Tribune* ran a devastating editorial when it heard about the problem,
and the local bureaucrats soon reversed course. Levitt was breaking new
ground, and the result of doing things differently is often resistance from
those used to a previously prescribed method.

The standard model in Levittown was the Cape Cod, priced to sell initially at $6,990 and then later at $7,990. It had two bedrooms, a bathroom, a living room and a kitchen in its 750 square feet. At the time a garage was not considered a necessity. The house was readily expandable into the unfinished attic upstairs or into the 60 by 100 foot lot. The house included a Bendix washer and an eight-inch television set for which Levitt organized joint advertising programs with the manufacturer of each.

The other key selling point at Levittown, which others copied as slavishly as they copied the construction techniques, was the financing. Levitt himself made good use of Federal Housing Administration (FHA) rules to get pre-approval for his construction costs to build Levittown. Then, for each buyer, he set up a buying-financing contract program that took only about a half-hour for each section. The houses were originally rented to veterans only with an option to buy after one year, but with the total mortgage payments being less than the rent, nearly everyone bought after the year was up. After that, houses were for sale only. With the help of the Veterans Administration (VA) and the FHA, low or no down payments were available, and loan payments were on the order of $58 per month, everything included. The price you were quoted was what you paid. No closing costs, no hidden extras, and you were approved and an owner in a period of about one hour. In March of 1949, 1,400 contracts were drawn on a single day. It was mass production and mass selling.

Levittown was a booming success. Levitt built over 17,400 houses on Long Island, and the community reached a population of 82,000 in the next decade. It was the biggest such development built to that date. *Harper's Magazine* reported in 1948 that Levitt undersold his nearest competitor by $1,500 and still made a $1,000 profit on each house. Architect critic Paul Goldberger of the *New York Times* said approvingly that "Levittown houses were social creations more than architectural ones — they turned the detached single-family house from a distant dream to a real possibility for thousands of middle-class American families."

Levitt and his building and financing techniques were copied all across the nation. It was the true impetus to the building of suburbia in the United States through the 1950s, and the country never looked back. Levitt put the nation on the road to suburbia just as surely — and in the same way — as Henry Ford put the nation on wheels.

Bill Levitt became the true head of the company, as his father Abraham retired and his brother Alfred sold his share of the company, as neither could continue working with the dynamo that was Bill Levitt. In the next two decades more Levittowns were built near Philadelphia in Bucks County, Pennsylvania, and Willingboro, New Jersey, and the Levitt Company became the biggest private builder in the nation.

However, as big housing construction companies became the norm, Levitt was bought out by the huge conglomerate International Telephone and Telegraph (ITT) in 1969. Unfortunately, Bill Levitt and big company procedures did not mix well, and Bill Levitt decided to move on. The housing part of ITT declined, and was eventually sold off in parts and pieces. In that sense, the leading pioneer of the mass production suburb left no trace, and his legacy was the three Levittowns he left behind in New York, Pennsylvania, and New Jersey. Like Henry Ford, his legacy was the descendants of the Model T of housing while he himself left the scene.

As a footnote, the Smithsonian Institute in 1997 decided to include among it exhibits a model home from Levittown, built 50 years earlier in 1947. The Smithsonian considered Levittown the most notable element of the early days of suburbia. So the Smithsonian dispatched a search group to the original Levittown in Long Island. But after a few months of searching, they were unable to find such a model. All of Levittown's original homes had been modified in some way. Most had been expanded in terms of extra bedrooms and the addition of a garage, but even those with less dramatic expansions had been modified to the point that an original was not readily available. The Smithsonian still considered Levittown the key souvenir of its time, but some other approach would have to be found to demonstrate it. As had its founder, Levittown had moved on.

APPENDIX 4.
THE BALLOON FRAME

Relatively few people are aware of a development in the construction of houses that had a major impact on the housing process and the ultimate growth of the suburbs in the United States. The development took place in 1833 (or well before) and was called the balloon-frame house or simply the balloon frame. In essence, the use of the balloon frame not only greatly simplified the process of building houses, but also made it possible for houses to be built by relatively untrained workmen. These two considerations made it much easier and thus much cheaper to build houses, even to the extent of having them built by their owners using standard instructions and precut lumber.

It must be said that there is considerable controversy about who, if anyone, developed the technique and first put it into practice. This element is not nearly as important as the fact that the balloon frame came into use and made a major impact upon the building of houses and ultimately the suburbs. However, we will address this controversy before discussing the details of why the balloon frame was so useful and so important.

The original story of the development of the balloon frame was that George W. Snow, a handyman and carpenter in Chicago in 1833, who also owned a lumberyard, invented the balloon frame to build St. Mary's Church in Chicago, the first church of the Catholic faith to be built in that city. Then a carpenter-architect of the period, Augustine Taylor, was given credit, then George Snow was credited, but his building was supposedly done in 1832, not 1833, and it was a warehouse, and not a church. Finally, this story was labeled a myth and the balloon frame was claimed to have originated in the colonial period. It evolved in a major way in the Chicago area. By the 1880s, there were companies producing ready-made houses in Chicago using the balloon frame.

But whatever its origin, the balloon frame was popularized in the Chicago area, where considerable building was going on in the 1830s. It spread across Chicago, then the Ohio Valley, then to the heavily populated Eastern part of the nation, where it was called "Chicago construction." Eventually it became the standard method to build a house. To understand what the balloon frame was, it is necessary first to understand what it was not.

The settlers who came to the United States in the 1600s brought their techniques for building houses from Europe. The prime consideration was durability, but it was only as the settlers developed and imported tools that they could begin to build houses here as durable as those they left behind. Except for log cabins (there was plenty of wood in the early United States), the most common type of home was the traditional New England frame house. Most often made of durable oak, the weight of the house was supported by thick horizontal beams in turn supported by strong vertical posts. The joints were made to fit together with various means of interlocking (including wrought nails).

But the beams were usually 8 inches by 8 inches and had to be assembled on the ground. Then a crew of men could raise them into position and continue the framing. The result was very durable, but it required much labor and much skill in terms of shaping the beams and the carpentry techniques used to make the joints. A number of experienced craftsmen were needed to build one house.

The balloon frame completely revised this technique. The balloon frame was given its name originally, by the way, as a sign of contempt. The house was expected to blow away like a balloon when winds struck, compared to the stability of the heavy oak frame house. But the balloon frame did not blow away, and it proved to be very stable. The balloon frame had a number of significant advantages compared to its hefty cousin. The key to the balloon frame was exactly its lack of heft and the techniques needed to assemble it.

The balloon frame used relatively thin 2 by 4 inch studs (actually 1.5 by 3.5 inches but generally called 2 by 4s by all carpenters). The studs were nailed together so that the strain went against the grain of the wood. The frame was like a box, requiring no heavy corner posts for stability, and it had lateral as well as vertical strength to withstand winds. The weight of the house was borne by the many 2 by 4 posts placed 16 inches apart, and also by the floors acting as platforms. There were also a few 2 by 8 and 1 by 10 studs, but the majority of the construction consisted of the ubiquitous two-by-fours. This technique spread the stresses of the house over a large number of light boards of a few sizes, and the balloon frame had strength far beyond the apparent capacity of the light studs. Further, each wall unit could be framed on the ground by one or two men and then lifted relatively easily into place. No special carpentry ability or craftsmanship was required, and no large crew was needed for heavy lifting.

Two men with very moderate carpentry techniques and some good tools could erect a structure using the balloon frame technique more quickly than could twenty men using the traditional heavy frame technique. The result was that many new immigrants could build their own homes and have a higher home-ownership rate than native-white affluent Americans who had to have their homes built for them by skilled carpenters. With the balloon frame, building of houses quickly evolved from a specialized craft into a real industry.

Part of this evolution was due to a parallel evolution in the nail industry. Before 1817 nails were hand-wrought and cost 25 cents per pound, even as late as 1825. But the invention of the nail-making machine, and the use of the balloon frame which proved that simpler nailed joints would withstand wind and other stresses, brought the machine-made nail into common use. The price was just over three cents a pound for the new nails compared to the 25 cents a pound for the hand-wrought nails, and the use of machine-made nails exploded. This made the use of the balloon frame even more attractive.

The advancement of different kinds of transportation made it possible to live farther and farther away from jobs in the city, and the farther away building lots were from the city, the less they cost. Housing developments using the balloon frame were built quickly and cheaply. Housing materials and plans were delivered to an appropriate railroad depot, and people who bought building lots on the cheap could then build their own homes on the cheap. Studs could be pre-cut to the proper size, and by 1872 prefabricated parts included windows and doors.

A number of known magazines included plans for people to build their own houses (or even to have them built cheaply by people having only minimal carpentry skills). So-called pattern books came into vogue with plans and styles for do-it-yourselfers, or as a crutch for would-be architects who could offer house-building services at very low prices because the self-styled architect was simply following the designs and instructions from the pattern books.

Cities like Chicago and San Francisco rose from small villages to good-size cities in brief periods thanks to the rapidity with which balloon-frame single-residences grew around the basic city. This was really the beginning of low-density suburbs in the United States, which were unthinkable in Europe, where such building techniques and low-priced land were not available.

In many ways the construction in the 1940s of such huge developments as Levittown owes a great debt to the balloon frame, even if the developers may have never heard the term. The balloon frame was the standard way to build a house by the end of the 1800s (or before), and no further thought was given to the evolution of the process. But the balloon frame was exactly what was needed to help in the mass production of houses, especially as Bill Levitt led the process of building houses on a concrete slab rather than digging out a foundation that provided an expensive cellar.

In addition, the simplicity of the balloon frame house made it possible to continue to reduce the need for skilled workmen to build houses as better and better power tools (and building materials) were developed. This was the key step that made the balloon frame the equivalent of the Model T. All the workman had to known was how to repetitively perform a number of simple steps to complete his portion of the house. In fact, he really didn't have to know he was building a house. This further reduced the cost of labor needed to complete houses in a large development. The march to suburbia became easier and easier as time passed, and a major contributor was the balloon frame house, a phrase that would draw a puzzled look from most people today.

APPENDIX 5.
FINANCING OF HOUSING

We have dealt in this book with the great technological advance of the balloon frame in constructing houses, and with many technological advances in transportation (up to and including the most significant, the automobile) that made it possible to live farther and farther away from the jobs in center cities, getting from houses in the suburbs to jobs (and from suburb to suburb). But the biggest single factor that has supported the continued boom in constructing houses in the United States (and the immense growth of the suburbs) has been the evolution of easier and easier financing for individuals to buy those houses. This appendix covers the changes in financing from the first great change with the coming of the Federal Housing Administration (FHA) in the 1930s to the almost anything goes atmosphere of the early 21st century, where monthly payments are often the main item of concern to home buyers rather than the kind of house being purchased.

The Federal Housing Administration (FHA) was literally an invention of the administration of Franklin D. Roosevelt. As in most of his key programs, the main purpose of the FHA was to get people back to work. The construction industry was a key target because it was estimated at the time that one-third of the unemployment in the country was involved with the building trades in some way. But Roosevelt wanted to create a system that would get private capital involved in putting people back to work rather than always relying on government funding.

Mariner Eccles, a close friend of Roosevelt, led a committee from 1933 into 1934 trying to find just the right solution. But Winfield Riefler, an economist and a statistician on the committee, is credited with making the major contribution towards creating the FHA. The majority of the inputs the committee received from witnesses favored a system of government insurance guaranteeing private investments in the construction industry. That's what the FHA did when its recommendations were announced and subsequently signed by Roosevelt on June 27, 1934. The FHA revolutionized home financing and was a smashing success.

The FHA increased guaranteed mortgage loans to 93 percent of the appraised value compared to the average of 58 percent previously required. This step alone decreased the required down payment to less than 10 percent from the previously required minimum of over 30 percent (often 40 percent). Further, mortgages were made available with repayment periods of 25 to 30 years at a fixed (low) rate of interest. Not only did this greatly reduce the monthly payment amount, it protected the homeowner from having to re-negotiate the mortgage in only 5 years or so when interest rates could be higher. All of this sounds normal today, but it was revolutionary at the time. A further dramatic improvement was the concept of the self-amortizing mortgage, i.e., when the final payment was made the homeowner owned the house. No additional hidden or previously undisclosed charges.

Much of this was an adaptation of the Home Owners Loan Corporation (HOLC) bill that had been passed in June of 1933, but the net result of the FHA was that home mortgage foreclosures in the nation fell from 250,000 in 1932 to 18,000 in 1951. Housing starts rose from an all-time low of 93,000 in 1933 to 332,000 in 1937, 619,000 in 1941 just before World War II started, and to a regular level of between one and two million per year after the war.

The FHA helped 11 million people own homes in its first three full decades, returned a constant profit to the Treasury after its startup, and showed that the housing industry could regularly be jump-started by further infusions of capital responding to more generous loan terms. The FHA would eventually be surpassed in volume by private insurance companies later in the twentieth century, but until then it would remain the prime loan source in the nation, both to developers of housing communities and to the people who bought houses from those developers. The Veterans Administration (VA) would offer many similar advantages at slightly better terms after the GI Bill of 1944 (and subsequent versions afterward) was signed in 1944.

The downside to government financing such as the FHA was that it was originally a program to increase unemployment, not one necessarily to have social benefits such as equal opportunity in housing or to help decaying cities. Insuring loans to build and buy houses meant a number of new standards were required to be sure the loans were a good investment (FHA approvals were initially so important that builders would advertise (correctly) that they met FHA standards even if they weren't using FHA loans). A key result of this aspect of the FHA was that loans were generally not made in mixed communities containing blacks or other ethnic groups because the data showed clearly that such real estate normally did not hold its value. The result was that blacks and other ethnic groups did not participate in the housing booms of the second half of the 20th century. Preference was also given to the suburbs rather than urban areas because the suburbs were superior in terms of holding real estate values.

When complaints were raised about these issues, FHA officials replied quite correctly that their charter from Congress was to reduce unemployment in the construction industry at a critical point in the Depression. They were not chartered to, nor could they at the same time, address social issues or plan to help cities. When Levittown, the model for the great suburban boom amid the national housing crisis after World War II, was built with much FHA help in 1947, the non-mixed real estate protocol was applied so stringently that by 1960 Levittown held 82,000 people without a single black. Complaints were answered in the same manner. The national housing crisis to meet the needs of returning veterans was the key issue of the times, and the Levitts responded that "we can solve a housing problem, or we can try to solve a racial problem. But we can not combine the two."

It was the classical problem of the results of good intentions. But the FHA and the Levitts in their time (and in 1947 together) both were addressing the overwhelming issue of the day, and in that they were quite successful. But the law of unintended consequences left blacks and other minorities out of the positive effects of the housing boom in the 1950s, and also left these groups concentrated in the cores of declining cities and out of the suburbs. Later legislative attempts, especially in the 1960s, were made to try to correct these problems, but there was much to be made up for, and there is still a long way to go to achieve full equity in housing opportunities.

Another problem connected with the negative results of good intentions that affects our discussion of home financing concerns the nation's Federal Reserve Bank, or the Fed as it is commonly known. The Fed sets short-term interest rates, and is nominally expected to be the referee for such rates, setting them as it seems best for the national economy (especially in terms of avoiding inflation) and letting the stock market and mortgage interest rates, for example, adjust as best they can in a way that reflects market-driven forces. The Fed has long been criticized for doing too much or too little, depending on the view of the beholder. There is general agreement, however, that the then relatively new Fed did the wrong things at exactly the wrong time at the end of the 1920s, and had a strong negative effect on the stock market crash of 1929 that preceded the Great Depression. So the actions of the Fed need to be taken very seriously.

In recent times the Fed has become the subject of much discussion. Alan Greenspan became the commissioner of the Fed in 1987, the year of the great stock market crash of that era. His immediate effort was to switch from the inflation fighting efforts of his predecessor, Paul Volker, to flooding the market with money to offset the effects of the stock market crash. Greenspan did the right thing at the time, and was generally well regarded until he stepped down in 2006. However, many critics felt that 1987 left an indelible mark on Greenspan, and thus over the years he became viewed as a proponent of the stock market rather than the neutral referee he was supposed to be. "Uncle" Alan always was seen as trying to calm and shelter the stock market from any international problems, and he adjusted Fed policy according.

The result in the view of many was the great stock market bubble of the 1990s that burst in early 2000, and, in the case of the Nasdaq, is still 60 percent below its peak six years later. Even the Dow has only managed to climb back to close to its peak of six years ago, but it is still below that level. In the eyes of his critics, Greenspan then tried to fix his errors by embarking on a series of rate cuts in the next four years that devastated anyone living on variable interest rate investments, and in the meantime built a potential real-estate bubble, as rates hit historic lows of 1 percent in 2003-2004. In the 2001–2005 period, housing prices started their great rise, being driven by low interest rate mortgages and the assumption that exotic mortgages, of which we will speak in a moment, would always find a safe haven in ever-increasing housing prices. Such a cycle, of course, cannot go on indefinitely. This is the background against which many persons are waiting to see if the housing price bubble will burst and make many mortgages unmanageable as their previously liberal terms adjust to a new reality.

Greenspan reversed himself in June of 2004, and for the next two years rates slowly increased as the Fed professed to be concerned with inflation, once its key task. As noted, Greenspan left (by retirement) the Fed in early 2006, but by then some trends had been established that may yet come back to haunt homeowners. It is not clear how new Fed chairman Ben Bernanke will handle this issue, but the Fed paused in its series of rate increases in August of 2006 after 17 straight increases over 26 months. Many people are not aware of how Fed policy can affect their future, but another trend that has developed in recent years is that the Fed may have lost the ability to affect mortgage rates while it was off running rates up and down almost irrationally.

The Fed controls only short-term interest rates. These rates directly control such things as the prime rate and the short-term costs of doing business. Normally long-term rates rise as short-terms rates do, but such has not been the case in recent years. The interest rate curve that shows the amount of extra interest one gets for taking a longer-term risk of loaning money has become inverted. That means short-term yields now exceed long-term yields.

This is historically a sign that the marketplace suspects a recession is coming and short-term yields will fall once again.

But in this globalized world, it may also mean that there is so much money around the world looking for long-term investment, especially in such preferred things as United States real estate, that the Fed's attempt to push up long-term rates by raising short-term rates no longer drives the long-term market. Even Greenspan complained about this inversion, for which he could offer no firm reason or solution. For example, as of August of 2006, after more than two years of short-term rate increase by the Fed from the historically low 1 percent to 5.25 percent, the long term 10-year bond, on which mortgage rates are often based, is practically unchanged at about 4.75 percent (now lower than conventional short-term rates). This may be good news for homebuyers fearing a big jump in future mortgage rates, but it may not help much those with exotic mortgages about to reset to new conditions. This has many federal bank regulators and many standard mortgage loan companies concerned.

In the 2001–2005 period, as housing prices approximately doubled across the nation due to the liberal mortgage terms created in response to the historically low interest rates set by the Fed, critics complained that homebuyers began to buy monthly mortgage payments to get in on the boom almost regardless of their financial circumstances. Independent mortgage companies, anxious to profit from the fees they get from writing mortgages, proliferated everywhere. Many such companies sold their mortgages to other companies (or even government agencies), not wishing to take any further risks after having captured their fees. But in some cases they may be forced to buy those mortgages back if the quality is not as presented, and the stock prices of many of these sub-prime lenders are falling. The rising price of housing, caused in large part by such mortgages, kept everyone afloat in a cycle that seemed to go on forever, as all such bubbles do — until they burst.

The "greater fool" theory holds sway in such an atmosphere. This theory states in essence that the equity being purchased is overpriced, but if a greater fool comes along who will pay an even higher price, all is well. Many responsible mortgage lenders and governmental advisory groups have decried the risky mortgages being issued, but their voices have been drowned out by those chasing what they see as easy profits.

Critics complained that as the Fed continued its stock-market recovery stance, the mortgage industry became nearly unmanageable. An industry that once required reasonable down payments of at least a few percent now often requires none. A mortgage payment plan based on one's ability to pay and one's credit history to demonstrate reliability has changed to one requiring payments of interest only — or payments based on adjustable rates starting as low as 1 percent which in many cases do not amortize the mortgage, leaving the mortgage amount to grow (negative amortization) instead of slowly declining.

The savior of such mortgages is ever-increasing home prices or ever-declining mortgage rates. Thus, potential problems are pushed off into the future, but for many over-extended mortgage holders the future is about to arrive right now. The adjustable rate mortgage (ARM) marvels of a few years ago are about to reset starting in about 2007 or even before. If one has a non-conventional mortgage, as do two-thirds of all people who made mortgage loans since the second half of 2004 in the United States, problems involved with increased mortgage payments lie just ahead.

Whether it is called an ARM or an Option ARM (which permits even lower monthly payments), interest-only (which as it sounds permits lower payments that build no equity), 100 percent financing (no down payment), or some variation thereof, potential problems exist in the opinion of many industry watchers and government agencies. It doesn't help that many lenders have greatly relaxed their credit standards, offering loans to customers with limited or no income or asset documentation ("no doc loans"). Some lenders insist it is a new era and old standards no longer apply. Critics point out these lenders sound just like investors in Internet dot-com businesses sounded immediately before the dot-com stock market crash of 2000. These are the same lenders who have steadily objected to the proposals of various governmental regulatory agencies over the past several months to tighten rules on such liberal mortgages.

Some independent liberal loan companies have already failed or cut back their activities as new mortgage requests have slowed dramatically as noted in the chronology. Many analysts feel that this coming payment reset problem is contributing to the present real estate market stalemate, where home sales are falling steadily across the country but prices generally continue to remain high. In the opinion of many, this is because homeowners refuse to accept that the market is finally declining and refuse to finally sell. Refinancing of an existing mortgage, once a large part (up to 50 percent) of the mortgages written, has also fallen off because many of its advantages disappear when prices cannot be predicted to be going up or rates predicted to fall. In the view of these analysts, many of these owners will be forced to sell when their liberal mortgage resets and higher payments are required. That will further depress a declining market in the classical way that happens when bubbles finally burst.

The bottom line is that this is a very dangerous time to purchase real estate, and more than normal care should be taken in the process. There are still many kinds of mortgages available, but people should be careful not bite off more than they can chew. Some highly unethical loan sources have made "loan to own" loans. In such cases loans are made to persons whose situation indicates they will clearly fail to continue to make payments. The lender forecloses and takes over the house. If prices continue to hold, the lender resells the house and makes a profit on top of his mortgage fees even after encountering new selling costs. More than ever, it's buyer beware. If it seems too good to be true, one can be sure it probably is exactly that.

BIBLIOGRAPHY

This bibliography lists the key books consulted in putting together this chronology. By far the most useful book was *Crabgrass Frontier* by Kenneth T. Jackson. This is a very detailed analysis of the suburbanization of the United States and contains much useful information. The only defect of this book is that it was published in 1985. This means it misses all the additional items that have happened since 1985, and even though the author attempts to forecast what will happen next, he is much too conservative and thinks that the suburbanization must cease soon. Of course, it has increased dramatically since that date, and continues to do so. But other than this very forgivable shortcoming, this is an excellent book.

A second book that would be of interest to most readers is *The Fifties*, by David Halberstam. Of course only a portion of this book is applicable to my book, but that portion covers the details of the very important building of Levittown. Like most books by this author, it is extremely interesting to readers at all levels.

The book *Edge City: Life on the New Frontier*, by Joel Garreau, is an excellent discussion of what could be considered the final stage of suburbanization in the United States, and it is (apparently unintentionally) the fulfillment of the forecast by prior authors such as Frank Lloyd Wright in his 1958 book *The Living City*. Wright and other authors forecast what essentially became the edge city, long before that term had come into common use. The book by Garreau is an excellent description of the forecast of the edge city as the ultimate suburb.

The book *Building Suburbia*, by Dolores Hayden, even if it is not really favorable to the existence of suburbs, is a good, recent description of how the suburbs came to be. The book *Bourgeois Utopias* by Robert Fishman is also a good overview, but as noted in its subtitle, *The Rise and Fall of Suburbia*, this book, published in 1987, defines the end of suburbia simply because

Fishman's definition of suburbia is growth around a core city, and he believes such growth stopped before he wrote the book. In essence, he selects new names for suburbia, and ends up with ones analogous to edge city even though he doesn't specifically use that term. It is another unintentional support for the fact that edge cities are the new era in suburbs.

The book *Picture Windows* by Rosalyn Baxandall and Elizabeth Ewen contains much useful information about the so-called McCarthy hearings on housing in 1947-1948. The book is intended to be another description of how the suburbs came to be and it especially discusses Levittown. But by far its most useful contribution in this chronology was the detail of its discussion of the McCarthy hearings.

In addition to the books listed in this bibliography, the Internet has been a useful research source. No attempt has been made to compile a list of specific Internet sources for this book because most Internet-based material in the book is a combination of facts drawn from several different Internet sources. Also, Internet information constantly changes as it is updated. Anyone interested in obtaining more information on a specific aspect of this book will be able to do so using the Internet.

Baxandall, Rosalyn, and Elizabeth Ewen. *Picture Windows: How the Suburbs Happened.* New York: Basic Books, 2000.

Bridgewater, William, and Seymour Kurtz, eds. *The Columbia Encyclopedia.* 3rd ed. New York: Columbia University Press, 1963.

Fishman, Robert. *Bourgeois Utopias: The Rise and Fall of Suburbia.* New York: Basic Books, 1987.

Fogelson, Robert M. *Downtown: Its Rise and Fall, 1880–1950.* New Haven, CT: Yale University Press, 2001.

Foy, Jessica H., and Thomas J. Schlereth, eds. *American Home Life, 1880–1930: A Social History of Spaces and Services.* Knoxville, TN: University of Tennessee Press, 1992.

Fulton, William. *The Reluctant Metropolis: The Politics of Urban Growth in Los Angeles.* Point Arena, CA: Solano Press Books, 1997.

Garreau, Joel. *Edge City: Life on the New Frontier.* New York: Doubleday, 1991.

Hacker, Andrew. *Two Nations: Black & White, Separate, Hostile, Unequal.* New York: Scribner, 2003.

Halberstam, David. *The Fifties.* New York: Fawcett Columbine, 1993.

Hayden, Dolores. *Building Suburbia: Green Fields and Urban Growth, 1820–2000.* New York: Pantheon Books, 2003.

_____. *Redesigning the American Dream: Gender, Housing, and Family Life.* New York: Norton, 2002.

Holloway, Mark. *Heavens on Earth: Utopian Communities in America 1680–1880.* 2nd ed. New York: Dover, 1966.

Jackson, Kenneth T. *Crabgrass Frontier: The Suburbanization of the United States.* New York: Oxford University Press, 1985.

Linklater, Andro. *Measuring America: How an Untamed Wilderness Shaped the United States and Fulfilled the Promise of Democracy.* New York: Walker, 2002.

Mason, Joseph B. *History of Housing in the U.S. 1930–1980.* Houston: Gulf, 1982.

McGeveran, William A., Jr., editorial director. *The World Almanac and Book of Facts, 2006.* New York: World Almanac Education Group, 2006.

Radford, Gail. *Modern Housing in America: Policy Struggles in the New Deal Era.* Chicago: University of Chicago Press, 1996.

Thomas, G. Scott. *The United States of Suburbia: How the Suburbs Took Control of America and What They Plan to Do with It.* Amherst, NY: Prometheus Books, 1998.

Toobin, Jeffrey. *Too Close to Call: The Thirty-Six-Day Battle to Decide the 2000 Election.* New York: Random House, 2002.

Vale, Lawrence J. *From the Puritans to the Projects: Public Housing and Public Neighbors.* Cambridge, MA: Harvard University Press, 2000.

Waldie, D.J. *Holy Land: A Suburban Memoir.* New York: St. Martin's Griffin, 1997.

Wright, Russell O. *A Twentieth-Century History of United States Population.* Lanham, MD: Scarecrow Press, 1996.

_____. *Chronology of Education in the United States.* Jefferson, NC: McFarland, 2006.

_____. *Chronology of Labor in the United States.* Jefferson, NC: McFarland, 2003.

_____. *Chronology of the Stock Market.* Jefferson, NC: McFarland, 2002.

_____. *Chronology of Transportation in the United States.* Jefferson, NC: McFarland, 2004.

_____. *Presidential Elections in the United States.* Jefferson, NC: McFarland, 1995.

INDEX

175